moving WATER

moving WATER

A Fly Fisher's Guide to Currents

JASON RANDALL

STACKPOLE
BOOKS

Guilford, Connecticut

Published by Stackpole Books
An imprint of The Rowman & Littlefield Publishing Group, Inc.
4501 Forbes Blvd., Ste. 200
Lanham, MD 20706
www.rowman.com

Distributed by NATIONAL BOOK NETWORK

Illustrations by Thomas Barnett

British Library Cataloguing in Publication Information available

Library of Congress Cataloging-in-Publication Data available

ISBN 978-0-8117-1022-0 (cloth : alk. paper)
ISBN 978-0-8117-3907-8 (paper : alk. paper)
ISBN 978-0-8117-4881-0 (electronic)

♾️™ The paper used in this publication meets the minimum requirements of American National Standard for Information Sciences—Permanence of Paper for Printed Library Materials, ANSI/NISO Z39.48-1992.

To my father, Harold Randall,
who first introduced me to the outdoors,
and to my mother, Susan Randall,
who said, "Oh, all right, go ahead."

Contents

Foreword

Lefty Kreh

In my fly-tying room is a shelf full of books devoted to trout fishing, and I've read them all. With the exception of one or two, *Moving Water* has more information to help make you a better trout fisherman than any of the others. You'll have to read and reread it many times to fully absorb its contents so you can use it in pursuit of trout wherever there is current, be it a tiny brook, a tumbling mountain creek, a meandering limestone stream, or a large river.

I have a number of fishery scientist friends who have wonderful information we trout fishermen could use, but they lack the ability to communicate in our language. Not so with Jason Randall, whose text is clear and understandable to all.

Randall is a trout fisherman and a scientist who gives a startling new and comprehensive look at how current affects the stream's design, what lives in it, the trout's food, and ultimately the trout. If you absorb all of this, you'll be able to catch more and even bigger trout.

Once you read this book you will never look at a flowing river the same way again. With clear text and Thomas Barnett's excellent illustrations, Randall explains where and why currents flow through a pool at different speeds both horizontally and vertically. Understanding these different flows tells you where to fish and which places to avoid.

Unnatural drag on the fly, a result of the different flow rates, does two disastrous things: trout refuse the offerings and worse they are often frightened out of the area. Randall's advice on how to avoid drag in dozens of different current situations is some of the most revealing and instructive I've read.

Learning about the various currents makes you realize why you may need to get closer or change locations to make a good presentation. You may even need to wade across the stream and fish from the other side or change position and make the presentation upstream or downstream from the trout.

The section on nymph fishing is superb yet common sense, emphasizing that drag is most important when nymphing. Perhaps 90 percent of nymphs eaten by trout are taken underwater where they clearly see their prey—and can detect any drag. Randall's explanations of various nymphing methods and how to rig for different current conditions are informative.

Reading this book you will give new insight into how currents affect a stream's shape, speed, color, and height and bottom structure. You'll learn how weather and evaporation affect the stream and its temperature; how the fish cope with the varying currents to survive, hide, and feed; and why they change locations. You'll learn how trout respond to the seasons and changes within streams and how the rate of flow affects a stream and how you fish it.

Years ago it took me a few days to realize that many of the mountain brooks in the Great Smoky Mountains have a steep drop and water rushes downhill, scouring the bottom and leaving little trout food. After watching my hillbilly friends for a while, I realized they caught more trout because they fished many times faster than me, knowing few fish would be in any pool. They hit the best spots and went on. The reverse is true at the Letort in Carlisle, Pennsylvania, near my home. That stream is clogged with aquatic vegetation that holds incredible amounts of insect food, so a slow and very deliberate method is best. Had Jason Randall's *Moving Water* been around then for me to read, I could have been much more prepared for the high-gradient Smoky Mountain brooks. As it is, this book is indispensable for explaining in detail what's going on with these very different types of water.

It has been said many times that 90 percent of the trout are in 10 percent of the water—and Randall clearly explains why. I believe this is the most informative book about trout streams and their currents and how to successfully fish them. It belongs in every serious trout fisherman's library.

Acknowledgments

When I count my blessings, I am always thankful for my wife, Jo, for her strong support and encouragement, as well as for my kids, Erin and Evan, and their understanding while this work was in progress. The fact that they all share my passion for the outdoors in general and fly fishing in particular has made this task a lot easier. I also thank my son and daughter for allowing me to share some personal moments from their childhood experiences in this book.

Without Jay Nichols, whose editorial skills and vision have been instrumental in this effort from start to finish, this book would not have been possible, and to him I am grateful. I also thank the editorial staff at Stackpole Books for their commitment to education within the sport. I am grateful as well for the guidance and skill of other fine editors who have shaped my writing through their patience and dedication to excellence, particularly Steve Walburn and Russ Lumpkin at *American Angler* and *Gray's Sporting Journal*.

Finally, and most important, I am grateful for a wonderful and merciful God who created the beautiful places that trout inhabit—and the trout that we anglers enjoy so much.

Chapter 1

The Lotic Ecosystem

When we look at a river, we are often captivated by its beauty and tranquility. The sound of the flowing water and the light sparkling and dancing on the surface delight our senses. This is soul food of the most nourishing kind. The constant, reassuring flow gives us pause for reflection. Rivers have a mystical quality that has held the fascination of mankind from the earliest time. We view rivers with a bit of awestruck wonder as well, for rivers have a formidable quality, with raw power hidden under their beguiling veneer. Nevertheless, we are enamored, sometimes even spellbound, by their enigmatic beauty.

We are drawn to rivers and streams for many reasons. As anglers, we hope to catch a few fish. For most fly fishermen, the aesthetic aspect is also important: angling allows us to visit some beautiful places, which certainly adds a great deal to the overall experience. Too often, however, we overlook the vast complexity that lies beneath the surface. Fly fishing may be an art, but it is also a science. The more you learn about the scientific aspect of rivers and the details of their inner workings, the more success you will have in the pursuit of angling. And the more you know about rivers, the more you are reminded that you are just a visitor here. Only when you look closer do you realize that you have truly encountered a strange and foreign world.

A river is an intricate ecosystem with complex layers of life where the current is king. The movement of water is the predominant feature in rivers and streams, and it has modified and shaped the entire structure of this aquatic habitat. When you wade into a river, you brace yourself against the force of the water's flow, but you probably haven't thought about how strong of an influence it must exert on the lives of aquatic insects and trout. A current that feels strong to us must seem overpowering to organisms much smaller than we are.

Think about the last time you were outside in strong, gusty winds. Walking into the teeth of the wind was hard. You had to lean into it just to keep from being pushed over. Imagine for a moment that you lived in a world of constantly blowing winds, with no buildings in which to hide. Where would you seek refuge? How would you adjust? You would tire easily from fighting the strength of the wind, so you would find ways to reduce your exposure. You would change your behavior, find relief behind trees or other windbreaks, crawl on the ground, or sprint from place to place. You might find a depression or a ditch to settle into.

Imagine that at the same time, you had to snatch your food from the passing wind storm. You would have to sneak glances into the wind and learn to quickly identify the edible from the inedible. It would be like peeking out from behind a tree trying to snag a cheeseburger whisking by in a cloud of litter. You might occasionally snatch an unsuitable item from the passing milieu only to discard it after you had examined it close-up. But you would get better with practice. You would have to succeed, for in this world to fail is to die. All the while, you would have to constantly be looking over your shoulder, always on the alert for other predators roaming around, seeking to make a meal out of you.

What if a sudden spring storm came and the force of the wind doubled? How would you react? All of your normal established shelters might have been blown away or may no longer be safe because of the storm. You would have to find new safe shelters. They would have to offer ready access to food, because with the high metabolism necessary to survive in this hostile setting, you would need to eat regularly. What if your source of food suddenly changed or disappeared altogether? You would have to locate a new food source and find another place protected from the elements from which to examine the offerings. Such a harsh environment would not tolerate mistakes. Poor decisions would have dire consequences. The penalties would be death by predation or starvation. Would you be able to compete?

This scenario accurately describes the trout's world. They have adapted to the harsh demands of their environment. They do not see this situation as strange and unfamiliar; it is all they know. They are survivors and have adjusted to this routine. Even so, many are lost along the way. In fact, most of the trout sac fry that hatch from the fertilized eggs never make it to their first birthday. For this reason, trout that reach reproductive age lay an abundance of eggs. This is nature's way of offsetting the high attrition. Those that make it to adulthood have been selected for their survival skills. They have learned to compete and succeed in this unforgiving setting. Nature rewards efficiency and success. In light of this, it is no wonder that trout have developed elaborate mechanisms to compensate for the currents and incorporated them into their behavioral, reproductive, and feeding patterns.

LOTIC ECOSYSTEMS

Ecologists and biologists use the term *lotic ecosystem* to describe the biological environment created by flowing water such as rivers and streams. Like terrestrial ecosystems, they include all the organisms that inhabit them—vegetation, insect, and animal life—as well as their interrelationships with one another. Understanding the lotic ecosystems and the currents by which they are defined will provide you with insights into how trout relate to their environment, how they react to different situations, and other aspects of the world in which they live. If you want to beat the home team on its own turf, you need to understand the playing field. Anglers seek a quarry that lives in a complicated environment, and the trout are as familiar with their world as we are with our own neighborhoods. The more you know about their flowing-water home, the better you can understand and catch trout.

Lotic ecosystems can vary tremendously from one water system to another, from a small trickle of water from glacial runoff to a huge river like the Mississippi. Each stream or river is unique and has a completely different organic and inorganic composition than any other. Each is different in scale, flow, and character, but all share one common feature—current—that makes them different from stillwaters such as ponds and lakes, which are called *lentic ecosystems*. All of the key characteristics of lotic ecosystems are created by the current, either directly or indirectly.

In these ecosystems, water flows in only one direction. The stream originates at the headwaters and flows to its termination, whether it joins with another waterway or discharges into the ocean. Water may be lost or added along the way, but the direction is always downstream. Marine ecosystems differ in that the direction of water movement in oceans is variable. Water moves back and forth as the tides move in and out and ocean currents shift in response to the prevailing winds.

The Greek philosopher Heraclitus once said, "No man ever steps into the same river twice, for it's not the same river and he's not the same man." This is an accurate description of a river, and perhaps mankind as well. To put it simply, rivers are in a constant state of change, which includes both large-scale and small-scale changes. I think that Heraclitus said it better, but in the terminology of today's biologists, lotic ecosystems are spatially and temporally heterogeneous at all scales and levels.

To biologists, scale is an important consideration. Scale can be as small as a microscopic organism or as large as the planet. To say that rivers are heterogeneous at all scales means that there is no uniformity from the smallest point of reference to the largest.

Heterogeneous, the opposite of *homogeneous*, means that there is variation rather than uniformity. *Temporally heterogeneous* refers to variations that occur in the river from one point in time to another, and *spatially heterogeneous* refers to variations from one place in the river to another.

Temporal Variation

Rivers and streams are dynamic. They change over the course of time, whether that is one second or a millenium. Some of these changes can be fast and sudden, occurring over a short period of time, such as those resulting from heavy water flow during floods due to climatic extremes. Heavy spring rains can cause a surge in discharge, undermining banks and remodeling rivers to such an extent that they may alter their course. Even without flood conditions, local weather can produce an influx of additional water into the stream, creating a much greater volume of flow. If you visit the river during this period, sections of the river that were riffles before might now be unfishable whitewater. Periods of drought will have the opposite effect, creating low-water conditions. This presents challenges for us as anglers. Besides having to exercise caution while wading under different conditions, we also need to employ adaptive angling strategies.

Changes in the lotic ecosystem also vary in scale. These changes are often not as obvious on a smaller scale as large-scale changes. They can be as subtle as a heavier sediment load in runoff created by normal precipitation, which can temporarily change the composition of the river from one day to another by introducing this suspended material into the water, even if the volume of flow in the river is not tremendously increased. This may affect insect and trout activity as well as aquatic vegetation, because the turbidity decreases the amount of light transmitted through the water. Drought conditions can also lead to changes in water composition and clarity.

New structure or features in the river can introduce small-scale changes as well, which can result in entirely new habitat. Have you ever visited a river and found a new deadfall or logjam in the water? The river immediately starts to react by remodeling in response to the new feature.

The current may be deflected, flowing in a new direction. This can cause erosion or freshly undercut banks. Deposition of material creates sandbars behind the obstruction, and the shifting current can expose areas of riffles. The next time you see a new water feature in your favorite river, observe all the changes that have happened as a result of its presence. Notice the way the river has reacted and current flow has changed, even well downstream.

By altering habitat, these conditions can redistribute trout within the river and cause changes in their feeding behavior. From one season to the next, the river can fish quite differently. The trout may have shifted their location and feeding behavior in reaction to the changing circumstances. You will have to respond as well. You may not be able to rely on your favorite places. You have to be observant and react to the changes. Anglers face a different river each time we visit, and we have to be dynamic and responsive in our angling approaches.

Large-scale changes caused by flowing water may take thousands of years. An example is the Grand Canyon, which took eons for the river to carve out of the bedrock. Lowland floodplains and river deltas also formed over many years. A huge river like the Mississippi reflects large-scale changes from both temporal and spatial perspectives, as it involves both a long time frame and a large surface area within the environment.

Spatial Variation

Rivers also have tremendous variation from one spot to another, even when climatic factors and water-flow conditions are constant, and this variation is critical for the rich diversity of habitat characteristic of lotic ecosystems. Streams have areas where the current has removed looser material, exposing the rough and rocky substrate to form riffles, and areas where slower and softer water has allowed the sedimentary material to drop out of the flow and be deposited on the bottom to create an entirely different habitat in pools. Thus different habitats in the same stream often are only a short distance apart, such as a riffle immediately followed by a pool. Each of these water features creates an entirely different microenvironment within the ecosystem, providing a wide array of unique habitats for the diverse organisms that live in rivers and streams.

On a larger scale, there is great variation from one waterway to the next. Consider the differences between a glacial-fed mountain stream and an alluvial river such as the Mississippi. An alluvial river is a lowland river that flows over a riverbed made up of loose sedimentary material that was deposited during previous periods of high flows or floods. These water systems carry a high load of sediment from erosion upriver and deposit it in the floodplain. As a result, these rivers are constantly rechanneling and re-forming according to the deposition of that material. By contrast, glacial streams, especially near their headwaters, may be rich in inorganic minerals but very low in organic matter. Both of these are lotic ecosystems, but they are drastically different.

THE BIOLOGY OF WATER

When you are standing in a large river, the sheer volume of water may make it hard to believe that such a large and vast waterway has a single point of origin. As T. S. Elliot once said, "The River itself has no beginning or end. In its beginning, it is not yet the River; in its end, it is no longer the River. What we call the headwaters is only a selection from among the innumerable sources which flow together to compose it." It is possible to trace most rivers to their headwaters, but they usually have more than one source of water. Most rivers have humble beginnings but gain water and momentum along their course as other tributaries join and add their water to the flow. Water enters rivers and streams in three ways: through direct precipitation, surface runoff, and subsurface flow.

Direct precipitation is water that falls directly into the river or stream as rain, snow, hail, or other forms of precipitation, or as condensation falling from streamside vegetation or structure. This method contributes the lowest percentage of new water.

The next-largest contributor of new water entering rivers and streams is *surface runoff,* water that flows over the surface of the ground in the geographic region that drains into the river. This includes not only surface water from recent precipitation, but also water from melting snow or ice, including glaciers. This source is seasonally dynamic and fluctuates with the climatic activity within the region. Heavy rains and snowmelt can increase the amount of surface runoff, whereas periods of drought can eliminate any contribution at all. Some rivers that depend on surface runoff for the predominant source of water may dry up altogether in the dry season. Snow or glacial melt can form the headwaters for many mountain streams. For these streams, surface runoff constitutes a more significant portion of the total amount of their water, at least near the headwaters, although farther downstream other sources may contribute additional water.

Subsurface flow accounts for the largest water contribution for most rivers and streams. Subsurface water in storage reserves is known as groundwater. Water from the subsurface water table in the form of seeps,

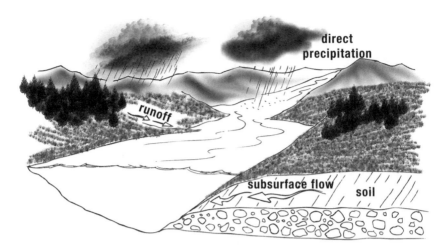

The water in rivers and streams comes from three different sources: direct precipitation, surface runoff, and subsurface flow. The proportion of input from each of these sources varies according to season, weather, climate, and geologic factors, such as slope and soil composition.

springs, and subsurface flow can serve as the headwaters for many waterways, as well as add water at many points along the length of a river. The temperature of the underground water that enters the river is fairly constant year-round, so trout frequently concentrate at the points of groundwater input, where the water temperature remains within their comfort range.

Most rivers have a combination of water from all three sources, the proportion of which varies depending on the season, location, and climatic conditions. Even though the headwaters of many streams may draw heavily on one particular source, all three can introduce new water at any point along the waterway. For example, streams that begin as runoff from melting snow or ice near the headwaters often receive contributions from other sources as they move into the valley. Those that draw their headwaters from springs or seeps receive additional water from surface flow during the spring thaw and heavy rains.

THE WATER CYCLE
Water is essential to all living organisms and is supplied by the continual recirculation of water within the global ecosystem in what is referred to as the *water cycle*—the constant interchange of water among three main ecological water storage reservoirs: atmospheric water vapor; surface water in the form of rivers, streams, lakes, ponds, and oceans; and subsurface groundwater. The atmospheric, surface, and subsurface reservoirs contain

vast amounts of water, and water can move among these reserves, which may require a change in its form, such as liquid to vapor or solid (ice). Although this interchange of water has been occurring for millions of years, the balance of water on the earth has remained fairly constant over time.

Rivers need a constant supply of water to remain viable ecosystems. Without the movement of water from watersheds to the oceans, which represent the largest surface-water reservoirs, rivers would run dry and the organisms that live there would perish. As Jacques Cousteau pointed out, "The water cycle and the life cycle are one."

A closer look at the water cycle is essential to understand the factors that regulate water input. To appreciate the current that is created by the flow of water, it is necessary to understand how that water got there in the first place. The flow of water, and thus the strength of the current, is directly proportional to the amount of water entering the waterway. Currents vary drastically at different rates of flow. This not only determines which waters are suitable for wading, but also influences insect activity, trout location, and their behavior and feeding patterns.

The entire geographic region drained by a river and its tributaries, including the area of land where runoff from precipitation or melting snow or ice drains downhill to join a waterway, is known as a *drainage basin*, *catchment*, or *watershed*. Each river exists as an extension of the drainage basin, which includes the terrestrial ecosystem characteristic for that area and climate. The landscape features influence the composition of water in the particular river, and thus the terrestrial ecosystem influences the lotic ecosystem. Slope and pitch of the landscape, the soil type, and hardness or porosity of the surface all affect water movement in the watershed. Rivers and streams connect each drainage basin with other waterways and eventually the oceans.

The water cycle plays a vital role in the maintenance of aquatic ecosystems. It is the constant movement of water among the three types of reservoirs that results in precipitation and replenishes the groundwater sources that serve as the headwaters of many rivers and streams, which carry the water to the oceans. The water cycle is also important in regulating the temperature of rivers and streams through the process of evaporation. In the warm summer months, as the water temperature of a river rises, evaporation of water at the surface lowers the temperature, just as our bodies cool when sweat evaporates from our skin. Evaporation from the surface is affected by the temperature and humidity of the air and the amount of wind present. More evaporation occurs on dry, windy days, keeping the streams cooler. On hot, humid, still summer days, there is less

Each river is an essential component and extension of the entire geographic area that it serves. The climate and terrestrial features shown in the right foreground produce an entirely different kind of river than those on the left. A mountain stream, shown in the background, is fed by glacial melt and is different from both of the others in terms of water composition, temperature, and flow.

evaporative cooling resulting in substantially higher water temperatures and creating uncomfortable conditions for trout.

The opposite reaction, condensation, frequently occurs when the temperature falls and water vapor in the air is cooled. As the air temperature falls, the saturation level is exceeded and the excess moisture condenses on exposed surfaces. As water changes from vapor to liquid, it has the opposite effect from evaporation, raising the surrounding temperature. The most common natural example is dew, which is important ecologically to both plants and animals, alike. In fact, condensation serves as a water source for several species of beetles, and in California's redwood forests, fog drip from condensation on trees is essential to that ecosystem.

The water cycle can be viewed as three financial banks where, instead of money, water is held in deposit. These three banks represent the atmosphere, surface water, and subsurface groundwater. Each bank is capable of storing large amounts of money but must be able to communicate with the other banks to ensure a constant back-and-forth flow of funds. The atmosphere can interface directly with the surface waterways, and the surface-water system can exchange directly with the subsurface groundwater, but the surface-water systems act as a mediator for the exchange of water between the atmospheric and groundwater reservoirs. Water must first enter the surface-water system from either the atmosphere or subsurface sources before it can proceed to the other depository. The mechanisms

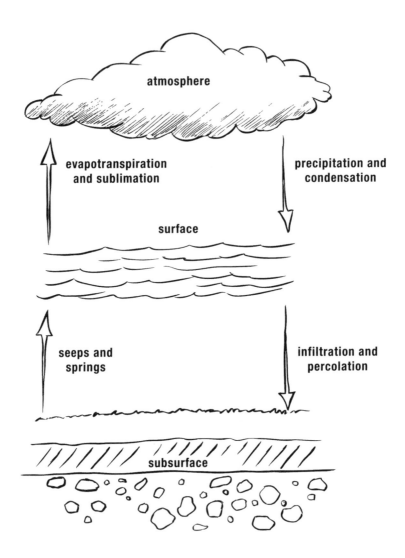

The water cycle consists of the three storage reservoirs and the paths of communication that allow the transfer of water among them. The illustration shows the interrelationships among these water reservoirs and the mechanisms that facilitate the transfer of water.

that exist to transfer funds from one reserve to another ensure a dynamic balance among these storage reserves.

The direction of water exchange is not always equal or constant. The water cycle is dependent on and affected by many factors, such as climate, weather, and geographic characteristics. For instance, in arid regions, there may be long gaps between periods of rainfall. Sometimes the recycling of water takes place over thousands of years, as in the case of water frozen as ice in glaciers and then returning to streams slowly as meltwater. Other times the cycle is very fast, such as when rainwater falls into a river one day and evaporates back into the atmosphere the next.

The Atmospheric Water–Surface-Water Relationship

The water cycle can best be understood by considering the interrelationships between two reservoirs at a time. This section looks at the relationship between atmospheric water and surface water, and the next section examines that between surface water and groundwater.

The atmosphere can store a large amount of water in the form of vapor or humidity, which can be transferred to the surface through precipitation that falls into the catchment, mostly in the form of rain or snow. Condensation also introduces a smaller amount of water into the catchment. This water can either remain on the surface as runoff, eventually entering a surface waterway, or join the subsurface water system by infiltrating through the soil and percolating downward under the influence of gravity to join the groundwater reserve. Many factors dictate how much water soaks in and how much becomes surface runoff. The amount and intensity of the precipitation are two important ones. If the soil becomes saturated, any new precipitation is more likely to become surface runoff. If the precipitation falls faster than the soil's ability to absorb it, surface flow will increase. The slope of the landscape and the presence or absence of vegetation also influence the ability of the water to infiltrate to the deeper layers. The soil composition of the catchment is another factor in water transfer. If it is hard and nonporous, the water is more likely to remain as surface runoff. If it is looser and more porous, the water can infiltrate and percolate into the deeper layers. If this happens, the water will pass from the surface-water system and enter the groundwater reservoir.

One early July afternoon, I was fishing the Green Drake hatch on the Elk River in British Columbia. The Elk winds between the jagged peaks of the Canadian Rocky Mountains, and the surrounding terrain is rough and rocky, with very steep slopes. I had just begun to fish when dense, charcoal-colored thunderclouds appeared from out of nowhere and made their menacing march up the valley in the abrupt way that seems to typify weather changes in the mountains. I hunkered down in the cover to ride out the squall, which arrived with all of the subtlety of a freight train. The gusty winds, driving rain, and dime-size hail had me a little worried. Being a flatlander, I half expected to see Dorothy go flying by with Toto. But the storm was over as quickly as it had begun, and I made my way back to the river and was soon fishing again, with sunshine peeking through the dissipating clouds. It seemed that the sides of the surrounding mountains took the brunt of the bad weather. I could still see misty sheets of rain pouring out of the black clouds farther up the valley. Before I could cast a dozen times, the water turned a muddy brown. The river had risen sharply and rapidly, and now it churned and raged against its banks. The torrential rains along the expanse of the mountainside had sluiced down into the feeders and blown out the river. In a matter of fifteen minutes, it had become unfishable. I left the river and headed to a nearby pub, where I swapped my rod and reel for a beer and burger. Instead of fishing, I spent the afternoon trading exaggerated fishing stories and worn-out jokes with the owner while a baseball game droned on from the corner television.

If that same rate and amount of precipitation had fallen in the watershed of another of my favorite rivers, the Pere Marquette in Michigan, I would have been able to fish the rest of the day. The river is surrounded by deciduous trees with a lot of groundcover vegetation, as well as gently sloping landscape features, so runoff would have been slower. The catchment's loose, sandy soil would have absorbed much of the rainwater, and thus the river would not have been substantially raised. But because of the Elk River drainage basin's steep terrain and hard, nonporous soil, the precipitation immediately washed into the river as surface runoff, and the resultant high water was nearly instantaneous.

Evaporation and transpiration are the two main mechanisms by which water can reenter the atmospheric reserve from surface-water deposits such as streams, rivers, lakes, and oceans. *Evaporation* is the means by which water is changed from a liquid within the surface-water reservoir into a vapor that joins the atmospheric bank. This can occur at any interface between air and water. There is a constant recycling of water over the oceans, where rain falls in one area and water evaporates back into the atmosphere in another. During the process, energy is absorbed, which serves as a thermoregulatory mechanism to cool the remaining water.

The moisture that reaches the soil as precipitation may begin to infiltrate into the soil, but some of it never reaches the groundwater layer. Before it can percolate very far, some of that water is absorbed by the roots of trees or other vegetation. Plants use a portion of the water that they absorb to sustain their life and growth, but some of it makes its way back into the atmosphere through release of water from the surface of foliage, called *transpiration*. Their leaves cause most plants to have a large amount of surface area exposed to the drying effects of sunlight and air, and much

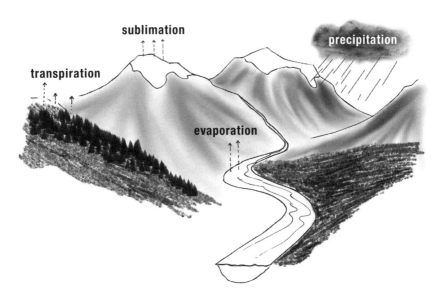

The water on the surface is in a constant state of exchange with the water in the atmosphere. Fresh water falls as rain or snow onto the surface landscape or waterways and returns to the atmosphere as water vapor, where it condenses to form clouds, which then repeat the cycle in the form of precipitation.

of the water that is absorbed by the roots is released back into the atmosphere by water loss from the surface of the leaves.

During the drying process, evaporation can also occur from wetlands and areas of saturated soils. This combined water transfer from the catchment back into the atmosphere is often called *evapotranspiration* and includes the release of water from evaporation from the surface water and the saturated soil as it dries and transpiration from vegetation. In some ways, this portion of the water cycle is akin to the respiratory cycle. Water enters or is "inhaled" into the catchment in the form of precipitation or condensation, and it is "exhaled" back into the atmosphere through the processes of evaporation and transpiration.

Some of the water that enters the catchment may be intercepted before it can either join the surface-water system or infiltrate through the surface to the groundwater reserve. When water enters the catchment in the form of rain, snow, or other forms of precipitation, some of that water never even reaches the soil. It can land on the leaves of vegetation, from which it can evaporate back into the atmosphere without ever contacting the soil. This most commonly occurs when snow is held in the boughs of coniferous trees such as cedars. It reenters the atmosphere as water vapor directly from the solid state of snow or ice. This transformation from a solid directly to a gas is known as *sublimation.*

Water can also be intercepted in its movement within the catchment by the formation of ice, snowpack, or glaciers, thus temporarily preventing it from joining either the surface or subsurface water system. This condition can last for a short period of time, as in the case of snow or ice accumulation on the ground or in the boughs of trees, which can be released in the spring thaw, or for thousands of years, as in a glacier. Although the water can reenter the atmosphere through the slower process of sublimation, most of it is released during the meltoff. The seasonal release of intercepted water can combine with spring rains to add a significant amount of new water to streams and rivers during the thawing period.

The Surface-Water–Groundwater Relationship
Below the surface of the land, successive layers of soil become increasingly saturated with water. The deeper the layers, the more water-saturated they become until the water table is reached, at which point the layers are fully saturated. This is the groundwater reservoir. Groundwater is typically held within the fissures, cracks, and spaces in porous rock formations in this layer.

Because of gravity, water moves within this saturated zone as it follows the natural slope of the terrain. Since the natural pitch is toward the bottom of the drainage basin, this subsurface flow often leads to rivers or streams, where this water can enter these waterways through seeps and springs. Subsurface flow can also occur during the infiltration process if the water encounters a layer that is hard and nonporous as it descends toward the groundwater layer. The nonporous rock prevents deeper penetration at this point, so the water flows along these interfaces, following the slope or pitch of the geographic land features toward the bottom of the drainage basin, where it may join with surface-water systems

Groundwater is replenished through the process of infiltration from the surface, which links it to the surface-water system. When rain falls on the soil, some moisture soaks through the surface layers and percolates downward to join the water table. Water also percolates through the bottoms of rivers and may continue its descent into the groundwater. The layer of substrate just below a river is saturated with water and interconnects with the water table. This layer, called the *hyporheos,* is alive with bacteria and other organisms and is a miniature ecosystem in its own right.

Within a catchment, gently sloping hills with trees and grass that discourage surface runoff promote infiltration and are groundwater recharge

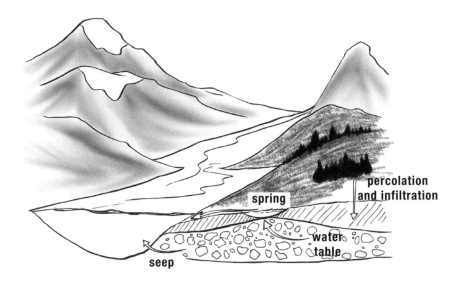

Water infiltrates the soil and percolates downward from the surface under the influence of gravity to recharge the groundwater reservoir. It returns to the surface at points where the water table discharges water in the form of seeps and springs.

areas. The loose, porous soils of recharge areas allow the rain that falls to soak into the soil. Gravity causes the water to percolate downward through the upper layers and eventually join the groundwater reserve.

Water returns to the surface from the groundwater reserve through springs, seeps, and subsurface flow in discharge areas, which are usually located along the valley floor in close proximity to the river. When the flow erupts to the surface as a single point, it is called a spring, whereas a flow that originates from multiple points is a seep. Seeps and springs can occur adjacent to the stream and trickle into it as a tributary, or they may erupt through the streambed or banks and contribute their flow directly to the stream. Since the temperature of groundwater is usually relatively constant from season to season, seeps and springs that join the river are important locations for fish during seasonal extremes when the river's water temperature is outside the normal comfort range for trout. In winter, when the rest of the river is too cold for comfort, groundwater input infuses warmth; in the heat of summer, when the water in the stream is too warm for trout, seeps and springs offer cool locations where the fish congregate to find relief. Seeps and springs offer trout more comfortable water conditions during the temperature extremes of the seasons and can be fish magnets in locating trout at these times.

The Constantly Changing River

The next time you visit your favorite river, consider a single drop of water in your hand. That drop of water in the river today may have been in a passing cloud or a groundwater rock formation the day before. Or, depending on where you are fishing, the drop of water may have even been trapped for thousands of years in a glacial formation or icepack.

Your drop of water might have fallen as rain or snow directly into the river. As such, its character might be slightly more acidic than the rest of the water in the stream. If it did not have contact with the soil in the drainage basin, it would not have acquired any of the compositional characteristics typical of the geology for that region. If, however, the drop came from surface runoff, it might have carried sediment and organic debris into the river. If it came from groundwater, it would likely be free of debris but would be influenced by the geological characteristics of the catchment.

If you were to follow that single drop of water in the river, from the point where it entered the river to the point where it departed, the average time is usually about ten days. Not all of the water in the river goes all the way downstream to the ocean or another body of water. Your drop of water may filter through the bottom of the river to enter the groundwater reservoir, or it may be lost by evaporation from the surface. It might even end up being carried out of the river attached to a fly line or waders. Some of the water flowing past you may have arrived after you did and may be gone before you get home. With all the millions of drops that go into making up the river, and the different origins and destinations of each one, it really is a different river each time you visit. Heraclitus was right—you cannot visit the same river twice!

THE INFLUENCE OF THE REGIONAL CLIMATE

The water cycle is different over the oceans than it is on the land. Since the oceans cover about 70 percent of the earth's surface and store about 97 percent of the surface water, they are an integral part of the water cycle. Over the oceans, there is a continuous cycle of exchange with the atmospheric water stores through evaporation and precipitation, and this cycle can be very short. Often the water moves back and forth quickly and frequently. Water may be falling in one area of the ocean, while at the same time in another area, direct sunlight and dry air are evaporating the water back into the atmosphere.

The water cycle over land is in a continuous state of exchange as well, but here the cycle may be a bit slower. Percolation and infiltration are also slower processes. Water continues to move but may reside in one reservoir for a longer period of time. If it is trapped in a glacier, it may not move between reservoirs for a significantly long time.

Within any geographic area, water moves from one reservoir to another, but not always in the same direction, at the same time, or to an equal extent. There is a global balance of water but tremendous temporal and spatial variation. *Temporal variation* describes the erratic variation in precipitation amounts from one season to another or between one year and another. In fact, water movement may be predominantly in one direction for prolonged periods. During a long wet period with heavy rainfall, which infuses a surge of new water into the surface-water supply, the movement of water will seem unidirectional. The ground may remain soaked, with standing water in low areas and depressions. The rivers may reach bank-full stage, completely filling their channels to the level of the banks, or overflow to produce flood conditions. Once the weather conditions change, much of this water will return to the atmosphere through the process of evaporation.

Spatial variation in the water cycle refers to the differences between geographic regions, such as a desert climate compared with a temperate rainforest. The local climate affects the movement of water from one reservoir to another, and the area streams and rivers are likewise affected. One river can differ tremendously from another just a short distance away if they are in different climates.

On a recent trip to the state of Washington, I was playing hooky while my wife attended a professional seminar in Seattle. I had a couple days to myself, so the first morning I drove east from the city and spent the day fishing in a few mountain streams in the Cascades. The native cutthroat trout were beautiful, already starting to show their fall colors that early September day. I wandered up and down a small stream all afternoon, enjoying the cool, misty mountain air. The stream cascaded down the rocky mountainside, forming plunge pools below each drop. Most of the streambank was blanketed in the shade of the forest, but I found a boulder in the sun and sat down to enjoy the moment. It had been a chilly day and the sun felt good.

The next morning, I was awake early and on the road again. By the time the sun was up, I was in Ellensburg having breakfast. After the requisite visits to the local fly shops, I was on the river. By 9:30 a.m., I was sweating from the heat, looking for a spot to rest in the shade. It was only an hour's drive between the mountain stream in the Cascades where I'd spent the previous afternoon and the Yakima River in Ellensburg, but in that short distance the climate changed dramatically. Instead of the lush terrain of the Cascade Mountains, the Yakima River valley was a semiarid landscape.

And how different the two rivers were! The small cutthroats that were abundant in the mountain stream were replaced with rainbows. The Yakima River was bathed in sunlight and was much warmer than the mountain stream just a short distance away. The two rivers fished entirely differently as well. The Yakima River trout were holding in deeper water in any sparse shade that was available, whereas the cutts had been in shallow water taking dry flies.

As a result of the influence of the climate, the water cycle in a wet region is different from that of an arid one, such as a desert. A wetter region has more precipitation and greater humidity, which reflects the increased amount of water stored in the atmosphere. The rivers here have a more consistent rate of flow from season to season, with new water added more frequently by precipitation. And because the air is more humid, there is less evaporative water loss from the streams.

Conversely, in the arid climate typical of most deserts, precipitation is scant and infrequent, temperatures are hot for much of the year, and the rate of evapotranspiration is high. The plants in these areas are those that can survive under these conditions, which favor those with less surface area exposed to the sun and thus have reduced water loss, such as cactus and yucca. Deciduous trees, with their numerous flat leaves, are generally absent. The scarcity of rainfall and high rate of evaporative loss have a tremendous impact on the lotic ecosystem. There is a large seasonal variation in flow volume of desert rivers, with surges following periods of precipitation. Some small desert rivers may be active only a few months of the year. Thus the desert streams in the Southwest differ greatly from the streams in the wetter climate of the Pacific Northwest, not only in their water cycle characteristics, but also in the way the water cycle affects their thermoregulation. For instance, since arid regions have a high rate of evaporation, desert streams stay cooler through the heat transfer that occurs during the process. This helps maintain a lower temperature than would otherwise be possible and allows organisms to exist in rivers that would otherwise be too warm. Nevertheless, with the exception of tailwaters, most desert rivers are too warm for trout.

INFLUENCE OF THE WATERSHED ON WATER MOVEMENT AND CHARACTERISTICS

The stream and its valley have an intimate relationship, and they need to be considered together. The river is an extension of the geographic region it serves and is influenced by the geologic and geographic characteristics of the watershed, both in the way the water moves through the terrain features and in the composition of the water. Environmental biologists say that "the valley rules the stream." Rivers vary in many respects, including their sources of water input, rates of flow, bottom composition, riparian (shoreline) habitat, mineral content, chemical composition, and thermal behavior, all of which are influenced by the surrounding drainage basin. These factors also cause them to be favored by different species of insects and even different types of trout, and thus you need to fish them differently.

The movement of water within a drainage basin is dictated by the terrain features of the watershed, including degree of slope, types of vegetation, and soil characteristics. Once the water enters the river system, the slope of the bottom of the river is the largest determinant of current speed and flow. Where the slope is gradual and mild, rivers flow slowly. Rivers located in mountainous terrain, on the other hand, flow faster. Wild whitewater rivers are not typically found in flatter landscapes. A bucolic stream flowing through the gently rolling farmland of southwest Wisconsin, for example, will be different from a small mountain stream in the Great Smoky Mountains in eastern Tennessee.

Water that enters a stream has been influenced by the organic and inorganic characteristics of the catchment from which it flows. Thus the character of the water reflects the geologic constitution of the valley. Each geographic area is unique from a geologic sense in terms of subsurface composition and soil characteristics. These features affect the clarity, turbidity, and composition of the water of the area's rivers, which in turn have an impact on insects, fish, and other organisms. The inorganic composition of the catchment influences the organic composition and population of a stream, which includes all living organisms and is referred to as its *biomass.*

The inorganic aspects of water governed by the catchment include its hardness, acidity or alkalinity (pH), mineral content, and chemical composition. Watersheds that are composed of igneous bedrock such as granite tend to impart a lower, more acidic pH to the rivers and streams. In watersheds that are predominantly based on sedimentary substrate, such as limestone, the rivers have a more alkaline pH. The famous limestone rivers of Great Britain and Pennsylvania typically have a high pH. The types of vegetation in the area also influence the pH. For instance, hemlock trees increase the acidity of the soil and hence the watershed's streams and rivers.

Water hardness and pH have a powerful influence on trout and insect populations. Hard-water, alkaline streams are able to support a higher biomass than soft-water, acidic systems. There's also a difference in the insect species each type of water supports. Streams with harder, more alkaline water tend to be favored by certain insect species, most notably mayflies, which are abundant in this type of stream. These conditions also create a more favorable environment for trout. One study on brown trout showed a much higher rate of growth under alkaline conditions with harder water. The differences in trout growth patterns are probably due to the variation in biomass. As a result, these streams may also have different sustainable populations of fish than would otherwise be possible. Streams with softer, more acidic water tend to be better tolerated by stoneflies. That's why a typical Pennsylvania limestone stream with hard water and a high pH, such as the Letort, is drastically different from a western freestone river.

Several years ago, I visited the Letort for the first time. Not only did I want to visit the home waters of many of the pioneers of angling, but I also wanted to compare a limestone stream to the midwestern and western rivers with which I was most familiar. At first glance, I have to admit that I was underwhelmed. Not that the river lacked beauty or fishability, but it was not what I had expected. It was a typical central Pennsylvania limestone stream, pleasant but unprepossessing and understated. Perhaps I had anticipated encountering notable anglers stalking the banks, carrying notebooks filled with wisdom and knowledge as they snapped pictures of riseforms and tested different presentations. Perhaps I expected to at least feel the presence of fishing legends or see the shadows of giants.

On closer inspection, however, the true character of the Letort came to light. It supported a much higher biomass than I had encountered previously in other rivers. The amount of aquatic vegetation was surprising. It was so thick in some runs that the current had cut channels through thick beds of watercress. It would be difficult to drift nymphs through entire sections of the stream without tangling in the plants, and the multiple channels through vegetation created threads of competing currents for dry flies. Even though the bottom was soft in many sections, the water remained clear and free of turbidity. I was also amazed at the amount and diversity of aquatic insects.

It was a day well spent. I never encountered the ghosts of anglers past, but I fished their home waters and fooled a few trout. I walked the shores where they had walked. I left with an appreciation for the tremendous variation among rivers. I would like to say that I experienced firsthand the larger trout often found in hard alkaline water, but the fish I caught that day were not very big. But my observations of the Letort in comparison to

The soft-bottomed stretches of the Letort are nearly choked with vegetation in many places. The high pH of a limestone stream is capable of sustaining a much higher biomass than streams with a lower pH.

the western rivers I was accustomed to reinforced the fact that each river is unique, because each valley is unique and the valley rules the stream.

The organic composition of a stream is also affected by the watershed's character in terms of vegetation type and density. If the surrounding landscape has large numbers of deciduous trees, there will be a seasonal influx of organic debris in the autumn when the leaves drop into the water. Surface runoff will also carry organic material from the catchment into the river during heavy rain, but if the surrounding landscape is grassy, the amount of runoff will be reduced.

WATER MOVEMENT AND THE SHAPING OF RIVERS

Once water has entered the lotic ecosystem, it begins to move downhill across the surface of the terrain according to the topographic features of the landscape. Any time water begins its journey from an elevation higher than sea level, it is loaded with potential energy that reshapes and remodels the terrain through which it travels as it flows back to the ocean. Just as a fully cocked and loaded crossbow stores energy that is let loose when the arrow is sent flying, the water in rivers contains energy that is ready to be unleashed in the process of its downhill trek. The higher the elevation from which a river flows, the greater the energy. During the time of transit, this energy creates hydrological force that is released in the course of the journey and is fully discharged when, back at sea level, the potential energy has been completely exhausted.

The hydrological force of a river is a powerful instrument of change. Not only does it help create features and habitats in the river that help sustain trout populations, but it also has the power to move mountains. One of the most impressive examples of the power of moving water is the Grand Canyon, carved out over thousands of years by the relentless hydrological pressure created by the Colorado River.

Potential energy is the energy of possibility. It's a little like having a million dollars to spend. Before you begin to spend it, you have unlimited possibilities and the needed resources to effect change. You can do a lot with that much money, and there are a lot of options as to how you might spend it. If potential energy is similar to the sum of all the things you might do with that money, kinetic energy might be viewed as the process of actually spending it. *Kinetic energy* is the energy of activity, and a stream's energy can be spent in a variety of ways—by creating new channels and meanders, carving out new pools, remodeling banks, undercutting the terrain to create new turns and curves, picking up sediment from an area to create riffles, or scouring out a softer area to create pools. Over a long time period, a stream might carve a canyon out of solid rock. The type of investment a river makes in these various activities depends on its type, the character of its substrate (bottom), the nature of its flow, and its location with respect to sea level. Thus the kinetic energy is the spending of a river's potential energy over the extent of its journey to the sea.

Every stream spends some of its potential energy to form its own channel by erosion, especially during floods or high flows. It carves out the streambed from the substrate over which it flows. As the volume of flow increases, the erosive and remodeling power also increases. During these periods, the stream may carry large loads of sedimentary material suspended in the water. Surface runoff washes much of this sediment into the stream. This suspended material may include soil, silt, sand, or clay from the landscape within the watershed. The rest of the sediment comes from the stream's own bed and banks, scraped away by the erosion of the stream's substrate by the hydrological force. The transport of this bed and bank material from one site in the river to another is important for creating and modifying fish habitat. Through this process, the stream makes its own changes.

Much of the remodeling of rivers and streams happens during floods or high-water conditions when the force is increased so much that in the worst cases bridges are washed out, houses are removed from their foundations, and cars are swept off of roads. The flow of water always has the ability to move material in the current, but any time water accelerates or flow increases, the capacity to move material from one place to another also increases. Usually the materials that are transported in the flow arise from the riverbed and banks, as the water lifts and carries rocks, sediment, and other debris from one section of the river to another. This remodeling process is called *bed-load transport*, and the greater the hydrological power of the river, the larger the sediment size and load it can transport. During periods of peak flow, even larger rocks and boulders can be moved, but as the river loses energy in the process of this work, the flow decelerates and power diminishes, and the material that has been lifted is strewn downriver and deposited according to its weight, size, and coarseness. In other words, the transported material begins to drop out of the current as the flow loses force, starting with the heaviest material, followed by the next largest in succession, and so on until all of the energy is exhausted.

Depending on the type of river system, the hydrological force of change can reshape and remodel the river in several different ways. Lowland, alluvial rivers that flow over softer soil tend to form series of bends and turns that are called *meanders*. Rivers at higher altitude that flow over hard bedrock show a pattern of remodeling that is characterized by the repetitive creation of riffles and pools. Most rivers display both sets of characteristics at different points along their course.

Meandering Rivers

Alluvial rivers are typically lowland streams flowing across a flatter landscape at or near sea level. They course over the layers of soft sedimentary material that they deposited previously, especially during floods or high flows. As rivers descend from their initial higher elevations in the hills or mountains, they often become or join with slower-moving alluvial systems near the confluence with the ocean. Sometimes these rivers form extensive deltas, with channels and branches that enter into the ocean separately. The rivers carve and recarve these alluvial plains as they alter their courses. In this type of river system, the hydrological force of moving water tends to create meanders, where the river loops back and forth.

The hydrological principles that govern how a river meanders also regulate the distribution of food in a river, which in turn affects where trout like to hold. Knowledge of current dynamics along river bends will aid in

A meandering river has a repetitive pattern of loops occurring at a consistent frequency that varies according to the width of the river. On wide rivers, the loops are wide and lazy. ED AUSTIN/HERB JONES PHOTO

your fishing strategies. Knowing where to fish is as important to success as knowing how to fish. The greatest angler in the world will strike out if his fly is swimming in a stretch of water that doesn't have any fish in it.

These lowland rivers generally have soft banks and bottoms that are easily eroded. This kind of river erodes the outer banks of its channels, creating accentuated, exaggerated bends and a wider river valley. The course is generally convoluted by twists, bends, and sharp turns that can nearly double back on other sections of the river. During periods of flooding, the old channels may be filled in with new sedimentary material, and new channels can be cut in the surrounding landscape that was previously terrestrial habitat. Meandering rivers seem, at first glance, to travel to and fro with no apparent rhyme or reason.

Under closer examination, particularly when viewed from an airplane or on a map, you can see that these meanders are not random. The loops have a consistent frequency of repetition, appearing at the rate of twelve or so times the cross-sectional width of the river. Thus larger, wider rivers have longer loops and bends, with fewer of them per river mile. Narrower rivers have more twists and turns within the same distance, and they are tighter and closer together.

A narrow stream has a series of tight switchback meanders with exaggerated loops that occur at high frequency. JIM PEACO PHOTO

So what causes these rivers to meander? It seems to be an inefficient way to get from point A to point B. Wouldn't a straight line following the greatest angle of slope be the simplest course in obedience to the law of gravity? There are several theories as to the exact mechanism that starts the meandering process, but once a river begins to meander, the power of erosion and bed-load transport takes over, which exacerbates the meanderings and creates additional river features.

The most likely theory as to why rivers begin to meander is based on the movement of water. Water and every other fluid move with a waveform nature and a variable frequency, just like radio signals and light. The frequency and oscillations of water movement begin the meandering process. Even under controlled conditions, the flow of water is not uniform. Many factors can disturb the uniform flow of water, such as the inherent instability of fluids in motion, which tend to pulse or vibrate as they travel. These vibrations are often due to shear stress at the point of contact with the air or another border, such as the banks of a river. This causes the flow to have a ripple or pulse, which eventually begins to resonate at one common frequency that depends on the river's width. Even on glacier icefields, as the sun warms the surface of the ice and rivulets of meltwater collect into larger flows across the surface, the channels that the water cuts into the ice tend to loop back and forth in a frequency relative to the width of the channel. The next time it rains, watch the rivulets track down the windshield of your car—they also tend to loop back and forth.

In a river, over the course of time, these oscillations in water movement cause the water force to strike against the banks at opposing points along the river. At the points of impact, the current erodes that section of the bank. This widens the channel of the river at the points of contact, as the river slowly begins to reshape itself according to the frequency or oscillation of the water movement. As the water swings outward into these newly widened channels, it is redirected more effectively toward the contact point on the opposite side just downriver. These new current paths continue to widen the bends of the meanders into the pattern we recognize.

The meanders are accentuated by centrifugal force over the course of time, forming bends in the river that begin to loop back and forth. Because of centrifugal force, as the water bends around the outer banks of a curve, there is an increased velocity in the corridor of the current adjacent to the outer bank. As it gains momentum, the increased force erodes the outer bank and deepens the bottom in this current pathway so that this becomes the main channel for current flow. The outer current path around the bend thus becomes the deepest part of the river. Just as centrifugal force sends a

The oscillations during the flow cause the water to strike repetitively against the same point on one side of the bank, which begins to widen it outwardly through erosion. This redirects the water toward a point on the opposite bank that is downriver of the first point by a factor of the river's width. In this manner, the meanders form to match the original frequency of oscillation.

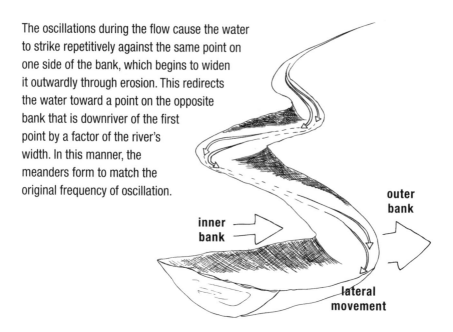

outer bank

inner bank

lateral movement

luge or bobsled high along the outer curves at the Olympics, the water also lifts as it sweeps along the outer bank of a curve. This occurs to such an extent that if a level line were stretched across the river at the bend, it would be obvious that the water level is higher along the outer bank relative to the inner bank.

As the water strikes the outer bank in the curve, most of it flows around the bend. The effect of centrifugal force causes some of that current to be directed downward toward the bottom of the river, immediately adjacent to the bank. When this downward water flow reaches the bottom, it is redirected along the bottom toward the inner curve of the bend. This creates a crosscurrent near the bottom of the river that travels from the outer bank toward the inner bank. Once the water reaches the inner bank, it rises to the surface and is redirected back toward the outer bank, which results in a crosscurrent at the surface of the stream that returns water to the outer bank. This forms a helical current in the deeper outer channel as the water bends around the curve, with the current traveling toward the inner bank along the bottom of the streambed and toward the outer curve along the surface. Imagine a Slinky toy that is pulled apart and then bent in a gentle arc. The wire spirals around and around as it bends around the curve. The current behaves in a similar manner.

This helical current lifts sediment that has been eroded from the undercut outer bank and carries it along the bottom of the stream toward

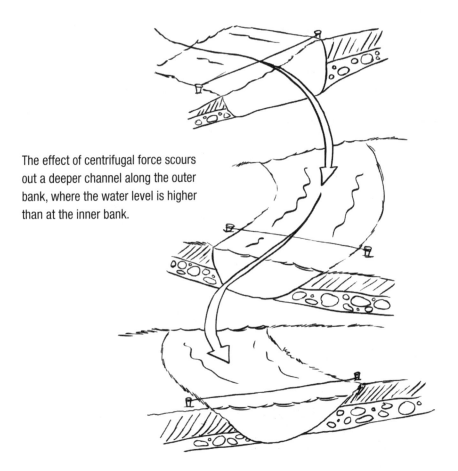

The effect of centrifugal force scours out a deeper channel along the outer bank, where the water level is higher than at the inner bank.

the inner bank, depositing it there. This combination of the buildup of sedimentary material along the inner bank of the bend and undercutting of the outer bank widens the bends and loops, further exacerbating the meanders. By the powers of erosion and redistribution, the channel pulls the river in a lateral direction at the curve, deepening the bends and causing the entire river to move laterally.

These helical currents create challenges for the angler. Dry flies on the surface are pulled toward the outer bend of a curve in the river, whereas weighted flies on the bottom drift toward the inner bend. These cross-currents also tend to concentrate food items toward certain areas in the river, both along the surface and at the bottom, and fish distribute themselves in the river along and after these bends according to the current seams and the channeling of food. The helical currents also cause a drift boat to float toward the outer bank at a bend in the river. Rather than track around the curve, the boat tends to move in a diagonal line toward the outer

The helical current that is created by centrifugal force as the water moves around a bend removes material from the outer bank and deposits it along the inner bank, deepening the channel at the outer bank while at the same time widening it laterally. The inner bank becomes shallower as a result of the deposition of this material, which also moves it laterally in the same direction as the outer bank. The movement of both banks laterally accentuates the meanders still further.

bend while still moving downriver. The oarsman has to row away from the outer bank to prevent the boat from grounding along the outer shore.

This current variation can continue for a short while downriver after the bend before it dissipates in the general flow. The helical current can concentrate food on the surface along the outer shoreline at the tail end of a curve and for a short stretch downstream after the bend. Look particularly for boulders or structure at the end of the bend or immediately after it to create a depositional zone where the current sweeps out the trash, so to speak. This can be a great place to throw a dry fly after a spinnerfall because of the concentration of dead insects in these areas. Crippled or dead emergers also can collect here after an emergence.

The initial stretch of the deep main channel in the straight section just after a river bend is a good place for nymphing. The area along the inner edge of this channel has received the crosscurrent deposition of materials and food particles that have been loosened by the erosive action of the water on the outer bank of the bend and funneled to this current seam along the inner edge. Trout take advantage of this depositional zone as an ideal spot to get an easy meal. Since this is often a deep trough, you may

Because of helical current, there is often a concentration of floating debris along the edge of the outer bank at the last bit of a bend and on the initial straight section that follows. Flotsam, foam, and insects accumulate in these depositional zones.

have to fish deeper. This is a great place to try a San Juan Worm, since the erosive effect of the current frequently dislodges worms and grubs from the soil, which the helical current then transports to this zone.

Through bed-load transport, much of the suspended material that was scraped from the outer bank of the river bend is deposited downriver in the straight section immediately following the bend, as the water loses momentum and energy after the remodeling process. The deeper channel created along the outer bend continues and crosses over the center of the riverbed as it prepares to follow the outer bend along the next curve in the river. As it crosses over, the current loses momentum and the ability to carry sedimentary material in the straightaway, and the rocks, loose gravel, and other material that the current picked up at the bend during the process of erosion begin to fall out of the suspended load of the river, creating crossover riffles. This explains why riffles are much more common in the straight sections of these rivers and seldom occur at the bends, while the deepest water is often found along the outer banks at the bends. Referring again to the photo of a meandering river, you can see the crossover riffles in the straight section and the deeper water along the outer banks at

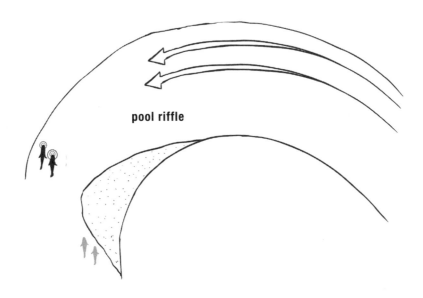

pool riffle

The outer bend of the river becomes a depositional area on the surface. After the inner bend, there is frequently a gravel bar or sandbar along the bottom, behind which is an area that collects food material from the crosscurrent. Both are depositional microhabitats and common feeding stations for trout.

the bends. The eroded outer bank at the river bend is clearly visible as is the shallow water along the inner bank.

The crossover riffles are composed of gravel and rocks that have been strewn out after the bends, having been dislodged by the current and then deposited here as the current slowed. The heaviest and largest boulders and rocks occur in the upstream portion of the riffles, with gradually smaller material as the stream flows downstream through the riffles. The finest, softest material is the last to drop out of the current as the river slows. *Downstream fining* is the term used to describe the transition from coarse and heavy substrate at the head of riffles to very fine material at the end.

The remodeling process leads to the formation of a main channel of deeper water that meanders back and forth within the river. Again, its path can be compared to that of a luge sled, riding high along the outside curves, crossing over in the straightaways, to wind up on the outside track going into the next bend. In the river, the channel that is the primary path of flow is called the *thalweg*. It is the deepest section of a stream and is like the river's superhighway. You will usually be able to identify the thalweg in most sections of any river. Sometimes in broad, flat riffles or slow glides of uniform flow, the thalweg may seem to span the river's entire

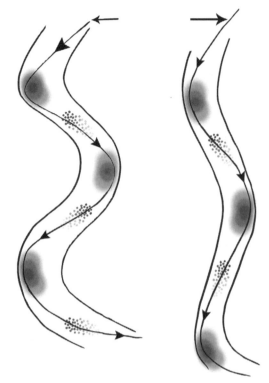

The thalweg wanders back and forth between the stream banks, following the same path as a luge sled at the Olympics riding high around the outer banks at the turns and crossing over in the straight sections. Deeper pools form at the bends and cross over riffles in the straight sections. Downstream fining is also shown with a coarser substrate at the onset of the riffles and a finer composition at the end.

width. But even in these sections, there is often a channel that can be identified as the thalweg.

Since the thalweg is the main conduit between the upper and lower sections of the river, it often carries the most food in its flow. Trout are aware of its significance, because often the best feeding lies are stationed along its path. Any constriction or choke point in the thalweg, such as a funnel or chute between boulders, creates an ideal lie for trout. Such points of restriction tend to narrow the feeding lane and concentrate fish along the edges in the short downstream section immediately following.

Interestingly, the rivers of the Northern Hemisphere tend to erode chiefly on the right side, whereas those in the Southern Hemisphere erode on the left. Although he was not the first person to investigate the cause of meandering rivers from a scientific point of view, Albert Einstein was certainly the most famous. In a 1926 article, Einstein described the hydrological forces that dictated the formation of meanders in rivers. He not only addressed the question of why they meander, but also went on to explain the difference between Southern and Northern Hemisphere rivers. The variance between the two hemispheres relates to the earth's rotational

This photo shows the crossover riffle between two bends in the river and the deepest part of the channel, the thalweg, following the outer bank at the curve. The riffles have been created by the deposition of debris in the straight section.

effect on centrifugal force, which Einstein explained by use of calculus, and even if he were here today to explain it to me in person, I would still not understand it.

Riffle-Pool Rivers

Riffle-pool streams and rivers generally occur at elevations well above sea level and are characterized by greater slope, as measured by the drop in elevation per unit of distance that the river travels. These streams often flow over a harder layer of bedrock, with a bottom substrate that is generally composed of rock, gravel, and sand. Many freestone rivers are of this type. Rather than traveling across soft, sedimentary material that can easily be remodeled into meanders, these streams often follow routes that are dictated by the layers of underlying bedrock, following the path of least resistance as directed by gravity, and therefore these rivers are less likely to meander. Their hydrology is more likely to produce a repetitive series of riffles and pools, spaced at a relatively even distance.

Called the *riffle-pool sequence* by biologists, the pattern can be seen in aerial photos as a repetitive cycle of alternating sections of shallow riffles

A riffle-pool stream follows the path of least resistance, and rather than repetitive meanders, it has a regular pattern of riffles and pools. The frequency of repetition in the riffle-pool pattern is a function of stream width, just as it was in the pattern of meandering rivers.

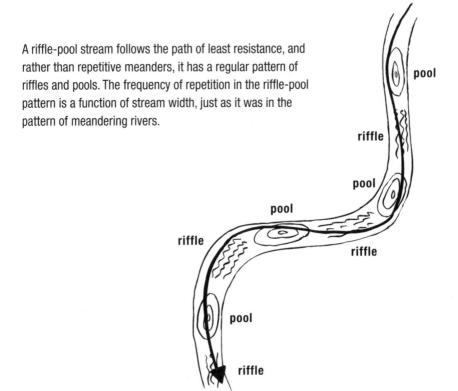

and deep pools, generally along the straight sections of river, separated by longer stretches of flat, less featured water. The frequency of this pattern is a relatively stable factor of five to seven stream widths apart.

Similar to meanders, the creation of the riffle-pool sequence also results from the hydrological force of erosion and bed-load transport. In its haste to return to sea level, the lowest-energy state in which it can exist, the water accelerates over certain sections of the stream, even without a corresponding change in slope. As it does, the water gains momentum and force until it has the power to erode the bottom, scraping off the finer sediment and carrying it along in the current. Through bed-load transport, the material that has been lifted will be strewn downriver and deposited according to its weight, size, and coarseness.

As the finer bottom material, such as sand and silt, is removed, the coarse substrate underneath is exposed, creating sections of riffles. At the head of the riffles, the bottom is characterized by large rocks that were too heavy to move or were only minimally transported. The riffles continue as the water accelerates, transferring more of its potential energy into kinetic

Streams with hard bottoms show a repetitive series of riffles and pools interspaced at a frequency that is five to seven times the width of the river.

energy, until it either gains enough momentum to scour out a depression in the substrate or encounters a softer bottom where it can scour away enough material to create a deeper pool, where it expends the remainder of its energy. It takes a great deal of energy to move the substrate. Through this process, the water exhausts its store of energy and momentum, which results in a long section of relatively slower-moving water after the tailout of the pool. The sedimentary material that the current picked up during its peak flow falls out of the water along the bottom of the pool and the section of river immediately downstream of it. This deposition of fine material creates a soft-textured bottom to the pool, especially near the end, and the flats that often follow.

As part of the bed-load transport process, the hydrological force of the river tends to concentrate the relocated material according to its size. Bed-load transport and the sorting of finer material in pools and coarser material in riffles has to do with shear stress. The highest shear stress occurs in the riffles, where the finer material, unable to resist this force, is washed away; it is then deposited in the pools, where the stress is lower. This happens not only as the river slows, but also at the point where it accelerates, as it picks up the finest sediment first, followed by the larger material as the current gains momentum and energy.

The next time you stand in a riffle, notice the consistency of the size of the rocks or gravel along the bottom. If you move to a different section, even within the same riffle, the size of the substrate may change from the previous location, but the size of the individual rocks will be uniform in the new area. You usually don't find gravel mixed in with softball-size rocks. The gravel will have been deposited in another area where the river lost momentum and its energy levels began to ebb. As a result of the loading and unloading of sedimentary material in the water flow, the substrate in the various zones within the riffle has been sorted according to size. Boulders and large rocks may occur at any point in the riffles and add variation to the uniformity of the substrate. These heavy objects may have emerged through the erosive action and been too large to transport. Neither is all of the fine sedimentary material removed from riffle habitats. Some is deposited in the backwater protection behind these boulders. These depositional microhabitats are fish magnets. After this energy-consuming activity of remodeling the stream, the water transits through slow sections of flats. As it does, it begins to store up the potential energy to repeat the process. Once it has reached sufficient momentum and strength, another sequence of riffles and pool formation begins.

In many rivers, the channel tends to be about 15 percent wider in the riffle section than in other areas, because of gravel bars—concentrated areas where coarse materials are deposited—that divert the flow against the outer banks. This process tends to carve out a wider channel at the riffle areas, while the rest of the sections of the stream remain unchanged in width. Since riffles occur most often in the straight sections of the river at the crossover point of the thalweg, the main channel can be split or braided, making it difficult to identify. Even when it is not split, riffles can become so broad and shallow that identifying the thalweg can be nearly impossible. In this case, look closely along either bank. Often one section has become deeper than the rest of the riffle. This is the thalweg, and it may very well be the most productive fishing stretch in the entire riffle.

The erosive forces working within these two river types—alluvial and riffle-pool—are powerful instruments of change and responsible for much of the variation in the lotic ecosystem. The hydrological power of the current is able to redistribute substrate material within the stream. Whereas alluvial rivers meander laterally, riffle-pool rivers are often described as meandering vertically, as the bed of the river undulates over sections of shallow riffles and into deeper pools, creating a stream bottom that alternates between shallow and deep.

Although the effects of erosion produce predictable results and patterns in the rivers we fish, nothing in nature is ever totally predictable. Variation is the name of the game in the lotic ecosystem. Every boulder, rock, log, or other obstruction can deflect the current and make new twists and turns.

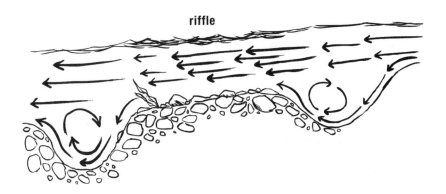

riffle

The undulation of the streambed in a riffle-pool river is often described as vertically meandering, because it changes in depth between riffles and pools. If viewed longitudinally, the streambed undulates or meanders up and down.

Change in the bottom substrate, new structure, or a sudden change in the slope of the streambed can form new riffles and pools. Riparian structure can create choke points. All of these situations and more add variation to rivers and streams. The next time you visit your favorite river, study the flow of water. Do you see a pattern of meanders or a riffle-pool sequence? Or do you see features of both? This will tell you how that particular section of the river has spent its energy in the remodeling process and the creation of fish habitat.

Longitudinal Zonation

Near the headwaters, the stream produced by its various water sources is vastly different than the river that eventually joins the ocean. Along its course, it changes in character and composition. The variation in the stream as it travels from its headwaters to its end is called *longitudinal zonation*.

At the beginning, where it occurs at the greatest altitude that it will achieve, its appearance is more representative of the riffle-pool sequence, with the bottom substrate features and erosive patterns typical of this type of stream. At its headwaters, the stream may have only a small trickle of flow. Through the addition of new water or the confluence of other tributaries, the flow increases along its course. Near its discharge, it may have joined with other waterways to become part of a larger river that terminates in an alluvial system. At this point in its course, it flows over a softer substrate with a more gradual pitch and is now a meandering river. Along the way, it may have areas where it gradually transforms and shares characteristics of both types of rivers.

The inorganic composition of the stream changes along its length, influenced by the land through which it flows or by other waterways joining it. The organic character of the stream also can vary a great deal as the water flows downstream. At the headwaters, the amount of organic content is usually lower, but this changes rapidly with the addition of organic material from the catchment. This variation affects the resident insect populations, and the upper reaches of the river support different insects than the lower reaches. Often filter feeders, such as net-spinning caddis, are the first to appear in the stream, with mayfly herbivores and shredding caddis appearing a bit farther downstream. As the river continues along its course, it becomes more organically diverse and the biomass tends to increase. The temperature and oxygen levels in the river can differ between the upper and lower stretches as well. This variation in the lotic ecosystem, even within the same stream, can be dramatic. This is part of the reason why some reaches of the stream can support trout, while other parts, often farther downstream, cannot.

Because the composition, temperature, and biomass of the river vary greatly from the headwaters to the lower sections, trout size and species and the presence of other fish may vary from one section of the river to another. The upstream waters may support brook trout, as is the case with the North Branch of the Au Sable in Michigan. This upper section is ideal habitat for these fish. Downstream, in the main river, brown trout flourish but brookies are scarce. With the larger biomass in the lower portion of the river, the browns in that area can get pretty large. At the ends of many rivers, trout species have disappeared and are replaced with warm-water species such as bass and catfish.

The first time I visited the Deschutes River in Oregon, I had long read about this fabled river and envisioned myself catching monster trout on the rough and untamed river. But when I met my guide for the day, he told me that because of the hot mid-August temperatures, if we were going to have a chance at catching any fish, we would have to fish the upper part of the river. During the long drive, I watched the river transform from the mighty river of my imaginings to a small, stone-strewn stream, which was beautiful but much different than the lower section. The guide was right, and we did catch a fair number of trout that day, but in a much different river than I had anticipated. Because of the effect of longitudinal zonation, even a river like the Deschutes has places where an angler can wade across comfortably.

Microhabitats

Besides the large-scale creation of habitat such as riffles, pools, and flats, the current also causes small- and medium-scale changes that break down the larger habitats into smaller segments called *microhabitats*, further diversifying the ecosystem.

Microhabitats can be dramatically different from one side of a boulder to another. The current blasts its full force on the upstream face of a boulder, discouraging most insects and vegetation from this area, although a few species of hardy plants and organisms can flourish in this environment. Behind the boulder, backeddies produce a pocket of calm water where there is often a recycling current that collects sediment and food particles. Certain species of insects gravitate toward these depositional microhabitats in search of the rich organic material found here. Trout, too, prefer these zones for feeding lies because of the concentration of food, the insects that dwell in this microhabitat, and the ease they find in the

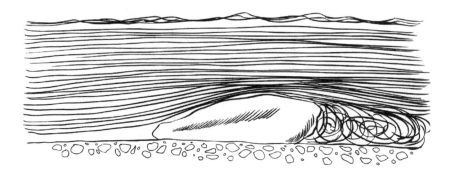

Behind rocks, boulders, and other obstructions are quiet backeddies that become depositional microhabitats. Silt, organic debris, and organisms such as insects are often whisked from the streambed in upstream reaches of the river and collect here.

current-protected location. Look for some of the best feeding lies for trout to be in depositional microhabitats within riffles and runs.

Microhabitats also form where detritus, leaves, and other organic material collects in areas along the river's course, often in backwater regions. These depositional zones, found in the slack water behind eddies or where material accumulates in logjams or other obstructions, attract certain species of insects and other organisms that break down this organic material. Many immature aquatic insects are detritivores, which, like miniature garbage disposals, feed on and break down the detritus and organic debris from other organisms. They flourish in these depositional zones.

ADAPTATION TO CURRENT AND SPECIES SPECIALIZATION

The current is the defining characteristic of lotic ecosystems, and the resident organisms have had to either adapt to its presence or find areas of the ecosystem where the effect is minimized. The result is a high level of species specialization, where the various organisms are highly adapted to their ecological niches. The rich variety of habitats and microhabitats created by the current within the lotic ecosystem allows for specialization of the diverse species that live along a river's course, so that each is ideally suited to its surroundings and fills its particular niche.

The current is a strong force that has shaped and molded the entire ecosystem. Trout and every other species living in the river have adapted and evolved according to the influence of the current. Those species that have successfully adapted have been able to thrive in this ecosystem and found a specific niche. Those that were not able to adapt were eliminated in the natural selection process. Other selective pressures were at work as well, such as predation culling the less wary trout from the gene pool, but the current created by the flow of water is the dynamic force that drives the constant changes and is responsible for the variation of habitats in rivers and streams.

Because of species specialization and the creation of niches, organisms are not uniformly distributed throughout the ecosystem but are concentrated in their preferred habitats. In other words, because they have adapted to specific habitats, they are found most commonly in these areas and less frequently in others. This concept applies to insects and trout alike. Many anglers have drawn the same conclusion when they state that 90 percent of the trout are in 10 percent of the water. The challenge for us as anglers is to know which part of the river is the right 10 percent. And compounding the situation is temporal heterogeneity, which means that the right 10 percent of the river on one visit might not be the same 10 percent the next time you visit the river. Aquatic insects and other invertebrates also are concentrated in their specific habitats, and as with trout, 90 percent of any particular insect species are probably found in 10 percent of the habitat. Many factors dictate trout feeding patterns and subsequently their location, such as variation in light from daylight to nocturnal conditions, season of the year, and food availability and location.

Because of the diversity of habitats in the ecosystem and the fact that each species has evolved and adapted to fill a particular niche, anglers can predict the location of certain insects within the stream according to their habitat preference. For instance, certain net-spinning caddis species need current for their survival and are frequently found in riffles. Other species of caddis have developed ways to thrive in areas with little or no current. Stoneflies thrive in faster current, as do clinging species of mayflies. Their flatter bodies reduce exposure to the current, allowing them to remain attached to the substrate where other species would be swept away. Burrowing mayfly species, such as the giant Hexagenia, prefer the soft bottom of flat, slow-moving sections of the stream. In this material, they can easily construct the burrows that are essential to their life cycle. Although Hex nymphs are good swimmers, you won't find them in fast riffle water unless they are there by accident, having been displaced and entrained in the current. In each case, these organisms have modified their behavior or evolved morphological (physical) characteristics in direct response to the current or the way it has shaped the ecosystem.

At the bottom of the food chain are single-celled organisms such as diatoms and algae, which are easily carried in the current. More complex aquatic vegetation has also adapted to life in the current. Most of these plants, unable to thrive against the full-force current of the riffles, have found suitable habitat in the flat sections of the river, with their slower water and softer bottom.

Trout have also adapted in response to the current. They are as familiar with their surroundings as you are with your own living room. As anglers, we seek a quarry that has evolved under the current's constant presence. Trout have also developed morphological characteristics and behavioral modifications to be well suited to life in the current. Their streamlined, muscular bodies are ideally designed to maximize efficiency against its force. Their fins and tails are engineered for aquatic propulsion. Even their feeding and reproductive behaviors have adapted to the effects of current.

In order to improve your angling success, you also must adapt to the current and take every aspect of its influence into consideration, from the way it has shaped the ecosystem to the effect it has on trout. It also affects the quality of your presentation of the flies you offer to tempt the trout. The current usually works against your presentation, not only when fishing dry flies, as has long been understood, but also when fishing below the surface. You must fully understand the effects of current in order to develop effective strategies to catch fish.

Chapter 2

Laminar Flow

A ngling involves salesmanship and duplicity: we offer a product that promises one thing but delivers another. Like the snake oil salesmen from long ago, we are trying to sell the trout something they're not sure they want by making hollow promises we won't keep, knowing full well that they're sure to be disappointed with the sale after it is completed. It's a tough sell, especially considering the wariness of our customers. Our goal is to make the offering so promising that it is irresistible.

Several factors affect the credibility of the merchandise we offer. Certainly, selecting the right fly as to color, size, profile, and type is important. But even more important than fly selection is the art of presentation, offering the fly in a manner that realistically portrays and mimics the natural insect. Often this is what seals the deal. An appropriately chosen yet poorly presented fly has less chance of success than an imperfect match that is well presented. One of the greatest detriments to presentation is an unnatural appearance or behavior of the fly. Most commonly, the unnatural effect is created by the current and the physical characteristics of water movement.

The movement of water has inherent properties that tend to degrade your fly presentations. When water moves in any manner, its velocity is not uniform. It is affected by friction wherever there is contact or an interface with any other surface. Whether water flows through a pipe, streams down the windshield of your car in a rainstorm, or moves as a river, friction alters the uniformity of the flow.

When you turn on a faucet in your home, the water moves as a circular column of flow inside the pipe that carries it to the faucet, filling the

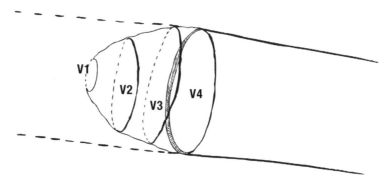

This illustration shows the layers of water that move at various speeds as it moves through a pipe. The velocity is strongest at V1 and slowest at V4, with a gradual transition of velocities in between.

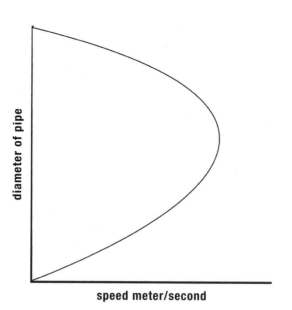

As shown in this graph, the water in the central zone, unimpeded by the force of friction, is moving at a faster speed than the layers of water near the inner wall of the pipe, where friction has slowed the velocity. This results in a circular column of water that has a three-dimensional shape resembling the nose of a bullet. The longitudinal velocity profile, when viewed in two dimensions, would be represented as a parabolic curve.

volume of the pipe. The friction from contact with the inner surface of the pipe slows the speed of the water at the edges of the column, while the water in the center of the pipe has less impedance to flow and moves at a faster velocity. Surrounding the central core of fastest-moving water are concentric layers of progressively slower-moving water, similar to the rings of an onion; this layered effect is called *laminar flow*. At the outer layer, where the water contacts the inner wall of the pipe, the effect of friction is the strongest and the water moves the slowest.

The effect of friction creates parallel layers of different velocities within the forward-moving water, which is characteristic of laminar flow. Even though all the water is still moving in the same direction, there are multiple velocities depending on the zone in which the water is traveling. If the speed of water movement is displayed as a graph, with speed indicated along the bottom in meters per second (m/s) and the cross-sectional width of the pipe along the vertical axis, the resulting curve represents the longitudinal velocity profile for the water movement.

Even though the movement of water in streams and rivers differs greatly from the movement of water in a pipe, the principles of laminar flow still apply. The effect of laminar flow in streams, with the variations in current velocity it creates, has consistently been one of the greatest obstacles for anglers to overcome and a challenge for newcomers to the sport. Many angling techniques have been developed to overcome its adverse affects, including different casting adjustments and corrections to presentation.

THE MOVEMENT OF WATER

The speed of the water, or current velocity, is measured in units of distance the water travels in a given unit of time. The standard unit of measurement is meters or feet per second. The total amount of water that is moving past any given point along a stream in a given length of time is known as the stream's *discharge*, measured in cubic feet per second (cfs). It takes into account both the amount of water as determined by the cross-sectional area of the waterway and the velocity at which the water is moving. Whereas current velocity measures only the speed of movement, discharge involves both the velocity and the volume of water that is moving. Larger rivers have higher rates of discharge than smaller streams, even though a smaller stream may have a greater current velocity. This is due to the river's larger width and depth. For tailwaters—rivers formed by the outflows of dams— the amount of discharge is determined by the amount of water that is released by the dam. These rivers can have dramatic fluctuations in discharge independent of natural causes such as precipitation.

There is longitudinal variation in the discharge of a river from its beginning to its end. Thus a river can present different challenges to the angler at different points along its course. Just like my experience on the Deschutes, it can almost be like fishing different rivers. What initially is a small mountain brook can be a significant river later. The discharge near the headwaters is usually less than near points of confluence with other waterways or the ocean because of subsurface flow and tributaries adding to the total volume as the river flows. Weather conditions that influence melting of water from glaciers, rates and frequency of precipitation, and regional temperature and humidity all affect the discharge of the river in a particular watershed. Since current and discharge are inherently linked, these factors also influence the strength of the current in the river. All of these factors determine the nature of the river you face as an angler.

Gravity causes water to flow downhill and thus imparts movement to the water in rivers and streams. Once moving, its natural tendency is to remain in motion, flowing downhill as it makes its way to the lowest level possible, eventually to merge with other waterways or bodies of water. According to Newton's first law of motion, however, an object in motion tends to stay in motion with the same speed and direction *unless acted upon by an outside force.* In this case, as in the pipe analogy, the outside force of friction impedes the downhill flow of water in the river. As the water flows over the substrate, along the banks and over the streambed, friction is created at the point of contact between the water and the substrate. Thus two opposing forces are at work here: gravity causes the water to flow downhill, while friction impedes it in its downhill journey. Just as with the water pipe analogy, friction slows the flow of water in the layers adjacent to the point of contact. As a result, the water in rivers and streams are governed by the same principles of laminar flow that also dictate the movement of water in a pipe, with layers and current threads moving at different speeds, sliding past one another.

If we look at an idealized stream from above, the interface that occurs as the water contacts the banks on either side produces friction. This impedes the flow of water exponentially closer to the shoreline. In the center of the idealized stream, the water is unimpeded by the effect of friction from the shores, so it moves at the greatest velocity. The velocity of the water decreases gradually as it approaches the bank on either side. Near the point of contact with the shoreline, the velocity is almost zero.

Just as in the pipe analogy, on a graph the horizontal velocity profile is a curve. The center of the vertical axis of this graph is the center of the idealized stream, with one bank at the top and the other bank at the bottom.

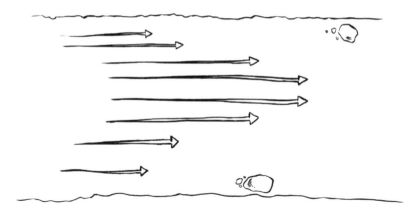

This overhead view of the stream shows the effect of friction that slows the water near the banks. In the center of the stream, the current is unchanged by the effect of friction and will be moving at the greatest velocity.

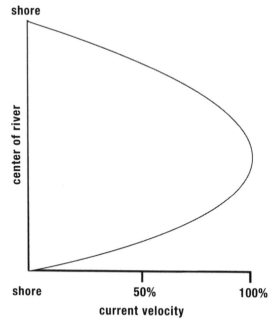

At the top and bottom of the vertical axis is the bank on either side of the stream, and the distance between these two points represents the total width of the stream. The stream velocity is displayed along the base line of the graph and is shown as a percentage of the maximum current speed. This will be different for each stream or river. If it were not for friction, all the water in the stream would be moving downhill at the same rate of speed.

On the horizontal axis, the speed of the current is indicated. In a real stream, however, the thalweg wanders from side to side between the riverbanks, and as a result, the fastest current thread may not always be centered as shown here.

In the idealized stream, the water section with the strongest current is in the center. The velocity is greatest here and drops off precipitously near the shoreline, with a sharp zone of transition between the two. This is the *slip seam*, where currents traveling at two different speeds slip past one another. This basic current profile holds true for any stream or river, but it will vary slightly according to the location of the thalweg, speed of the current, and characteristics of the banks. These horizontal laminations of different currents and slip seams have dire consequences to angling presentation and performance whenever you have to cast across them.

Many factors introduce variation into the horizontal velocity profile. The deepest part of the river is not always centered between the banks, depending on the location of the thalweg, and thus the strongest current may be to one side of the stream or the other. As a result, the horizontal velocity profile may be skewed away from the center. At bends in the river, the thalweg is compressed and is shifted closer to the outer bank of the bend; here the current in the main deeper, outer channel will be swift, while the flow along the inner bend, where the water is shallower, will be slower. In such cases, the greater disparity between the currents results in prominent slip seams and creates angling challenges if your presentation needs to cross these seams.

Around some sharp bends, there may even be current reversal. This may be evident toward the end portion of the bend, where the water moves upstream along the inner bend in the river. This is common whenever there is a sharp bend in a section of the river with fast overall flow. This is frequently a depositional microhabitat and creates feeding stations for trout. Sometimes the current reversal can be highly developed enough to create a small whirlpool with a circular flow.

At different current speeds, the horizontal velocity profile changes. With faster currents, the profile is a sharper curve. This results in a dramatic difference between the slowest-moving water in the buffer zone and the swift water in the main current. The slip seams are narrower and sharper, with a greater differential velocity on either side of the seam. The transitions are more drastic and abrupt than those in slower water. Crossing this current seam with a dry fly would indeed be a challenge requiring a great deal of adjustment and skill.

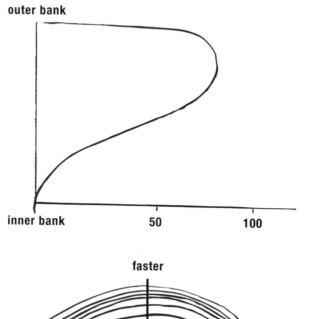

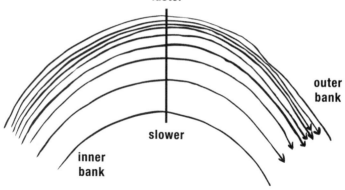

The velocity profile at a bend in the river shows the fastest current at the outer bend and slower current near the inner bend. Here the thalweg follows the outer bank, whereas along the inner bank the water is shallower.

With slower currents, the velocity profile is a gentler curve. In this case, the difference between the fastest water in the center of the flow and the slower-moving water at the margins is less drastic. As a result, the transition zones or seams are broader and less obvious, sometimes marked only by the concentration of foam or floating debris. Note that there is less difference between the fastest and the slowest velocities. A fly line lying on the surface in a section of water with this type of horizontal velocity profile will require fewer adjustments to achieve an ideal drift.

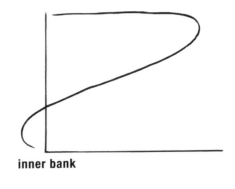

inner bank

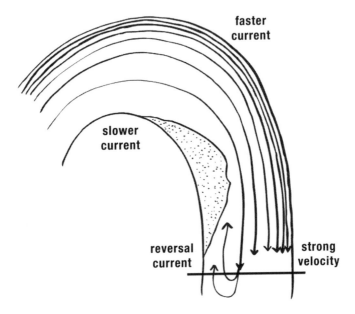

There may be current reversal along the inner bend, where the water travels upstream in a direction opposite to the general direction of flow of the river. In this illustration, the negative velocity to the left of the vertical axis on the graph represents upstream or reversed flow.

Since friction is the cause of the laminar flow of water, any factor that increases the friction will influence the dynamics of the current. More friction results from a substrate that is coarser and rougher than from one that is smooth and even. This occurs when the banks are broken and irregular. Rocks, boulders, logs, or other structure along the banks increase friction and its hold on the passing water. This extends the buffer zone of slower water toward the center of the stream and moves the current transition or

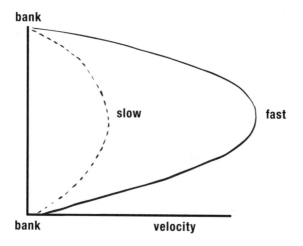

The horizontal velocity profile for rapidly moving water is shown in bold, and the velocity profile for slower current is shown as a dotted line.

slip seam farther away from the bank. It compresses the thalweg into a narrower width and usually carves out a deeper channel to accommodate the main flow of water, which then has an increased velocity. The resulting slip seams are more dramatic as a result of the sharper contrast between the currents.

This type of situation, with the concentration of current into a narrow area by the extension of the buffer zone, creates ideal habitat for trout. Optimal feeding lies are created on the edges of the thalweg and along the bottom of the trough wherever there is a break from the current, such as a rock, other structure, or depressions along the bottom. The compression of the thalweg also concentrates and funnels food material, so it becomes a feeding lane to the trout lying in wait in the current-protected feeding stations. Fishing this type of area, with its strong current differentials and prominent slip seams, is challenging, and you must often move to overcome the competing elements working against your presentation.

Sections of the river with smooth banks have less influence from friction. The buffer zone is thinner in width and closer to the shore. The current seams may be less obvious and less likely to offer ideal feeding lies for trout, unless other features are present. Without structure or other habitat features, this type of water has little to offer trout in the way of desirable feeding stations.

The discussion so far has been considering an idealized situation. Pure laminar flow is not a natural occurrence, however, because of the presence of turbulence. The random, mixed, and chaotic activity of turbulence tends to disrupt the integrity of laminar flow. Nevertheless, the features of laminar flow are still present in the movement of water in rivers and streams, and you need to understand them in order to make adjustments to your presentations to maximize their effectiveness. Although they may be blurred by the influence of turbulence, the seams of differential water movement occur in every section of the river.

DIFFERENTIAL VELOCITIES AND DRAG

Trout enhance their chances for survival and improve their rate of growth by maintaining the best net balance of energy. From the earliest point in their lives, trout seek the easiest meals, with the highest rate of energy return for the lowest energy investment and exposure to risk in the process of obtaining it. In order to accomplish this goal, they must maximize their energy input and minimize their energy expense when feeding. The less energy they expend in feeding, the more net energy will be available for growth. Nature's selective process favors the most efficient. Individuals that fail to meet this goal will be unthrifty and poor competitors compared to trout that are more successful. Therefore, trout have developed feeding behaviors that favor efficiency. They have learned to gravitate toward the current seams, where they can hold in the slower current, conserving energy by not fighting the stronger, faster current while they peruse the food offerings it delivers to their doorstep.

Since to trout, the thalweg is like a conveyor belt carrying food, they often establish feeding lies along its path. Current seams that offer protection from the force of the current but proximity to the thalweg are ideal to trout, and you need to target these areas when fly fishing. The zones of transition between the swifter current and the buffer zone of slower water are the current seams that anglers have come to recognize as ideal fish habitat. In order to catch these fish, you frequently must cast across these threads of different current velocities. As soon as you do, however, you encounter one of the most common problems in fly fishing: drag.

Drag is caused by the unnatural influence of the leader or line on the fly. It refers to the loss of the random, unrestricted movement of the fly that is characteristic of the natural, free-floating insects we try to imitate. The goal is for your fly to drift as if it were uninhibited by the presence of the leader or the fly line and influenced only by the whims of the current and random motion; it should behave as if it were completely untethered.

The best way to understand drag is to look at a common fishing scenario, where you want to fish a fly in a slow current but must cast across

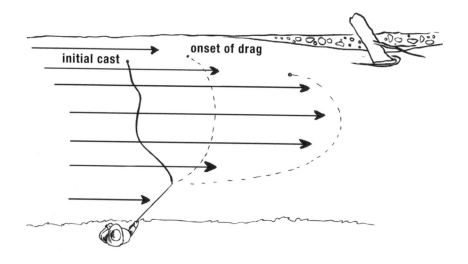

After the cast, drag occurs as the line assumes the shape of the horizontal velocity profile. Even though drag is most often manifested as an artificial speed of the flies relative to the current in which they are traveling, the effect of drag on the fly is not always visible.

faster currents to do so. When the line passes over and lies on the surface of the stream and crosses the different zones of variable velocity produced by the laminar flow of water, it assumes the curved shape of the horizontal velocity profile. Once the current eliminates any slack in the line or leader, drag results. This drag pulls the fly out of the ideal current thread and causes it to accelerate unnaturally relative to the movement of the water in which it is drifting. Once this occurs, your fly will now travel at the speed of the fastest segment of current and will look less like a free-floating insect and more like a miniature Jet Ski.

Since drag occurs anytime the flies move differently than the current in which they are traveling, you can also get drag when you cast across slower water into faster currents. In this instance, the opposite will occur, with drag preventing the fly from drifting naturally at the faster speed.

In some instances, the influence of drag can be subtle and difficult to detect, especially from a distance. Even when the flies are moving at the same speed relative to the immediately proximate current, there can still be interference with the random, capricious movement of the fly or its orientation on the water. To accurately portray the natural insect, the fly may have to follow small surface eddies and current variations. You may not notice these, but they may have a devastating effect on your presentation.

Any amount of tension on the leader inhibits this ability. No matter how slight, the effect of drag compromises the presentation.

In most circumstances, how you present the fly is more important than which fly you present. Certainly, there are times when trout are feeding selectively, focusing on a particular food item, and may refuse other types of imitations. But more often than not, trout are less discriminating as to the type of food they will accept and are more opportunistic.

There must be slack in the leader to avoid the influence of drag, but the balance between too much and too little slack is hard to achieve. On the one hand, you need to have enough slack to avoid drag, but too much will delay hook sets and strike detection. An excess of slack is what often accounts for beginner's luck. My first attempts at fly fishing were blessed with good fortune—I got a lot of hits! I failed to land them all, however. Disbelieving the fabled "beginner's luck" theory in favor of what, at least to me, was a more appropriate explanation—namely, my natural fishing prowess—it seemed to me that I was destined for greatness. Often my luck was so strong that the fish would actually try to bite before I was even ready. It seemed as if they wanted to jump right on my hook. My fishing buddies, well versed in the ways of beginner's luck, told me of its fickle favor and even laughed a little at my high regard for my newfound skills. I failed to see the wide, loopy casts that they certainly noticed, and hence I disregarded their mirth. These lazy casts produced piles of slack on the water. Beginner's luck actually had little to do with it. My poor casting technique resulted in an abundance of excess line on the water, which at least initially produced a drag-free drift as I frantically tried to gather the slack and regain control of the line. I got a lot of strikes, but the piles of slack that ensured a dead drift also condemned me to many failed hook sets.

Most of the strikes occurred while I was still pulling in the excess line. Once I had gathered all the line, this actually spoiled the drift, because I did not mend frequently enough after that point to maintain an ideal drift. So the only time the drift was free from drag and the trout were interested was while I struggled with the slack. It seemed to me that the trout had a sixth sense that told them I wasn't ready, so they chose that time to hit, but in reality, it was only during that part of the drift that I had truly tempted them.

After I improved my casting a bit, I actually caught fewer fish. I was casting better, more accurately, and greater distances, but I seemed to have lost my touch. I was really into showcasing my new casting skills, trying to dazzle my friends with the longest cast I could muster. Once the fly hit the water, however, I lost control of the drift. A drag-free presentation was out of the question, because the effect of drag was immediate, and it was impossible for me to mend with that much line on the water. It wasn't until I learned to eliminate the drag through proper line control that Lady Luck seemed to smile on me once again.

Dealing with Drag

Drag is not always the archenemy of presentation. In fact, there are times when you can use it to enhance the sale of your flies to the trout. Wet flies and streamers are often used to imitate an insect or baitfish that is swimming in the water. Employing the drag from the current and giving a twitching pulse to the rod can imitate these situations effectively. Skating dry flies on the surface or imparting motion to nymphs at the end of a dead drift are other examples of using drag from the current to add animation and movement to imitations. When nymph fishing, pausing at the end of the dead drift will cause the flies to tighten to the leader and elevate in the water column in the lifting style that James Leisenring made famous.

In most cases, however, you want to eliminate drag as much as possible. It is important to predict the onset and amount of drag in order to overcome its influence on presentation. Once the fly is affected by drag, at best it becomes unacceptable to trout and at worst it sends them fleeing away, reluctant to return to their feeding activity. Many trout have been put down by inept presentations. Before you cast to a rising fish or promising holding water, you need to have a strategy in mind for dealing with drag. The amount of drag you will encounter depends on the horizontal velocity profile for that section of the current and your position relative to the target. Try to predict the amount of drag by the current speed. If the current is swift, the effect of drag will be greater and quicker to develop than in a slower section of water, according to the shape of the velocity profile. Less correction for drag is needed in slower water, whereas in the faster part of the river, you need to be prepared to make adjustments early and often. Once you determine the current speed, you can then use in-air or on-the-water mends to defeat drag.

As your first means of adjusting for drag, you should consider moving to a better position from which to make a cast if possible. Changing your location is an effective method of reducing drag that is often overlooked by anglers. If a trout is rising in a place that is difficult to approach, simply move to a spot from which a presentation is easier. If you anticipate a large influence from drag in a particular approach to a target, study the situation to determine whether there is an alternative position from which to cast that will allow a presentation with less drag. It does require a little intellectual and sometimes physical exercise, but I like the problem-solving challenge it entails. If a fish is rising or I want to present a fly to specific structure or cover that likely harbors feeding lies, I analyze the situation before making the first cast. I select the most advantageous position by anticipating the amount of drag the cast would receive from each location. This can involve moving and maybe even crossing the stream. Repositioning often provides the best opportunity to offer an ideal presentation with a minimal influence of drag.

Casting from a location directly above or below the target has an advantage in that it allows the line, once it settles on the surface of the water, to lie in a thread of water that is moving at or near the same speed as the fly. If you can eliminate the zones of dramatic transition and avoid crossing sections of multiple current velocities, you can greatly reduce the influence of drag. A little excess slack should still be introduced into the line to allow for minor variations in current speed, but by avoiding casting directly across the current, the line needs less slack than if it were passing directly across multiple current seams.

This lesson was reinforced to me on a trip with my family to Rock Creek in Montana. We drove from Missoula and made our camp at the public campground along the banks of Rock Creek. The stream is postcard picturesque as it sprints down the rugged terrain. We had stopped at the fly shop by the interstate to stock up on flies and information before we made our way up the winding road to the campground. The early August sky was washed-out blue with faint whispers of clouds. The fly-shop owner had assured us of an evening caddis hatch, so we set out at a leisurely pace. My son, Evan, and I headed to the river while the girls set off on a hike in the woods.

Rock Creek shall forever be known in our minds as Slippery Rock Creek. From the moment we entered the water, the slimy, slick, rounded, rolling rocks challenged us to stay upright in the strong current. Evan, ten years old and a whopping 75 pounds, was only one of many victims of the precarious footing. He had walked just a short shout upstream from me as I set up to fish a promising run. I had no sooner made my first cast than I looked up to see him pass by, bobbing in the current like a cork. He gave a nonchalant little wave and an unabashed smile. In his other hand, he still clutched his fly rod. Being a smart-alecky sort of kid, he asked me how the fishing was. Being a concerned father, I asked if he needed any help. He replied that he had it under control. With the complete fearlessness of a ten-year-old, he crawled to his feet, got up, and kept on fishing. He wasn't even very wet because, with his small frame, the wader belt was just below his armpits.

The caddis hatch arrived as promised. Soon a nice trout was rising in a backeddy behind a log across from where I was fishing. Separating us was a wide run of fast water. I could cast that far, but I would never be able to mend that much line in time to hold the fly in the backeddy where the trout was feeding. I tried anyway. I cast a few times, but the current whipped the fly out of the eddy before it could tempt the trout. With total disregard for my efforts, the trout keep feeding. He was so confident in his invulnerability that he didn't seem to notice my poor attempts at mends and reach casts. This I took as an affront. Or perhaps it was his disdain of my skills that offended me. Either way, I was determined to catch this fish.

I walked downstream until I found a slower area where I could manage to wade across the river, wobbling my way through the water over the slick rocks that tried to dislodge me. I soon made my way back upstream to the trout, which was still nonchalantly feeding in rhythm, overconfident of the superiority of his position and inaccessibility. I approached him from directly below where he was feeding, so that my line would lie over the slower water close to the shoreline instead of crossing the fast current as it had when I cast from the other side. The cast was easy from this position and landed gently on target. After a pause that made me think that my journey had been for naught, the trout took my fly. Experience must have taught him to wait a moment before attacking to see if the fly was just an artificial that would suddenly zip away.

It was the only fish I caught that entire afternoon. Evening had fallen by the time I had released him and made my way downstream to where I could cross back over. It gets dark pretty fast in the mountains. The stream crossing had been merely treacherous in the light of day, but it proved unmanageable in the dark. Slippery Rock Creek claimed another unfortunate victim on my way back across the stream. Evidently, it is more difficult to wade at night—another lesson I learned there.

Even if you cannot position yourself to be directly up- or downstream of your target, repositioning can at least provide you a better angle on the fish. The approach most influenced by drag—and therefore the most difficult from which to properly present—is the cast directly across the stream. If you can move somewhat up- or downstream from the target, some of the potential drag can be alleviated. Changing the angle from 90 degrees across-current to 45 degrees up- or downstream can help immensely to reduce the effect of drag. It will also make mending more effective, requiring fewer mends. Before trying to combat drag with slack line, mends, and fancy casts, always assess the situation and determine whether a simple change in position might be the easiest and most effective answer.

If you can't find a better position from which to cast, sometimes you can lift up the line and prevent it from contacting the swiftest thread of current by holding the rod high above the water and over the section of current that is most likely to produce drag. In this manner, you can eliminate the section of current with the strongest velocity from influencing the presentation. It will be easier to maintain a drag-free drift when the section with the strongest current is not affecting the line. An 8- or 9-foot rod held at arm's length can keep the line from contacting the water for quite a distance and thereby eliminate any influence the current might have on the presentation. Often you can reach over narrow runs or sections of faster-moving water to ensure that the line will travel in sections of softer current and not be affected by the drag produced by the rapid current. Many other angling methods have been developed to compensate for drag, including both casting and mending techniques.

Casting Corrections

Any time the cast crosses multiple layers of current, the line adopts the shape of the horizontal velocity profile for that particular section of the stream, and drag results accordingly. In slower-moving water, where the curve is flatter, fewer corrections are needed. In faster water, where the transition zones or slip seams are drastic, more compensation for drag is needed, and a corrective cast can begin the drift in a proper manner and allow you the time to reintroduce further corrections as the drift continues. If you anticipate substantial drag in presenting the fly in a particular situation, you can incorporate adjustments for this drag in the form of mending casts. Thus, when you combine the cast with a corrective mend, the line settles on the surface of the water and initiates the drift with a correction for drag already in place. The basic goal for these casts is to introduce an upstream bow in the line so that the fly lands downstream of the line. You can accomplish this with either reach casts or in-air mends. The current soon works to reverse the arc, from an upstream orientation at the onset of the drift to a downstream bow. The speed at which this occurs depends on the horizontal velocity profile. The correction you have made will delay the onset of drag, or if the velocity profile is gradual, it may be sufficient to prevent drag from occurring throughout the drift.

One type of casting correction I often use, particularly when I have to cast across stronger currents, is a reach cast, which is one type of mending

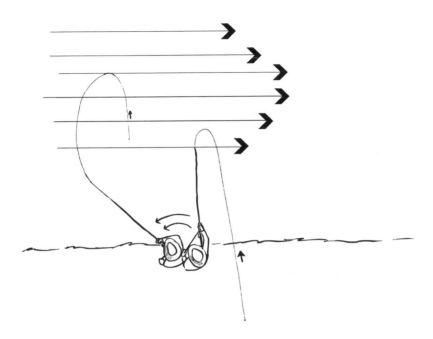

A reach cast is used for a presentation where substantial drag is anticipated. It creates an upstream bow in the line as it settles on the water, in a shape that is opposite to the velocity profile. During the forward cast, as the line unrolls from the angler, the rod hand is firmly and quickly moved in an upstream direction to create an upstream bow in the line, with the fly in a position that is downstream of the line.

cast. The reach cast lengthens the period of drag-free drift before mending is needed. Other casts, such as in-air mends and curve casts, can achieve this same goal. Since the purpose of this book is not to teach casting techniques, but to address the impact of current, I have not included each individual cast by name, but rather by the goal of the method. For simplicity, I have incorporated all the mending casts in the same category.

Another type of corrective cast is known as the pile cast, puddle cast, or stack cast. This cast is used for upstream presentations and introduces a few loops or coils of slack in the leader at the onset of the drift. It seems that every author who has described it gave it a different name and slight variations in the method. According to Lefty Kreh, the cast is directed in an upward manner so that after the line extends fully, it falls gently on the water with slack in the leader. This also gives it a soft landing. The cast is slightly underpowered so that the leader does not reach full extension.

Other methods can accomplish the same goal, including a gentle tug on the line as it reaches full forward extension. As the forward cast is nearing its completion, a light jerk at the end causes the line to spring back slightly and results in a small amount of slack in the leader as the line settles on the water. Sometimes these casting modifications require casting a little farther beyond the target than normally would be needed to allow for the line springing back, which shortens the cast somewhat. Do not send the first cast so far beyond the fish that the fly line splashes on the water directly over his head. This may send him darting for cover.

All of these methods introduce a small amount of slack, which absorbs any slight variation in current speed without tightening the leader to the fly. It is important not to introduce too much slack so that a failed hook set results. You need to achieve a balance whereby enough slack is placed on the water to prevent interference in the natural drift, but not so much that hookups are compromised. This cast or modifications thereof can also be used to fish in a downstream setting, introducing just enough slack to account for minor current inconsistencies.

Often enough correction can be incorporated into the cast to overcome the effects of drag completely, or at least delay the onset of drag considerably. However, if the mending cast does not completely alleviate drag throughout the entire drift, mending the line further can ensure a drag-free presentation until the conclusion of the drift.

Mending

"Mend! Mend! MEND!" You can hear these words from many of the guide boats as they pass by on the river. Mending to correct the fly presentation is one of the first things anglers learn in the sport of fly fishing. It takes experience to know when to mend and how to get it right. Most beginners usually do not mend early or often enough. The word *mend* is uttered so often by guides that it seems to have become their mantra.

One of my earliest fly-fishing experiences occurred when our family spent a week on vacation with another family in the Rocky Mountains of Colorado. It involved a beautiful river, an amazing guide, and a prolific caddis hatch. On the second day, the moms had planned a quiet morning and proposed that the dads take advantage of it. A casual suggestion from the other father, my good friend Dan Pesavento, launched my lifelong love affair with fly fishing. I had fly-fished a couple times previously in Wisconsin, but I'd had no instruction and walked away from those streams in frustration. This was to be my initiation. Little did I know then what we would set in motion that morning.

The first thing that impressed me about this whole experience was the relaxed pace. All of the guides met their parties at the fly shop around 8 a.m., which gave us ample time for a leisurely breakfast and a second cup of coffee. This was in sharp contrast to my experiences bass fishing with my father as a child. He had me up hours before the sun rose, shivering in the dark on an aluminum boat while I ate a breakfast of sticky donuts and drank tepid hot chocolate.

Once we were under way, our guide stopped for more coffee en route to fish the Upper Blue River. I have since come to learn that all fishing guides are caffeine junkies. Back on the road, the guide regaled us with stories of the area's history. He seemed in no particular hurry to get to the river. He told us about the trappers, Indians, and early settlers who lived in the region well before our lifetimes. In a pull-off near the river, he appeared to be wasting more time as he leaned on the side of his Jeep and continued to talk about the geology of the area and how the mountains were formed. It was kind of like listening to a James Michener book on audio, where he discusses a region starting with the Jurassic period. I kept checking my watch, wondering why I was paying this guy for a history lesson. I could hear my dad's voice in my head: "We're wastin' daylight!" It seemed to take forever to string a few rods.

I finally asked if we should get to the fishing. My memory may be a little cloudy on the next part, because I have surrounded this guide with an aura of transcendental powers, but I seem to recall that he looked up at the sun and said, "Nope, we got about an hour before the hatch. Plenty of time to teach you the basics. Then we're gonna catch a lot of fish." Maybe he checked his watch, but viewed through the rose-colored glasses of nostalgia, I like to picture him as squatting to sift the dust through his hand, sniffing the wind, wetting his index finger in the stream and holding it in the air, and then saying, "Relax, pilgrim, there's plenty of time."

"The first thing I'm gonna teach you is how to cast," he said after stringing the rod.

At least I now had a rod in my hand. He was a good teacher, and I was able to get the basics down fairly quickly. It was a nearly perfect morning, with only a light breeze, just right for a beginning caster.

"The second thing I'm gonna teach you is how to mend," he said. This was harder, but after some practice, I got a few drifts that were acceptable. Just about the time I had achieved some degree of proficiency, a cloud of insects began to erupt from the stream, right on time. It was magnificent! I looked at the clairvoyant guide with a sense of awe and wonder. No bass-fishing guide had ever proved so intuitive. We even caught a few fish.

I never saw this guide again and don't even recall his name. But I remember him well. He left a lasting impression on me, and I learned a lot from him that day. I learned to practice patience. I gained an appreciation of the harmony and balance of angling with the beauty of nature. And I learned a bit of history as well. I went to bed that night with visions of wild trout dancing in my head—and the mantra of fly fishing ringing in my ears: "Mend! Mend! MEND!"

The art of mending is an essential skill in fly fishing. It is a technique that you must master in order to be successful as an angler. If casting is the first skill you need to learn, then mending is the second. Appropriate mending will ensure a drag-free drift, whereas inappropriate mending will be nearly as detrimental as no mending at all. At first beginners often have to be reminded to mend. After a while, though, it becomes second nature.

Each circumstance is unique and thus requires different degrees of correction. The need to mend is based on the laminar flow of water, and the frequency and strength of mending is dictated by the horizontal velocity profile. Each mend has to be modified to fit the situation. It is a technique that is developed with experience. As far as the strength of the mend, you don't want to under- or overcorrect. If you overdo it, the fly might be lifted from the water and replaced in a current thread or path that is less desirable. The mend may also produce more noise, commotion, or splashing on the water than is necessary. At first it's difficult to mend the entire line without relocating the fly, usually pulling it toward you, but with practice and patience, you can improve your technique. If you undercorrect, the drag will still be present and all you will have accomplished is to introduce nonproductive slack in the line in the form of a large S curve or double wave. This excess slack will make hook sets more difficult. Mending is an art form that is developed and refined only with experience and patience, as you learn how much to mend without overcorrecting.

Timing the mend properly is as important as your mending technique. You need to start mending before the onset of drag, in order to position the line and leader upstream of the fly before drag can influence the presentation. If you can accomplish this, further mends will require less effort, and it will be easier to maintain a drag-free drift. Once the line develops a large downstream belly, it's hard for even experienced anglers to effectively mend without changing the drift course and relocating the fly into a different current thread. Many anglers, especially novices, wait too long to mend, doing so only after the drift is already compromised. When they finally do mend, they find it difficult and frustrating. If they had simply mended earlier, the whole process would have been much easier.

After the line is on the water, mending is accomplished by lifting the line and sweeping or flipping it to reposition it upstream of the fly. The

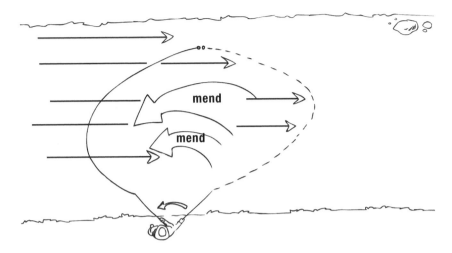

Mending is accomplished by lifting and tossing the line upstream in a rolling maneuver that creates an upstream arc in the line as it lands back on the surface of the water, reintroduces slack in the leader, and allows the fly to precede the line as it continues to travel downstream. The bow in the line created by mending prevents drag from pulling the flies at the speed of the faster current seam.

mended line should have an upstream bow or arc that mirrors the velocity profile, but in an opposite orientation. This bow allows the line to lie in faster water while the fly remains in the slower current, unaffected by drag from the line. If the line is a current seam that is moving significantly faster than the fly, a downstream arc will once again develop and the line will start to overtake the fly. If this occurs, you need to mend again to restore the proper drag-free orientation between the line and the fly. It is important to initiate successive mends before a large belly develops in the line and drag begins to spoil the presentation.

The goal is to mend in such a way as to avoid repositioning or even moving the fly. If the mend is too strong, the fly will be pulled toward you and usually out of the desired drift path. On the other hand, a mend that is not strong enough will not overcome the effect of drag, and the presentation will be spoiled. A shorter cast is easier to mend than a long one. When there is a large amount of line on the water, it's more difficult to lift and reposition the line with an appropriate and effective mend. Most mends of long lines end up being only partial mends that accomplish little in eliminating drag.

The horizontal velocity profile determines the amount of mending you will need to do. Where there is a sharp velocity profile, the effect of drag can be so strong that you need to make a series of mends, called stack mends, to ensure a drag-free drift. Multiple small, rapid roll casts can create a sufficient upstream bow in the line to overcome the stronger current. When mending cannot eliminate the effect of drag, it is time to recast and start over.

Fishing in current certainly creates challenges, but for many anglers, this and the many other challenges in the sport of fly fishing are what make it so appealing. The realization of the impossibility of achieving perfection in our technique keeps most anglers humble, no matter what our skill level might be.

Chapter 3

The Three-Dimensional River

Whereas dry-fly fishing incorporates only two dimensions of the three-dimensional river, with nymph fishing the situation becomes even more complex. When you fish below the surface of the water, all three dimensions come into play and the influence of current is even more profound.

On a Bow River float trip a few years back, I introduced my daughter, Erin, to fly fishing. She had fished a little previously on family vacations, but never in a serious way. When she was younger, she had enough interest to pick up the rod and cast for a while, but her attention would wander before she had a chance of success. She had always been content to spend an afternoon on the river with me, as long as she could do other things. When she was really little, she would splash and play in the water and collect bugs. But those days are long behind us, although I like to remind her of it now and then. A few years ago, however, she agreed to go with me on a full-day float trip. It would be her grand introduction to a lifelong passion, I was sure. All she needed was to catch one fish.

How this agreement came to pass was really quite simple. Like all good parents, I bribed her, though after we were done negotiating, this float trip cost me a great deal more than the actual price of the guide. We had been talking about our annual father-daughter trip for quite a while and decided that Calgary and Banff, in Canada, would be a fun area to visit for a week. We agreed that she would plan the activities for both of us for the first half of the trip, and I would do the planning for the second half. The first day, I found myself hanging around the shopping malls in Calgary, shuffling my feet and drinking expensive iced coffee. The second day, she had us checked into a four-star resort in Banff. We walked the beautifully manicured grounds. We lounged and luxuriated in the spa, where we had hour-long backrubs that cost more than the entire eight-hour float trip. We spent three hours eating tiny but beautiful portions of overpriced food that night. This is what it cost me to get her on that float trip.

Finally, the day of our float trip arrived. I began the morning with nervous anticipation and a little trepidation. I wanted Erin to share my love for fly fishing. If this day didn't go well, it could throw cold water on her lukewarm interest in my favorite sport. I held on to the fervent hope that she would be able to cast her flies far enough to get them away from the boat, that she would be able to make an acceptable presentation, and if we were extremely lucky, that she might even land a fish. She had brought along a book and her iPod just in case, but my goal was for her to be totally absorbed in the moment so that they would remain tucked away in her bag. I had subjected her to fly-casting lessons in the backyard and drilled her to the point of exasperation, which for Erin, took about fifteen minutes.

By the end of our first few hours on the water, with each of us fishing a pair of nymphs under a strike indicator, Erin had outfished me five to two, even landing the largest fish—a 21-inch rainbow. I compared my long, perfectly drag-free drifts with her style of presentation. She seemed to play more with her strike indicator, pulling and twitching it, and then replacing it back on the water. The trout responded enthusiastically. She also employed various chants, dances, and one limerick that went something like "Here fishy, fishy—you're my wishy, wishy." I don't think that had anything to do with it, but I might try it sometime if I'm really desperate and no one is looking.

Erin ended the day a proud and passionate angler. She is now willing to go fly fishing with me any time. Of course, some bribery would still be involved, but she now enjoys the sport and is excited about it. She learned quickly that day, but I learned something as well: I experienced firsthand the profound negative impact the current has on our presentation when nymph fishing with a strike indicator, and that there are techniques to overcome it. Little did Erin know that by pausing the indicator, twitching or pulling it slightly upstream, she was imparting a more natural presentation and authentic animation to the flies.

NYMPH FISHING: PAST, PRESENT, AND FUTURE

Even though nymph fishing has recently soared to new popularity, the technique has been used from the earliest days of angling, and the pioneers of nymphing represent a "who's who" of fly fishing. Over the years and centuries, it has evolved, nearly disappeared, and reemerged like a phoenix to attain its rightful place as a valued technique to catch fish. What was once considered a "minor tactic," even by some of the founding fathers and strongest advocates of nymph fishing, has now evolved into a common and successful way to fish. With the advent of strike indicators, nymph fishing has reached new heights of success and widespread use. Many types of indicators are produced by a variety of manufacturers. New tackle, innovations in fly design, and new variations in styles and techniques seem to be introduced every year.

Although George Edward MacKenzie Skues is probably the name most often linked to the development of nymph fishing, he was not the first to describe subsurface insect activity and techniques to present artificial flies to these fish. The beginnings of nymph fishing reach back quite a bit farther. Two centuries earlier than Skues, observant anglers were aware of the activity of nymphs and also aware that trout often fed on them and other food sources below the surface. In the early and mid-1600s, John Taverner described an accurate account of underwater insect activity and emergence. Shortly afterward, Robert Venables discussed detailed techniques for "angling at the ground," as he called fishing under the surface. In 1662, Venables wrote in *The Experienced Angler; or, Angling Improved* that careful observation was an indispensable characteristic of the serious angler. His advice included taking time to observe before beginning to fish. "When you come first to the river in the morning, with your rod beat upon the bushes or boughs which overhang the water, and by their falling on the water you will see what sort of flies are there in greatest numbers." Venables went to great lengths to explain how to make tackle. He described the use of a different rod for nymph fishing than that used for dry-fly fishing. He may have made the first reference to the use of sinkers when he proposed in 1662, "Get a musquet or carbine ball, make a hole through it, and put in a string twist, hang this on your hook to try the depth of a river or pond." Today, three and a half centuries later, most of his deductions and observations are still just as relevant as when he first made them, although the use of musket balls as sinkers is not recommended.

Throughout the evolution of nymph fishing, new information has been presented, scrutinized, and incorporated into the modern style of nymph fishing that we know today. Many methods and styles exist, in part because of the various proponents. Ernest Schwiebert, Joe Humphreys, Doug Swisher, Ray Bergman, Gary LaFontaine, Carl Richards, and many others have made additional contributions and developed various techniques that now embody the modern art of nymph fishing. The original English style of nymph fishing generally involved casting the nymphs upstream, similar to the dry-fly techniques of the day. Under the influence of James Leisenring, among others, American anglers later adapted the English methods to better fish the North American rivers. Leisenring, famous not only for his lift but also for the flymph, which is a hybrid cross between a nymph and an emerger, was among many to advocate a more downstream approach to nymphing.

Charles Brooks was perhaps the first angler to appreciate the variation in the velocity of the current in the vertical water column and the effect it has on nymph fishing. He expressed a need for the flies to remain in the slower water near the bottom and noted that the faster current in the layers above creates a bow in the line. He recommended letting the flies drift until the bow in the line is completely gone and the flies have reached the full extent of the line and leader. This allows the flies to rise in the water column like an emerging insect. According to the Brooks method, the angler makes the cast upstream to allow the weighted flies to drop to the bottom, with the intention that they would stay in that layer. As the line passes even-stream with the angler, the rod is elevated and then lowered as the line continues downstream.

A technique that's a relative newcomer, Czech nymphing, has gained widespread popularity. A close cousin to high sticking, this technique involves short upstream casts in rapid current. The presentation usually involves three heavily weighted, thin-bodied nymphs that sink rapidly to the bottom at the onset of the drift. The flies are allowed to drift to a point even with the angler, at which time a new upstream cast is made. The casts are very short, often involving just the leader and perhaps a short section of line. The rod is lifted to keep the slack line off the water. The goal is to fish turbulent water that might otherwise be inaccessible. Large trout often make their feeding lies in this environment, hiding from the current in the rocky substrate along the bottom, poking their noses into the current only to catch a tempting food item whisking by.

The main disadvantage of this technique is that it requires close proximity to the fish. Water that is too clear or a section with a surface that is smooth will allow the fish to see you and flee to the security of deeper water. Under the right conditions, however, it can be extremely productive. Choppy runs or riffles with obstructions that create backeddies of deeper water are well suited for this style. Pocketwater situations present an ideal opportunity for this style of presentation. Taking a position below the area, you can make short casts upstream into the pocket where trout are likely to be holding.

Although tight-line techniques have been described by several author-ities as far back as the 1950s or possibly even earlier, these techniques have enjoyed renewed interest in recent years. Glen Blackwood introduced me to the Pennsylvania tight-line technique when he invited me to visit his family's retreat in that state several years back. He outfished me with it one afternoon on the Slate Run, and he graciously showed me how it's done. By altering his leader length and adjusting the weight, he was able to drop his flies through the current complexities into the depositional microhabitat behind boulders and in other pocketwater to deliver effective presentations to fish in those feeding stations. The technique also incorpo-rates short upstream casts to these pockets. A tight line is maintained to "walk" or draw the flies back to you, keeping a steady tension while the weighted flies bump along the bottom. The lack of slack in the line helps you detect subtle strikes that you might otherwise miss.

Strike indicators have taken nymph fishing to new pinnacles of popu-larity and encouraged more widespread usage. Nymphing with indicators has become the mainstay and staple of fishing guides everywhere. New-comers to the sport are able to learn this style quickly and can manage the drifts from float boats. The wide casting arc, using the water to load the backcast, is relatively easy to accomplish and tangles are reduced. Although some of the strikes are often subtle, most anglers quickly learn to recognize the strikes well enough to have some success. Guides can rely on each fisherman catching, or a least hooking, a few fish, which makes their trips more productive and enjoyable.

In addition to aiding in strike detection, indicators also suspend the flies at approximately the same depth, which can be changed by adjusting the length of leader below the indicator. This can be advantageous when fishing water that has a relatively uniform depth. To fish water that varies in depth, you need to adjust the indicator frequently to allow the flies to hold at different depths.

Certainly, the ease with which anglers can catch fish using strike indi-cators has helped contribute to the success of this technique. However, this ease and convenience can lead to an overreliance on them. You need to understand their strengths and weaknesses. The improper use of strike indicators can inhibit your skill development by fostering a false sense of confidence in your strike detection capability. They should not replace your instinct or feel for nymph fishing or serve as the only means of strike detection. They should not be used as the only method of nymph fishing. If they are used incorrectly or for inappropriate circumstances, they can actually be detrimental.

Each nymph-fishing strategy has its own variations, and the advantages and disadvantages of each can be appreciated through an understanding of the subsurface properties and effects of current. The more you understand the nuances of current, the better you will be able to refine and develop new techniques that will continue to enhance the art of nymph fishing. From those who have gone before us, we have received a tremendous endowment of wisdom and also a responsibility. Isaac Newton once said, "If I can see farther, it is because I stand on the shoulders of giants." We must build on the present body of knowledge in order for our new strategies to be effective and to advance the success of angling. And then, if it is possible for us to see farther toward the distant horizon, it is because we also stand on the shoulders of giants.

VERTICAL STRATIFICATION

Many anglers view the river only from a two-dimensional perspective. They know that if they cast a dry fly across the surface, they will immediately see the effect of drag and thus they compensate for it. They often fail, however, to envision the three-dimensional aspect of nymph fishing and lack an understanding of the impact it has on presentation. In order to maximize the potential of your nymph fishing, you need to have a three-dimensional perspective of the stream. You must learn to see beyond the obvious to understand the situation beneath the surface. From what you can see of the surface, you must be able to infer what's going on below. Gaining an appreciation of the three-dimensional characteristics of moving water will help you not only improve your presentation, but also understand trout preferences for location and feeding lies.

Just as there are horizontal zones or threads of current with different velocities, there are also vertical layers of water moving at different speeds, stacked upon one another in a laminated manner. Slip seams of velocity transitions occur between the fastest current and the slower current under the water, the same as between currents on the surface. When you fish nymphs and other subsurface imitations, the same features of laminar flow that could spoil your presentations while dry-fly fishing also can negatively affect your subsurface presentations. To improve your success, you must understand and address the intricacies and nuances of the current beneath the water. On the surface, you need to address only two dimensions: parallel to the current and crosscurrent. In nymph fishing, however, a third dimension comes into play: the vertical water column.

If you could view the vertical water column of a stream, you'd see that the surface tension at the air-water interface produces a small amount of

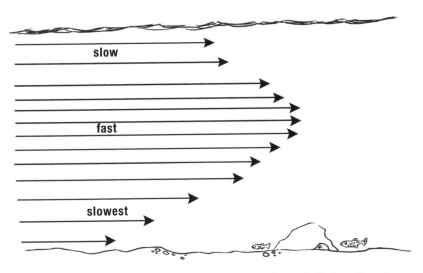

The friction both at the surface and at the bottom slows the water in the adjacent layers of current and creates vertical stratification of current velocities, with the swiftest current just below the surface and the slowest current near the bottom of the stream.

friction as the water contacts the air. This friction slows the current velocity of a thin portion of the upper layer of water. Depending on the speed and turbulence of the water, this layer may be so thin as to be virtually nonexistent. If the surface is broken or choppy, any surface tension is negated, and there will be no friction or velocity reduction at this interface. Just below the surface are successive layers of faster water. In the layers closest to the bottom of the river, friction is produced at the point of contact as the water flows over the substrate. This friction dramatically reduces the velocity of the water adjacent to the bottom. The effect is so profound that a narrow layer of water at the bottom has a water velocity close to zero. This is called a *boundary* or *border layer* and can sometimes be 1 centimeter to several centimeters thick, depending on overall current and bottom composition.

The speed of the current affects the shape of the vertical velocity profile. In a stream with swift current, the velocity profile is characterized by a sharp acute angle, which reflects a greater disparity in the speed between the zones of faster and slower currents. In slower-moving sections of the river, the vertical velocity profile is a gentle curve corresponding to the reduced current differential. The speed of the current still drops off precipitously near the bottom regardless of current speed, but in the slower section, there is less of a gradient between the fastest and slowest portions of

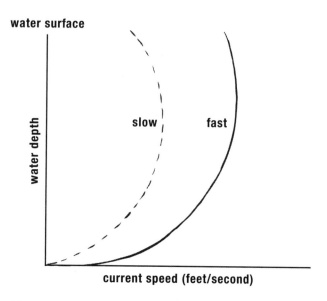

water surface

water depth

slow   fast

current speed (feet/second)

The dotted line shows the gentle curve of the vertical velocity profile in slower-moving water, resulting from less velocity variation in the vertical water column. The swifter current creates more dramatic velocity variations, as indicated by the solid line.

the vertical water column. When the leader passes vertically through these different stream sections, as is the case while nymph fishing, the swifter current produces the most dramatic impact and requires the largest adjustment to compensate for it.

The vertical velocity gradient indicates an area of transition, or seam, between the nearly static velocity of the boundary layer and the swiftest current overhead. The character of this transition zone is determined by the same principles that determined the slip seams in the horizontal profile. In fast current, the slip seam of transition is strong, narrow, and well defined. In slower current, the seam is broader and less sharply defined. The distinction will be blurred, however. Envision a stretch of slow-moving water as viewed from the surface. You will be able to distinguish the faster and slower zones, but the seams are more subtle and less defined. This also describes the vertical water column in slow-moving stretches. The transitions from fast to slow current zones are more gradual. In fast current, the sharp seam in the vertical water column serves as a barrier that makes it difficult for a weighted fly to penetrate.

The character of the substrate also determines the vertical velocity profile. In sections with a rough, broken substrate, such as rocks or boulders, the buffer zone of slow water is extended higher into the vertical water

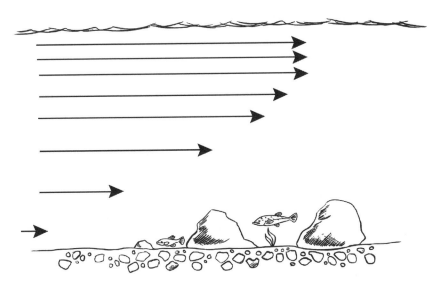

A rough, irregular substrate on the bottom of the streambed shifts the vertical velocity profile, extending the buffer zone higher into the main flow of the stream. This usually accentuates the slip seam, which creates a barrier that is difficult for nymphs to penetrate.

column and the body of the stream. Trout can hold in the thicker buffer zone along the bottom while perusing the food offerings passing overhead, which fits the criteria for an ideal feeding lie. This is why fish can be found in feeding lies within some of the fastest, roughest water in the river. Underneath these fast runs, because of the broken substrate along the bottom, protected shelter is available, and trout can be found and caught from these locations, provided you can suitably present your flies through the layers of current and the barrier of the slip seam. Where the current is swift over a rough and rocky substrate, the slip seam is dramatic. The seam delineates the quiet buffer water between the rocks where the fish are holding and the current flow rushing overhead. This might be the equivalent of hiding in a ditch while a tornado passes over.

While fishing the Oldman River in Alberta, Canada, with my wife, Jo, we found cutthroat trout holding in a stretch of the river that would challenge a whitewater kayak fanatic. This was an untamed part of the river that flowed out of the Canadian Rockies between jagged peaks that stood like ageless sentinels. We parked by the road and hiked far enough down the river that we needed a break to slow our heart rates and catch our breath in the thin mountain air. I told the guide that I wanted to stop to take a picture, but he knew the truth when it took too long for my gasping to subside. I took the picture anyway. I like to hike as well as the next guy, but I was pleased when we dropped our daypacks and set up to fish below a beautiful falls.

I looked at the stretch of river the guide had chosen. The river slowly gained momentum over a series of small drops before, in one final assault, it cascaded over a 7-foot waterfall and landed in a furious turmoil of froth and spray. Afterward, it continued on as a rock-and-rolling run of rough water. Thinking that I needed no guidance, I turned to walk downstream toward the tail of the run. As a gentleman, I planned to leave Jo the benefit of fishing with the guide. Before I had taken a few steps, however, the guide tapped me on the shoulder with the rod he was stringing for my wife. I was a bit surprised when he pointed the rod at the base of the falls and told me to cast into the churning water. I did so skeptically but was rewarded on my third or fourth cast by a beautiful cutthroat painted in nearly luminescent hues of sunset red and orange. Again and again I cast into that spot, lifting several fine trout from the frothy whitewater. Evidently, they didn't get the memo that this water was too rough for trout.

As my wife and I ate our lunch, I studied the stretch of river that had given up several nice trout that morning and tried to imagine how the fish could withstand the full force of the strong current. It wasn't until later that I realized that they weren't facing its full force at all. Like hiding in the eye of a hurricane, the trout were protected from the gale force of the current in subsurface pockets of relatively calm water while they waited for a steady supply of groceries to pass by overhead. They would dart from their calm recesses to intercept a passing morsel of food and quickly return to their lair like a moray eel shooting out of its hole to catch a damselfish. Their frequent excursions for food often carried them downstream from their original positions, after which we could see them slipping back upstream along the bottom to avoid the current. This allowed the trout to hold in water that otherwise would have soon exhausted and depleted them.

A closer examination of the vertical velocity profile can provide you with still further information. If we overlay the curve on a graph, the depth of the stream can be indicated on the vertical axis, represented as the percentage of the vertical water column. The bed of the stream would be 0 percent of the total vertical height of water above the bottom. At the top of the vertical axis, the surface of the stream would be 100 percent of the water column. The horizontal axis indicates the velocity of that stretch of the stream, shown as a percentage of the fastest current speed for that particular section of the river. The actual speed of the current is

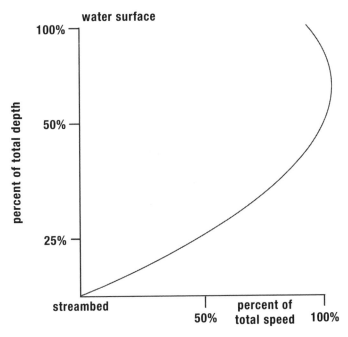

In his landmark book, *The Ecology of Running Waters*, H.B.N. Hynes uses this graph to illustrate the property of velocity stratification. The graph shows the relationship of current speed to the depth of the stream. The steepness and shape of the velocity gradient depend on the overall speed of the current and the roughness of the bottom substrate, but the ratio between the bottom and middle current threads is fairly consistent.

not displayed, but the relationship depicted on the graph would hold true regardless of actual current speed. Therefore, the fastest speed would be indicated as 100 percent. If any particular thread moved at half the speed of the fastest water, it would be shown as 50 percent. Looking at the graph, the lowest 20 percent of the water column has a velocity approximately 50 percent of that of the fastest current near the middle of the vertical water column. Thus in a river that is 5 feet in depth, the lowest 12 inches of water moves with half of the velocity of the water that is nearer the midpoint in depth. Fish take advantage of this fact as they move about the river, sliding along the bottom as they travel from place to place. Rarely do they swim in the middle current.

Where I fished in the Oldman River, I would guess that the water was several feet deep at the base of the falls and in the fast run that followed. The velocity profile of the current there likely had a layer of water at least 10 to 12 inches thick above the bottom where the velocity would have been half that of the current I could see at the surface. Allowing for the coarseness of the rocky bottom, this layer might well have been thicker. This would have provided the trout with adequate relief from the current as they moved about the bottom, and sufficient feeding lies would have been located behind the rocks and boulders. This location, with a slower current, well-oxygenated water, places for concealment, and a steady supply of food items, offered everything a trout could hope for in a feeding lie. It's no wonder I hooked so many trout in this stretch of the river.

Under natural conditions, laminar flow does not occur as precisely as in the idealized description above. At higher rates of flow, turbulence is introduced. Rocks, boulders, and other structures in the stream also cause turbulence. This disrupts the pure integrity of laminar flow, adding chaos and more variation to the movement of water. The principles of laminar flow still persist, however, just as was the case with the horizontal example. The vertical stratification of current, with slip seams between different speed zones, will be a characteristic of moving water in streams even in the presence of turbulence, and if you don't address it when nymph fishing, it will cause problems in your presentations.

To better understand the vertical water column and the layers of different velocities, imagine standing in the center of the river, where the flow is the fastest. Looking across the surface of the water toward shore, you can see the slower buffer water near the banks and the faster water in the center near your feet. The slip seams of transition are generally evident and easily recognizable. These seams may be disrupted occasionally by shoreline structure such as rocks, boulders, and logs, which temporarily alter the flow of water, but a short distance downstream the flow returns to the familiar pattern. Even when turbulence and structure alter the flow, you can still see the properties of laminar flow in the persistence of the zones of different velocities and the slip seams that separate them. Now imagine if the river were turned on its side, rotated 90 degrees so that one of the banks was now the bottom and where you stood in the middle of the stream was now the surface. What had been the horizontal axis would now be the vertical axis, and looking toward the bank from the center would be the same as looking from the surface to the bottom. The buffer zone of slow water is now flowing right above the streambed. Just above this is the slip seam separating the buffer zone from the zone in the middle depth of the vertical water column, where the velocity would be the greatest. This is an accurate picture of the vertical water column. It has a buffer zone at the bottom, and a slip seam of transition separates it from the fastest current above it.

THE THREE-DIMENSIONAL RIVER

By combining the vertical and horizontal flow profiles, the resulting flow of water is a three-dimensional composite of parallel current seams and layers sliding at different speeds, but in the same direction. The velocity of current is fastest in the center zone, with subsequent layers of progressively slower-moving water radiating outward from that point until, at the point of contact with the substrate, both at the banks and the bottom, the velocity is slowed to nearly zero. The three-dimensional composite velocity profile of current, created by friction, is a physical characteristic of water flow in rivers and streams. An object will float much slower close to the bottom than in the middle depth, and it will float slower near the banks than in the central current. Thus the variations in current will dramatically affect your fly-fishing presentation.

The three-dimensional velocity composite as illustrated here is an idealized representation. The deepest part of the river is not always at the center of the stream, and the slope of the banks is not always uniform. At bends, the three-dimensional cross section would show an entirely different appearance. The deeper thalweg would be along the outer bend, with shallow water along the inner bend. Approaching the crossover point, the thalweg is more toward the middle, as in the diagram. However, since the crossover riffle section is usually wider than other stretches of the river, the three-dimensional cross section of this region might be characterized by a shallow, flat-bottomed profile with gradual slopes, making the thalweg less identifiable. In this case, the profile would be flattened.

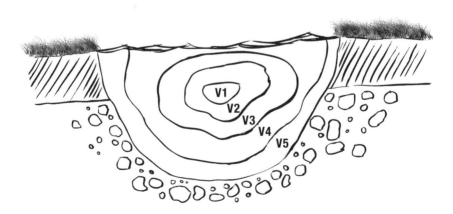

This illustration shows the three-dimensional velocity composite, with the highest velocity at V1 and the slowest velocity at V5.

Another factor to keep in mind is that there is more combined relative friction along a bank that has shallow water than along a bank that has a deeper bottom. Where the water is shallow, there is friction not only from the shoreline, but also from proximity of the streambed. Thus, since the force of friction slows the flow of water, the current speed along a bank with a shallow bottom will be slower than if the bank had more depth. In the deeper sections, the current along the bank will have less frictional influence and tend to flow more rapidly.

THE BENTHIC BOUNDARY LAYER

The the zone of water closest to the substrate, where the current velocity is nearly zero, is called the *benthic boundary layer*. This layer at the bottom exists in all types of water, in every stream or river. The thickness of this layer depends primarily on two factors: the substrate of the bottom and the swiftness of the current. A bottom with fine substrate has a thinner benthic boundary layer, while a coarse bottom such as rocks or boulders produces a wider layer. Additionally, faster current has a thinner layer, whereas slower current has a thicker layer. Thus in a riffle with a fine gravel bottom, the fast current and finer substrate minimize the benthic boundary layer, but in a riffle with a coarse bottom of rock and boulders, there are pockets of reduced velocity and a highly developed buffer zone. This not only allows fish to hold in sections of the river that appear—at least from the surface—to be unsuitable, but also provides a protected layer for other organisms, including insects, crustaceans, and other aquatic invertebrates.

The current-protected layer and the substrate beneath it are vital components of rivers and streams because they are home to the benthic community. Within this narrow, fragile habitat along the streambed is the richest abundance and diversity of life in the stream. Were it not for the stratification of current velocity in the vertical water column, this layer would cease to exist. If the current at the bottom were the same as the current in the middle depth, this fragile habitat would be scraped off by the force of the water and the entire ecosystem would be shattered.

Both lower- and higher-order organisms depend on this habitat. Water-filled nooks and crannies within this current-protected environment are home to aquatic vegetation, as well as insects and crustaceans. Much of the activity in the life of aquatic insects takes place within the benthic community. The vegetarian nymphs forage among the crevices. Swimming nymphs dart from place to place, while crawling nymphs scurry about as they hunt for food. Immature caddisflies make their nets and cases here, and marauding scuds forage for food. Without the velocity reduction of laminar flow, the insects and other organisms that reside in this layer would perish. They would no more be able to withstand the steady blast of the current than a butterfly could withstand the full force of gale-strength winds.

By providing habitat and sustenance for the lower-order organisms at the base of the pyramidal food chain, the benthic layer is the living foundation of the stream and vital to the sustenance of the entire lotic ecosystem. The insects that live here are routinely available to trout as food, especially as the nymphs or larvae mature and molt on their way toward winged emergence. The trout take advantage of this grocery store of plenty and rely on this layer for the bulk of their nutritional needs. The benthic community has such importance to the health and maintenance of the stream and the provision of food to trout that an entire chapter of this book focuses on it.

VERTICAL DRAG

Here is a scenario that all anglers can probably relate to: Cast a dry fly over fast water and well into a stretch of slower water. Do not mend or correct for drag in any way. What happens to the presentation? As soon as the current eliminates the slack from the line, the fly is abruptly accelerated and whisked out of the slower current into the slip seam, where it is held at the speed of the fastest current. The slip seam serves as a barrier preventing the fly from returning to or remaining in the slow water. Now envision a nymph presentation where you want the fly to bounce along the bottom like a natural insect. In this case as well, as soon as the slack is removed from the line by the swifter overhead current, the fly is abruptly accelerated to the speed of the fastest current thread through which the line passes. The fly is yanked out of the ideal, slower-moving section of water and lifted into the faster current at or above the slip seam, which now serves as a barrier that prevents the fly from penetrating back into the zone of slower water.

Just as different currents on the surface of the water can produce drag, the stratification of current below the surface has a profound effect on subsurface flies. The layers of differing velocities in the vertical water column produce vertical drag when the leader, as it passes through the various depths, assumes the shape of the vertical velocity profile. The faster the water, the faster the onset and greater the effect of drag. This drag can move the fly unnaturally fast, prevent it from reaching or staying on the bottom, and affect its orientation—all things detrimental to the presentation of your subsurface flies.

In the same way that drag affects presentations on the surface of the water, vertical drag restricts the freedom and randomness of movement

Vertical drag is created as the leader assumes the shape of the vertical velocity profile. It can cause the flies to zip above the trout at an unnatural speed relative to the current, spoiling the effectiveness of the presentation.

necessary to imitate the natural insect. Many of the immature aquatic insects that we imitate with weighted flies lack the ability to swim. It's important for these presentations to be free from the influence of drag. Stonefly nymphs, caddisfly larvae, and many mayfly nymphs are poor swimmers. If they are dislodged from the bottom, they are easy prey for trout. They float along, twisting and turning as they struggle to regain their hold on the bottom, where they can once again find protection. They may be whisked into the strong current, but they are anxious to regain their footing on the bottom. The tumbling, drag-free movement of a lightly weighted fly imitates this behavior very well as it bounces along the bottom. Affected by drag, however, the fly will no longer behave in this natural, unrestricted manner, and the speeding nymph will appear just as unnatural to the trout as a dry fly Jet Skiing across the surface of the water.

Vertical drag not only speeds up the fly so that it looks unnatural, but also prevents the fly from reaching or staying in the slower currents closer to the bottom, where the immature insects or other food sources we are trying to imitate spend most of their existence. If vertical drag affects the presentation, the fly will be yanked upward to ride well above the slip seam. It will be out of contact with the bottom currents where trout are most frequently feeding. In slow to moderate water, fish feed throughout the water column, but in fast water, they focus most of their attention on the bottom 20 percent of the water column, because traveling into the fast water is simply not an efficient use of energy. That doesn't mean that they won't occasionally chase a natural insect or minnow into the faster-moving water or that they won't take a fly from this layer once in a while. They are not flawless in their decision making, a characteristic we often ascribe to them, or we would never catch any of them!

Vertical drag may also create an abnormal orientation to the fly. A caddisfly larva, for instance, usually drifts head-down. This is usually well imitated by a bead-head fly. Vertical drag, however, will lift the head of the fly upward and give it an unnatural appearance. Most natural insects prefer to head into the current, particularly during emergence, but vertical drag will cause the fly to face in a constant downstream orientation.

The onset of drag depends on the acuteness of the velocity profile as determined by the speed and strength of the current. In water with slower current, vertical drag is slower to develop, whereas in faster water, the effect is quicker and more dramatic. The length of the leader below the indicator also determines when drag will affect the drift. By adding a longer leader below the indicator, you may be able to delay drag until the slack is removed. If you add too much length, however, many strikes will go undetected. Trout can expel a fly quickly on discovering your deception, often without your awareness that it was even taken. Even with minimal slack, the subtle nuances of a take can be difficult to distinguish. Too much slack will reduce hook-setting efficiency as well. The additional slack will also create a delay in setting the hook, giving the trout time to spit out the fly.

The effect of vertical drag is more profound with longer drifts. This is most evident when floating in a boat. The long drifts that can occur in this case are radically subjected to vertical drag and require frequent correction to reestablish a desirable drift. This may, in part, explain the success of the Czech-nymphing, high-sticking, and tight-line methods, which all share many similarities. The shorter upstream casts that are characteristic of these techniques produce a drift that is simply too short to allow vertical drag sufficient time to influence the presentation. In these methods, often only the leader or a short section of line is cast and is on the water, while the rest of the line is held above. In all of these instances, the effect of vertical drag is minimized, ensuring a more natural presentation. By avoiding vertical drag, the flies are free to drop behind rocks, boulders, and other structure to target fish holding tight behind these obstructions, instead of whisking high overhead. Once they are in the target layer, the flies are frequently led through the drift to completely eliminate any slack that may otherwise impede strike detection and result in failed hookups. This makes these techniques ideally suited for pocketwater, where it is vital for the flies to drop into these zones. However, when fishing from a drift boat or making longer casts from a stationary point, it is necessary to overcome vertical drag by other means.

Evidence of Vertical Drag

It was during a float trip on the White River a few years ago that I first observed the effect of vertical drag. The water was clear enough to see my lightly weighted, bright pink egg pattern on the bottom as I watched it drift nearby. I carefully kept some slack line between the tip of the rod and the strike indicator. There was no drag that I could see, and I was confident of a good presentation. But when my colorful fly passed by close enough to see, I noticed that it was trailing well downstream from the strike indicator. I also saw that it was nearly a foot above the bottom and moving faster than it should be. I picked it up and dropped it again, this time right next to the boat. It settled quickly on the bottom and bounced along happily for a few moments, but then it lifted and accelerated.

By repeating this a few times, I was able to determine the exact point where the drag occurred. My fly would stop its erratic movement, accelerate, and lift from the bottom the moment the drag began. The behavior of the fly also changed under the influence of vertical drag. Even though I had slack in the floating line between the rod and indicator, the leader below the surface created drag as it was affected by the vertical currents. Subtle changes in the indicator also coincided with the onset of vertical drag. In water that was calm enough to allow me to observe, I noticed that the indicator often dropped slightly in the water at the point of drag and began to float at a slightly lower level. With the onset of drag, it would slow slightly as if it were pulled backward. It also became apparent that vertical drag affected my drift even without the strike indicator. The line floating on the surface acted in the same fashion as a strike indicator, by keeping the end of the line fixed on the surface while the leader passed though the velocity gradient. The drag became so strong that it pulled the end of my floating line underwater. If the drag is strong enough to submerge the end of a floating line, which is made to be buoyant, think of the impact it has on the tiny flies.

Experimenting further, I found additional evidence that illustrated the power and effect of vertical drag. You can try this experiment the next time you are drifting in a boat. Take off the indicator and tie on a team of weighted nymphs, such as Beadhead Prince Nymphs or Pheasant Tail

Nymphs. Use 50 percent more leader than depth of the river and begin a drift. Notice that at first the line floats on the surface of the water. After a few moments, however, the tip of the line begins to sink. As the drift continues, more line appears to sink. The longer the drift, the more line disappears below the water. It is as if some unseen force is below the surface pulling the line under. If you sustain a long enough drift with these flies, eventually a substantial section of your line will be underwater. This is not because of a defect in the floating line, but rather it's an illustration of the strength of vertical drag.

Looking at the physics of the phenomenon, we have to apply Newton's third law of motion, which states that for every action, there is an equal and opposite reaction. When vertical drag sets in, the lifting and acceleration of the flies underwater produces a slight deceleration and dropping of the strike indicator on the surface. As the flies resist the lifting and acceleration, the opposite force lowers the strike indicator or, in its absence, pulls the tip of the line underwater. If the entire vertical water column were moving at the same rate of speed, this effect would be absent. The flies would settle on the bottom and drift there, right below the tip of the line. They would float down the river in a more or less vertical alignment. There would be no pull on the indicator or the tip of the line, and it would not disappear underwater. However, since the vertical velocities are stratified, drag is created, and the force of the vertical drag is strong enough to pull the floating line under the surface. The longer the drift, the greater the effect, which results in more line being pulled under the surface. As a contrast, try cutting off the leader and letting the line float downstream by itself. You'll soon discover that there is nothing wrong with your line. It does float, unless it is very old or damaged. This proves just how strong a force vertical drag is capable of producing.

While you're experimenting, you can test my original observation as well. Tie on a brightly colored, highly visible weighted fly, like a bead-head egg pattern. Put your strike indicator back on the leader with 50 percent more leader below the point of attachment than the depth of the river. Allow this rig to float next to the boat in water that is fairly clear and not too deep, so that you can see the fly. Observe the relationship of the strike indicator relative to the fly. First the fly settles to the bottom. Very soon after the drift begins, the slack in the leader is used up and vertical drag sets in, after which you will see the strike indicator drifting forward and downstream of the fly, which seems to trail behind. Notice how slowly the fly tumbles along the bottom prior to the effect of drag, and then how it accelerates, lifts, and loses random motion once the leader tightens and vertical drag sets in. This is what the trout see—a fly that is being pulled along artificially. Ask yourself, does this look like an insect that has been dislodged from the substrate, tumbling freely, wriggling and struggling to reattach itself to the bottom? I know it doesn't look convincing to a trout.

Another effect of vertical drag I noticed had to do with the timing of strikes that occurred while I was nymph fishing from a standing or stationary position. I like to be in the water as much as possible when I fish, wearing water shoes or waders. As much as I like to drift in a boat, for me wading seems to capture the essence of the sport, allowing the most intimate relationship with the river. When nymph fishing from a stationary point, I noticed that most of my strikes were occurring at the onset of the drift, just as the flies settled on the bottom or as they began to rise at the end of the drift. This was especially the case if I made a long cast and set up a long drift. The middle portion of these long drifts, however, seemed to be the most unproductive.

The reason for this phenomenon is vertical drag. At the onset of the drift, the flies sink freely to the bottom and begin a short period of true dead drift. Tumbling along naturally, they are attractive to trout. As the leader tightens and drag sets in, however, the flies no longer behave like natural insects, and trout are not as easily fooled by this unnatural presentation. At the end of the drift, as the strike indicator reaches the end of its course, the flies pass underneath the indicator until the slack is removed from the leader. During this period, they are once again free from the influence of vertical drag and are attractive to trout. Once the leader tightens, the flies turn into the current and rise just like natural insects. This accounts for the increased productivity during this later portion of the drift.

Think about it. If the entire vertical water column were moving at the same speed, bead-head flies would quickly sink to the bottom, just as they would in stillwater. You would then be able to feel them in constant contact with the rocks or gravel as they drifted along in the current. The ticking and bumping would be obvious. Steelhead anglers can attest to just how much weight it takes in order to feel the bottom during the drift. The stronger the current, the more weight is needed. Is this because sinkers don't sink to the bottom in rivers as they do in stillwater? If you think this is the case, drop one overboard and watch how fast it sinks. However, once you connect the flies or sinkers to the surface with the leader, they are subject to the effects of vertical drag as well as the force of gravity. Gravity causes the sinkers to sink, but this is offset by the lifting and propelling effects of vertical drag, which is created as the leader passes through the areas of faster velocity in the vertical water column. The stronger the current, the more vertical drag and the more weight it takes to maintain contact with the bottom, just as any steelheader knows.

According to tradition, Galileo demonstrated that objects of different weights fall at the same rate of speed by dropping two balls of different weights from the Leaning Tower of Pisa long ago. Research by Galileo and others led to the development of the equivalence principle of gravity, which states that acceleration due to gravity is a constant and independent of the mass of the object. To apply this principle to nymph fishing, an 8-ounce and a 2-ounce lead weight will sink in water at roughly the same rate. This assumes that the effects of resistance in the water are equal; a slight allowance needs to be made for increased resistance if the heavier object is substantially larger in size. If, however, they are fairly equal in size, they should end up on the bottom at roughly the same time. In a river, the current would carry them slightly downstream from the point where they entered the water.

Therefore, adding more weight won't necessarily sink your flies faster, but when fishing the bottom, additional weight helps keep them there once vertical drag sets in. If the entire vertical water column were moving at the same rate of speed, there would be no vertical drag, and it would take minimal weight to keep your flies in contact with the bottom. But in stronger current, the vertical velocity profile is sharper and the slope of the gradient steeper. Thus it takes more weight to maintain contact with the bottom, not because the effect of gravity is less, but because the effect of vertical drag is greater. It takes more weight to offset the lift and acceleration effects created by vertical drag.

If you use shooting line for steelhead or salmon, if the water is clear enough the next time you fish, notice the arc your line assumes as it goes into and under the water. It looks just like the vertical velocity profile. As the line passes through the water column, its shape reflects the various velocities of the current at each depth and assumes the parabolic curve characteristic of the vertical velocity profile.

Each March and November, when the steelhead return to their natal waters, I, too, migrate back to the Manistee River in Michigan. In synchrony with their natural biological rhythm, my trip is timed to coincide with the steelhead movement into the river from the open waters of the Great Lakes. Twice each year, I spend several days chasing chrome-bodied torpedoes of steel in the frigid wintry waters. Steelhead fishing is way of life throughout the winter for the purist who gets up in the dark of night, brews a thermos of coffee, and dons a snowmobile suit to go fishing. It is not for the faint of heart.

Jamie Clous has been my steelhead-fishing guide for nearly double-digit years. He makes a decent cup of coffee and an epic shore lunch. He has a sturdy aluminum boat for my damaged knees and is one of the finest steelhead fishermen I have ever met. In the winter, he stalks the rivers of Michigan in search of this quarry. In the summer, he prowls the same rivers at night for large brown trout during the Hex hatch.

One frigid November morning, my friend Dan Pesavento and I joined Jamie on a quest for steelhead on the Manistee. There was frost on the deck of the boat and ice in the guides of our rods, and by the time we motored to the first spot, there was ice in my coffee cup as well. But we didn't mind, because the chase was on! Dan was already fishing from the front of the boat as I stepped up on the rear platform to fish. The rest happened in the blink of an eye, and I relate it now only through the recollection of others. One moment I was stepping onto the deck. The next moment I was dangling over the side of the boat, clutching on to the cowling of the motor. Apparently, I skated across the frost-covered deck like Scott Hamilton at the Winter Olympics. It was just like stepping onto an ice-skating rink, minus the skates. If it hadn't been for the motor, I would have shot off the back of the boat like a different kind of Olympian, minus the skis and poles. According to eyewitnesses, I was a comic picture of slipping, sliding, and pinwheeling arms as I desperately lunged for the motor. I perched precariously on the treacherous deck, waited for the laughter to die down, and collected my dignity as well as the rod I had nearly lost over the edge of the boat. No worse for wear, I managed to make the first cast. I tried to work the reel while wearing gloves that afforded all of the dexterity of a catcher's mitt.

We were fishing a stretch of fast water. At first we could not feel our flies on the bottom, even with a lot of added weight. Jamie kept adding weight until we could finally feel the flies bouncing along the riverbed. This required a surprising amount. The next location had much less current, but it was quite a lot deeper. Even with the greater depth of this new stretch of water, the weaker current required less weight to maintain contact with the bottom, so we removed some of the weight we had added while fishing the fast current. More weight had been required in the faster current to overcome the lift from the increased vertical drag that was produced. Without the additional weight, the fluorescent pink egg patterns were elevated out of the optimal strike zone. Throughout the day, we continued to add or remove weight as the conditions warranted. It was worth the effort, because we had a pretty decent day. We landed a few nice fish and I dodged a bullet on the slippery deck, avoiding the cold water and a visit to the orthopedic surgeon.

In my quest for greater knowledge about current and its effect on presentation, I finally bought an underwater camera and set out to document the effect of vertical drag. I stole some yarn from my steelhead tackle box and fastened several small patches of the bright material every 6 inches along a leader. My plan was to use the marked leader under a strike indicator, with a weight at the bottom to simulate a weighted fly, and photograph the effect of the current. To ensure adequate visibility for the pictures, the clear water just below the dam on Tennessee's South Holston River seemed ideal, so Jo and I packed the Suburban and headed south one April. Along with my new camera and the marked leader, I also packed my scuba gear and wet suit for good measure.

The idea was fairly straightforward: Jo would stand in the water in a position upstream of where I would be. She would have a rod with the lightly weighted, marked leader and strike indicator. We used a length of the leader that was appropriate for the depth of the water. She would dead-drift the apparatus to my position, and I would attempt to follow it long enough to get a good picture or two.

The first thing I learned in Tennessee was that the water is very cold just below the dam in April. I don't know what I was thinking! I had brought along a light wet suit, more appropriate for warmer water. My high school geography teacher would be mortified, since I apparently must have assumed that Tennessee was somewhere near Bermuda. I didn't last

The design was simple: the leader was marked with a piece of bright yarn every 6 inches to ensure visibility below the surface.

The leader quickly assumed the shape of the vertical velocity profile, which accelerated the flies and elevated them from the bottom of the streambed, illustrating the profound effect of the current on nymph presentation.

long in the water before I was chilled to the bone. Sometimes my hands were shaking so badly that I was sure the pictures would be blurry. Maybe that's why Jo volunteered to stand upstream in her waders while I swam below in my wet suit.

But it was all worth it when I downloaded the photos onto my laptop. The results were amazing. Under the strike indicator, the leader marked with the bits of yarn is clearly visible. In many of the pictures, the 5X tippet is also clearly visible, much more so than I would have thought, and the strike indicator on the surface is often visible from underneath. The approximate depth of the water was 2¹/₂ feet and the length of the leader was about 4 feet. The current was fairly brisk, but not quite what I would call a strong run. The chop on the water surface was visible from below and gave some indication as to the speed of the current. The leader took the shape of the vertical velocity profile, and the weight was lifted off the bottom into the center of the vertical velocity column. You can't tell from a still picture, but the weight at the bottom along with the entire setup of leader and yarn was moving the same speed as the fastest current in the vertical water column.

We moved to a second location to photograph the effects in a section of the river where the current was stronger but the depth was shallower.

This photo shows the vertical velocity profile for a section of shallower water. Even with the same leader in the lesser depth, vertical drag still prevented the flies from the staying in the ideal current seam at the bottom. Notice the two small sinkers that we needed to get the presentation down nearer the stream bottom.

Even using the same length of leader in the shallower water, vertical drag prevented the flies from making contact with the bottom for most of the drift. The two sinkers that we used to simulate a weighted fly are clearly visible in the photo, elevated from the streambed as they approach a drop-off or ledge. If we had used only one sinker, it would have ridden much higher in the water column. The photo also shows the extension of the buffer zone upward into the water column because of the rough bottom.

Though this experiment is not flawless, it does illustrate the power of vertical drag to elevate and accelerate the flies when nymph fishing. The yarn may have introduced some small margin of error by increasing the surface area exposed to the current, but it did so evenly throughout the vertical water column, so for the most part this should have canceled out the effect. Some degree of buoyancy also may have been introduced by the addition of the yarn to the leader, but its influence was minimized once it became saturated with water.

We finished the experiment in time for a quick lunch, followed by a visit to a downriver stretch of the Holston for a few hours of fishing. I set up one rod for Jo to use and started rigging a second rod. Before I could even begin to fish, she had caught several nice trout, including one about

16 inches. Being the gentleman that I am, I helped her land it. It was a small price to pay for her help all morning with my experiments.

These experiments dramatically demonstrated the powerful effects of the current and the vertical drag it creates. These effects are greater in stronger current but are present in every river situation. Therefore, it's important to keep in mind what the current is doing to the flies at the end of your leader and the impact it has on your presentations.

Defeating Vertical Drag

When the strength of vertical drag is the greatest, you need to make more adjustments or corrections to maintain contact with the optimal strike zone. One possible option would be to add length to the leader below the indicator. While this would delay rather than eliminate the effect of vertical drag, it may be sufficient for shorter drifts. But for longer drifts, in order to reach the optimal strike zone, you need to use corrective mending or add more weight to overcome the lifting force created by vertical drag.

A combination of fast current and rough water is a frequent occurrence in many riffles and runs, and in such situations, added weight is necessary to get the flies to drop through the faster overhead current and into the recesses where fish are frequently holding. In slower sections of the river, vertical drag will have less of an effect, as evidenced by the gentle curve of the velocity profile. Although vertical drag will be slower to develop and require less frequent correction in this type of water, you will still need to make adjustments to your presentations. Fishing in these areas also generally requires less added weight to keep the flies in the optimal zone. When these adjustments are not sufficient, however, other corrections are necessary, such as mending or rigging to combat vertical drag.

Mending to Defeat Vertical Drag

Back when my daughter and I were fishing on the Bow River, unbeknownst to Erin, she was using a form of mending to defeat the effects of vertical drag on her presentation, which allowed her to catch more fish. By lifting and repositioning her strike indicator, she was mending for drag, which allowed her flies to resume a dead drift, at least for a short while. Just as mending corrects for drag when fishing dry flies, it can also correct for vertical drag on weighted flies. Watching her, I noticed that many of her strikes occurred as she lifted the indicator or shortly afterward as it resumed drifting.

The goal of mending, in all forms of angling, is to reinitiate a drag-free drift in order to get as natural a presentation as possible. Mending alleviates the pull from the leader, eliminating the effects of acceleration and lift. It also ensures that the flies are free from the inhibition of movement caused by drag. Lifting the line, flipping it upstream, and replacing it above the fly usually accomplishes this for the dry fly. A slightly different tactic, but with the same goal, is needed for the nymph presentation.

In nymph fishing, since the strike indicator is pulling the flies downstream, the mend needs to change the orientation and allow the flies to lead the way downstream, just as in dry-fly fishing, or at least let them catch up to the indicator. While mending, you need to achieve a balance between slack and drag. If you create too much slack, this will make it harder to detect strikes and you will miss fish. The ideal balance is to have just enough slack to avoid or minimize drag while maintaining contact with the flies. With practice, this becomes a little easier.

Mending can be accomplished in two ways, depending on whether you are fishing from a stationary point or a drift boat. After you make an upstream cast, retrieve line as the drift passes you, and then let it back out to drift downstream below you. As the line passes by or nearby, you can make an upstream mend to correct for vertical drag. This mend is accomplished by stopping the downstream progress of the indicator temporarily so that the flies, which are drifting in slower water below, can catch up to and pass the indicator on the surface. It can be as simple as holding the indicator in check for a brief moment while the flies below continue their downstream drift. This allows the flies to pass under the indicator to a position ahead and downstream of it. If the flies are drifting too far away from your position as they pass by, a roll cast that lifts the strike indicator slightly up off the water and pulls it upstream will have the same effect. Mending reintroduces enough slack into the leader to reestablish a drag-free drift. After you replace the indicator on the water to resume the drift, the flies once again are leading the strike indicator downstream. Because the strike indicator is moving faster than the flies, it will soon overtake the flies again, at which point you will need to mend yet again. On extremely long drifts, you may have to mend several times.

I have found it advantageous to mend just in front of structure, lifting the flies slightly off the bottom right in front of a likely feeding lie. This lifting of the flies headfirst in the current mimics the natural as it rises during an emergence, much in the same way as the Leisenring lift. It is often productive in eliciting a strike.

At the end of the drift, it is also a good idea to pause before recasting. The indicator is stationary at this point, just as it was during the mend. This allows for an ideal presentation as the flies continue to the extent of

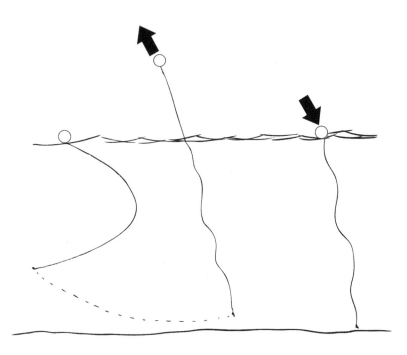

In nymph fishing, mending is accomplished by holding the strike indicator in a stationary position or pulling it slightly upward while allowing the flies to continue along the bottom. With practice, and by adapting to the specific conditions, you will learn to find a balance between too much and too little slack, improving your presentation while still being able to detect subtle strikes. Shown on the left in the illustration is the orientation of the leader under the influence of vertical drag. Once the leader is lifted or paused, the flies pass downstream, as shown in the center. After the strike indicator is released and the drift is resumed, the slack created will ensure a dead drift until the effect of vertical drag once again reasserts its effect.

the slack in the leader. As was first described in the Brooks method, developed by the late Charlie Brooks, this pause also allows the flies to bounce along the bottom beneath the indicator to the length of the leader and then rise at the end. Hurrying into the next cast robs you of an ideal opportunity to increase your success. Sometimes at the end of the drift, you can pull the strike indicator slightly upstream and reposition it in the current to repeat this last drift opportunity multiple times. By maneuvering the rod, you can use this technique to fish likely structure in different current seams below you.

The McCloud River in northern California has several long, alluring runs with nice plunge pools and is one of the most beautiful places to fly-fish. On the second day of my trip here with my friend Joel Ludwig, I was standing on the edge of a trough of fast-moving water that was too deep to wade. The fishing had been a bit slow, so I began to experiment. I was nymphing below a strike indicator and using the longest rod I had brought on the trip. I made a cast upstream and slightly across the current, into the fastest water, and held the rod held at arm's length. As the indicator passed under my rod, I stopped its downstream progression in the middle portion of the drift to allow the flies to tumble downstream of that point and even rise a bit on the leader as it tightened. After this brief pause, I replaced the indicator on the surface and allowed it to float again with the current. This mend corrected the presentation of the flies and started to produce more strikes. During the pause, as the leader tightened and the flies turned and rose in the current, this was a point of particular interest to the trout. The longer rod worked better for me, as it allowed me to work both sides of the trough. This type of presentation seemed to combine the benefit of the Brooks method with the advantages offered by the short upstream techniques such as the Czech style of nymph fishing.

I began to add a lift with a gentle twitch. I repeated this cycle—pause, twitch, and resume—several times through the fast water. After a few passes through the stretch, I caught a nice trout. The pause introduced just enough slack to allow the extra weight to get the flies down into the feeding lies where trout were holding, and the twitch added a bit of animation to the flies reminiscent of Frank Sawyer's induced take technique. Frank Sawyer, renowned English river keeper from the early 20th century, described a technique to entice trout to take the fly by adding a lifelike animation to the presentation. His method allowed his newly invented Pheasant Tail Nymph to sink during the initial portion of the drift and rise in front of trout feeding lies by lifting the rod at the end of the drift. To the trout, the rising nymph appeared to be an escaping insect and would elicit a strike. Using this technique, I caught a few more trout as I worked the entire stretch of water.

It can also be advantageous to mend in front of the cushion water upstream of boulders and rocks. If you can time the maneuver to lift the flies in front of these lies, you'll likely induce more strikes. It is also a good idea to drift your flies along both sides of every in-stream structure, such as rocks and boulders, which allows the flies to travel in the current seams on either side. This can be done from an upstream position by lifting and pulling the rig upstream and replacing it on the other side of the structure, allowing it to drift there. You can then reposition the flies again to fish the pocketwater immediately behind the obstruction. If the situation allows, this can often be better accomplished from a downstream position, making short upstream casts into the seams and pocketwater. However, sometimes you won't be able to fish from the downstream position because of heavy current or other unfavorable water conditions, and in such cases an upstream location may be a better alternative.

If you are casting directly upstream without the intention of drifting the flies below your position, mending will seldom be needed, unless the upstream cast is longer than customary. The drift of the flies is usually short enough to resist the effects of vertical drag. You recast the flies before vertical drag affects the presentation. This is often the case when fishing pocketwater if you are stationed just below the target area, making short casts into these regions.

A second method of mending for vertical drag is useful from a drift boat. These long drifts are very sensitive to the adverse effects of vertical drag. It is difficult to hold the strike indicator in a stationary position to mend when you are also drifting along at the same speed. In such cases, a slightly more aggressive correction is needed. You have to lift and pull the strike indicator upstream to allow the flies to swing downstream before resuming the drift. If the indicator is too far away to lift from the water, a gentle upstream pull will do the same thing. For long drifts, this mending will need to be repeated more than once to ensure a drag-free drift. It's important to do this with minimal disruption. A gentle pull of a few feet is often all that's needed, but you may need to do this several times during the drift.

During a mend from either a drift boat or a stationary position, a slight twitching of the rod can often impart animation to the flies, as I discovered on the McCloud River. This is especially effective if you add the movement near the end of the upstream mending pull. First draw back on the rod as is done for a normal mend. This allows the flies to freely tumble under and downstream of the indicator. Pause for a brief moment. If you twitch the rod but don't pause, it will accomplish little in the way of adding animation to the flies, since there is still slack in the leader. In the mending process, once the leader has tightened to the flies, which has turned them into the current and begun to elevate them from the bottom, a twitch or light shaking of the rod can make the flies appear to swim with a natural undulation as they rise in the water column like an emerging insect. This is a point in the presentation that is attractive to trout anyway, and this natural-looking animation can be the stimulant that seals the deal with a wary fish.

There are two rules of thumb in determining when to mend to correct for drag. The first rule is to mend before the onset of drag, which is more of a challenge in nymph fishing than it is for dry-fly fishing. A major difference between vertical and horizontal drag is that you can see the moment when horizontal drag spoils the presentation. The timing and frequency of mending are dictated according to need, and in dry-fly fishing the need is readily identifiable, since it is visible from the surface, and corrective mending can be done prior to the onset of drag. In dry-fly fishing, you can even estimate the extent of anticipated drag, assess the need for corrective procedures, and make a corrective cast before the fly hits the water.

When subsurface fishing, assessing the current can allow you to anticipate the amount of drag and implement a corrective plan. You can even employ casting corrections such as the tuck cast to initiate a drag-free drift and mend accordingly afterward. The tuck cast allows the flies to drop into the water in a more vertical alignment with the leader and strike indicator. This lets the drift begin without the detrimental effect of vertical drag. The tuck cast is made in an upstream fashion by elevating the handle of the rod at the end of the cast. Once the cast is made and the drift has begun, you must adjust the frequency of mending according to the conditions that prevail. As with horizontal drag, it is ideal to mend before vertical drag begins to spoil the presentation. For this reason, it is better to correct more frequently than less frequently.

Since the onset and strength of vertical drag can be influenced by the speed of the current, the depth of the water, and the length of the leader relative to the depth and the character of the bottom substrate, different conditions may require different approaches, and how often you'll need to mend will vary accordingly. Since the roughness of the bottom compresses the vertical velocity profile, the force of vertical drag is affected by the composition and character of the bottom. In situations where vertical drag is strong and quick to affect the presentation, such as in fast-water runs and riffles over rough bottoms, you will need to mend more often. In slow glides and flats with a relatively uniform bottom, you will encounter less vertical drag, and as a result, mending will be required less frequently. Thus the first rule of mending to combat vertical drag is that you need to mend more frequently in rougher and faster water.

If the river area you are fishing is characterized by broken, rough water, you should drop your flies behind rocks and boulders on the bottom, which is exactly where the fish will be holding. If you do not correct your presentation, the flies will not get where you want them. If you merely cast your nymphs into the swift current and allow them to be swept along at the same speed as the strike indicator, they will remain in the middle layer of the water column and never fall out into the slower current below. They will speed over the top of almost all the good lies, and the trout will not notice them or will not react to them if they do. In extremely deep water, vertical drag may already be pulling the presentation forward before the flies reach the bottom of the river. You can compensate by adding more length to the leader below the indicator and more weight.

The second rule for the timing and frequency of mending is that you should always mend before presenting the flies to an ideal section of the stream or structure. The Pere Marquette River is known for logjams and riparian structure and was a perfect place to experiment with this concept. When I fished there with Alan Ott several years ago, we caught several fine trout holding in logjams, by deadfalls, and under sweepers. Pausing the drift in front of such structure allowed the flies to proceed under the wood and get to where the fish were. Previously, I usually stopped the drift when the strike indicator got close to the deadfall, but in so doing, I never allowed the flies to show to those fish. Because vertical drag had caused the flies to be trailing well behind the indicator, they never got close to the trout. Stopping the drift just in front of the logs and pausing for several seconds gave our flies the opportunity to entice fish we otherwise would not have caught.

A nymph-fishing strategy for structure is particularly important when fishing from a boat. It is always wise to mend when approaching ideal cover in a float boat. If you see a nice run, riffle, or pool ahead as you float along, mend just before arriving at the ideal water. In a river such as the White in Arkansas, the flat, rocky shoals provide ideal trout lies. These are often widely separated by sections of slower water. While you drift in the slower water, your mending can be done more leisurely and less frequently. In the shoals, where the speed of the water is much faster, vertical drag is quicker to develop. While you're floating through this section of ideal cover, mend more rapidly and even reposition your presentation to drift over the most appealing portion of the shoals. In these sections, I frequently switch from side to side to present the flies to the best lies. I try to keep my flies in the best run through the shoals, which is often near the main channel. I also try to cast to allow the flies to present in likely holding lies, such as behind boulders, in backeddies, and in riparian habitat as the boat moves through the run.

When you are nymph fishing, it's important to target the ideal water. Avoid just letting random chance or the flow of the water dictate the course of the drift and hence the quality of your fishing experience. You need too determine the best places to present your flies. In each section of water, choose targets or flow paths that will optimize your presentations in the most advantageous positions. Once the drift has passed the ideal structure or seam, select your next target and cast there to establish the next drift. Do not fish the river as if all water were created equal. If 10 percent of the water holds 90 percent of the fish, then it is logical to assume that the remaining 90 percent of the water holds very few fish. This is never truer than in fast water, where the majority of the vertical water column has current that is just too strong for the fish to fight. The only suitable lies in these environments are in areas protected from the current, and this is where you need to present your flies. If you choose the path and water structure for your drift based on your interpretation of the river structure, holding lies, and what is most appealing to trout, you will catch more fish.

Most of the time, there will not be any visible clues for the need to mend. While drifting in flat, slow water, I have noticed a change in the orientation of the strike indicator that indicates the point of onset of vertical drag, but this is not usually apparent unless you have deliberately chosen such calm water for an illustration of its effect. Under normal fishing conditions, little change is apparent. With time and experience, you will learn to determine in various situations when you first should mend and how frequently thereafter.

Inadvertent mending can occur naturally during the drift. There are times when the presentation may correct on its own. The strike indicator may be affected by current variation, perhaps caught in an eddy or delayed in its progression by crosscurrents. Features that introduce turbulence, such as rocks, boulders, or other objects, may lift and jettison the flies ahead of the indicator in a maneuver that corrects for vertical drag. Regardless of such occurrences, however, it is essential to correct your presentations actively so that you will more frequently achieve a drag-free drift.

Rigging to Defeat Vertical Drag

Anglers can combat vertical drag and improve presentation in many different ways. Besides mending, the amount of vertical drag can also be affected by your rigging. Variables such as different styles of arranging the flies, leader length, and more or less weight all can increase or decrease the effect of vertical drag. These variables are under your control, and thus you can modify them to correct the presentation depending on the fishing circumstances.

Most types of strike indicators can easily be moved up or down to change the amount of leader below the indicator, which allows you to vary the depth of the presentation. Most anglers tend to have a "one depth suits all" mentality, however, and do not adjust their leader length as often as they should. Ideally, you should adjust the length of leader below the indicator whenever there is a change in the conditions you encounter. The length should be modified in response to changing depth, and it also may need to be adjusted when there are changes in current velocity.

How much leader you should use below the indicator depends on the fishing circumstances. A general rule is that your leader should be one-third to one-half longer than the depth of the water, depending on the amount of weight you plan to use and how fast the water is traveling. A shorter leader, closer to one-third more than the total depth, may be appropriate in slower water, but for faster water of the same depth, you need a longer leader below the strike indicator. If the leader is too short relative to the depth of the water, it will require more weight to maintain the flies in the optimal strike zone, or else the lifting effect of vertical drag will elevate the flies well above the strike zone. When the water current is swift, the vertical velocity profile is a sharp curve. Since the line or leader will assume a similar shape, it logically follows that you need to have more leader below the indicator for the flies to target the optimal zone.

With this in mind, you might be tempted to add an excess of line to ensure that there's always enough available as the situation changes throughout the course of fishing. If you do this, however, strike detection will be impaired. There will be too much slack between the flies and the indicator to signify a strike. Hook sets will be difficult as well, resulting in lost fish. It is essential to reposition the indicator frequently to reflect changes in both depth and current velocity.

In very fast water, simply adding more length to the leader will not counter the effect of vertical drag. Even though the additional length below the indicator will delay the drag somewhat, the drag that does develop will not allow the flies to drop out of the current into the best feeding stations. It will become necessary to add more weight as well as to mend more frequently. The addition of weights will resist the lifting force of vertical drag and help maintain contact with the bottom. When I fish for steelhead, I add and remove weight frequently, as well as change the length of the leader, to ensure contact with the bottom. Every time we move to a new location on the river, I make adjustments to the weight and length of leader. My first cast is an experiment to determine the right settings.

To add weight when nymph fishing, you can either build more weight into the fly during its construction or add weight to your rigging. When tying your fly, you can add a bead head or wraps of lead wire around the hook shank before building the rest of the fly. Many patterns are commercially available with bead heads, but custom-tied flies are generally the only ones with lead wrapping around the shank. You can either tie such flies yourself or order them from a custom commercial tier.

A lightly weighted fly, especially when the weight is added in the forward portion of its construction, offers considerable advantages. When the fly is displaced from the bottom by microcurrents, the weight will cause it to return to the bottom, thus imitating a natural insect that was detached from the substrate. The weight at the front of the hook gives the fly a lifelike head-down attitude as it drops back down to the streambed, like an insect that is trying to return to the shelter of the bottom. In situations where drag is minimal, this type of weight may be sufficient to get the fly down to the bottom on its own. In fast current, however, the fly will not have the capacity to fully withstand the elevating force of vertical drag without additional weight.

Avoid building too much weight into the flies. A fly that is too heavily weighted will no longer behave in a natural manner like the nearly weightless insect you want it to mimic. The insect that the fly imitates has a small intrinsic mass. A fly with a weight more consistent with that of the natural insect will allow the current to affect it in a similar manner.

An alternative method for adding weight is to fasten it directly to the leader. You can add one or more sinkers to the leader ahead of where the flies are attached. Another option is a narrow, metal hobby-style tube with a small-diameter hole bored down the length through which you pass the leader. More than one of these can be used at a time. Often several small sections are used along the length of the leader, which ends in a barrel swivel. From this, a section of tippet connects to the flies. The weight can also be added as an extension with a short section of tippet dangling from the leader, often from a swivel. This is a common style when steelhead fishing. From this extension, several different weighted devices can be attached, including several sinkers, the number of which is determined by the amount of weight needed for the situation. Some anglers use a device known as a slinky, which is a row of sinkers encased in a mesh fabric to prevent them from lodging between rocks. Pencil weights and coiled lead are also frequently attached to the swivel as additional weight.

Adding weight ahead of the flies offers several advantages to the presentation. It allows the flies to remain in the lowest layer of the water column, which is the optimal strike zone, provided that you add enough weight for the situation. It also interrupts the linear force of vertical drag that is transmitted down the leader to the flies by placing much of that force on the sinkers or another weighted device, rather than on the flies. When the added weight makes contact with the bottom, it effectively

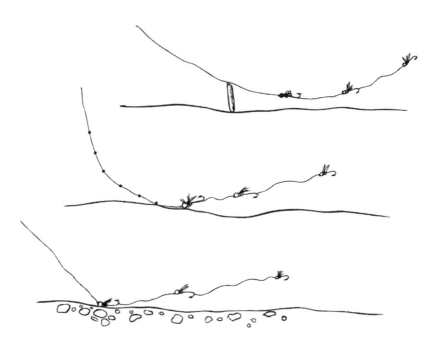

A common style of adding weight is from a short section of tippet tied onto a swivel attached to the leader. The flies are also attached to the same swivel by a short section of tippet. A series of evenly spaced sinkers is another common method of adding weight. Using an anchor fly also reduces the impact of vertical drag and may preclude the need for additional weight where the effect of vertical drag is less dramatic.

reduces the lifting effect of vertical drag on the flies. This allows the flies to be less weighted and permits them to range more freely within the optimal strike zone without their movement being hampered.

Other styles of adding weight have been advocated by various anglers. The use of a series of several small weights spaced evenly along the leader above the first fly creates an elbow or right angle near the bottom of the leader that allows the flies to track behind. Some proponents of this style maintain that it decreases the effect of drag while keeping the flies near the bottom. Other theories use a single point for the attachment of weight on the leader. A common midwestern steelhead technique is to use a tube weight on a snap hook that slides on the leader above a barrel swivel that connects to the first fly. This allows the transfer of the vertical drag force to the weight, which maintains contact with the bottom, while sliding up and down the leader to improve the detection of subtle strikes.

Another favored method is to use an anchor fly. One fly of a team of flies is heavily weighted, and this anchor fly pulls the entire group to the bottom, while allowing the other flies to be minimally weighted and thus appear more natural in their behavior. The force of vertical drag is transferred to the anchor fly, which allows the other flies to be free from its detrimental influences. The placement of the anchor fly in the team of flies varies according to the desired effect; sometimes it's the first fly, and other times it's the middle of three.

Neutral buoyancy is a term used in scuba diving to describe the relative tendency of the diver to rise or drop in the vertical water column while below the surface. If the diver has neutral buoyancy, he will remain at the same depth in the water, neither rising nor dropping. It is ideal for the diver to remain at the same depth through achieving neutral buoyancy in order to avoid expending energy to do so. If he is negatively buoyant, the diver will tend sink deeper. He will have to add air to his vest to achieve neutral buoyancy and remain at the same depth. When the diver is positively buoyant, he will tend to rise toward the surface. This relationship has to do with the density of the diver relative to the water at that depth.

These terms can also be used to describe the way artificial nymphs behave in the water column. If they are positively buoyant, they will tend to float to the surface. If they are negatively buoyant, they will sink to the bottom. If they are neutrally buoyant, they will tend not to rise or sink. The ideal construction of nymphs should be such that they are slightly negatively buoyant. The fly should have a tendency to sink, since this will cause them to imitate the behavior of natural immature insects that have been displaced from the substrate and are trying to return to the bottom. Too much weight, however, will give the fly strong negative buoyancy, and some natural animation of the fly is sacrificed. Our flies must navigate a myriad of microcurrents and eddies. At each point in the drift, they are pulled and pushed by these current influences. Tiny swirls will draw the flies into their vortices, just as they would the natural insects. A combination of a lightly weighted fly and added weight attached to the leader will allow you to present the flies in the optimal zone while letting them behave in the current in a natural manner.

New concepts in tackle design have been introduced to overcome the effect of vertical drag and improve a dead-drift presentation. Rio and other manufacturers offer level-taper leaders with a thinner diameter, which offer less resistance to the force of current from the faster water in the center of the vertical water column through which these leaders must pass. Other manufacturers have introduced ultrathin wire leaders that have a high sink rate in order to sink faster and have less resistance to drag once they reach the bottom.

Many other factors go into the attachment of the flies to the leader for nymph fishing, including knot preference, the manner in which the flies are attached to the leader, and how additional flies are added. Personal preference dictates whether you tie additional flies to the hook shank or eye of the preceding fly or as a dropper from the tag of the knot above the fly. There are as many opinions as there are anglers, and each tends to follow familiar habits that have proved successful in their experience. Experience is an effective teacher, and the lessons taught tend to have lasting value.

As with most anglers, many of my earliest lessons in fishing came as a boy standing by my father's side. He taught me fishing knots and casting techniques. His casts arced across the water with precision and grace and set standards that my youthful casts could not at first achieve. He had mastered the art of natural imitation. He taught me to fish to structure. And I was with him on the oars on what was perhaps his last fly-fishing trip. R.B. McCallister and I had taken him on a float trip down the Watauga River in Tennessee. At the end of the first day, we shot through a stretch of rough water that left us all with white knuckles, clutching our seats. R.B. was in the front, pointing out the rocks right before I hit them. Dad was in the back with a life preserver. We figured that at eighty-two years of age, he should have one readily available. Fortunately, he did not need it.

We came upon a pod of rising trout as the chute emptied into a large pool. The fish took an Elk Hair Caddis. After our harrowing adventure, it was a nice way to end the day. Each year, Dad fishes less and less, and mostly from the stability of the pontoon boat on the lake in front of his cabin. He is content to sit in a chair on the sunny side of the porch and listen to me tell of my latest angling adventures. He tells his own stories of long ago, friends long gone, and the fish they caught.

Chapter 4

Variations in Current

T here is tremendous variation in the flow of water. Because of the effects of friction, the velocity of the current is not uniform. As a whole, water flow behaves predictably, but on a smaller scale, it is less consistent. When viewed as individual current threads, they are not moving perfectly parallel to the banks or even parallel to the other current threads. All of the water ends up in the ocean sooner or later, but these small-scale influences give streams their subtle variations. Not all of these variations are small in scale, however. Sometimes the variant features are large in scale, which cause disruptions to flow and have much larger implications.

Several years ago, I developed a fascination with the current and movement of water in streams. When fishing, I would take a break to walk the banks and study different sections of the river. As I did, I began to notice many unusual variations to the current. I watched leaves floating on the surface of the water. Although the overall movement of a particular leaf was downstream, the path was not always linear or directly parallel to the general flow of water in the stream. There was often a tendency for a floating object to drift toward one side or the other as it progressed downstream. This movement was independent of the tendency of the thalweg to wander from side to side, because I also observed this phenomenon in slow-moving sections where the thalweg was the entire width of the stream from bank to bank. When I dropped a leaf in the center of the stream, sometimes it would remain in the center, drifting in the same current path, until it reached a bend in the river, at which time it began to migrate toward the outer bank. Other times, it would be carried to the edges before it reached the first bend. Still other times, there seemed to be a force that tended to move floating debris from the edges toward the center.

These observations indicated crosscurrents moving within the downstream currents. Even while the water moved downstream, these crosscurrents developed in certain sections of the stream and tended to carry debris either toward or away from the center. They did not directly oppose the main flow of the stream, but merely added a cross-directional element in some sections that resulted in a net movement on the surface that was diagonal, either from the bank to the center or from the center toward one bank or the other. In spite of these crosscurrents, the overall movement was always downstream. These crosscurrents indicated that other factors were at work besides the principles of laminar flow. While the properties of laminar flow were still evident, I was seeing irregularities that indicated other forces at work.

With further observation, I began to notice that there were areas along the surface of the stream where floating debris tended to accumulate. Following spinnerfalls, I observed how the dead insects tended to gravitate toward certain regions in the stream and collect there on the surface. They accumulated in larger concentrations within these depositional regions than in other areas in the stream. It was almost as if the stream, following the festivities of insect procreation, had swept the leftover debris into the alleyways of the ecosystem. These dumping zones were often away from the main thread of the current, sometimes in stillwater backeddies, but smaller regional collecting areas could be found alongside the course of the thalweg, if I looked closely enough. Depositional microhabitats were formed in small pockets and zones where they might not be expected. The trout, however, were well aware of these food collection points and frequently used these smaller depositional areas as productive lies where they could feed abundantly following all the spinner activity.

THE INFLUENCE OF RIVER FEATURES ON CURRENT

Water flows downhill, but it does not always do so in an organized and uniform manner. Crosscurrents, spiral currents, helical currents, eddies, vortices, hydraulic features, standing waves, and other physical phenomena result from the natural movement of water. While these features do not negate the properties of laminar flow or the overall tendency of the water to continue its downhill journey, they add character and variation to the ecosystem and serve a vital role in its health and maintenance. They also affect the resident trout and insect populations, as well as their behavior. Sometimes these variables have minimal effects and the river flows quietly and uninterrupted. The flow appears uniform and the properties of laminar flow are readily evident. Even under these circumstances, however, a closer examination reveals small variances. Other times, the entire course of the river may be altered by various features, and one section might bear little resemblance to another section a short distance upriver.

Large scale hydraulic features can be very dangerous. On our maiden voyage in a brand new drift boat, we had a close encounter with such a feature on the South Fork of the Snake River. A number of years ago, when our son, Evan, was still in high school, Jo and I planned a trip to Idaho so that Evan could visit a college he was interested in and I could pick up a new drift boat I'd purchased online. If all worked out as planned, we would be pulling the new boat back home behind the SUV. We arrived in Idaho Falls filled with the joyful anticipation that is normally reserved for the night before Christmas. At least, it was an exciting moment for me. I'm not sure the rest of the family viewed it in the same light that I did. Perhaps they had not been sleeping with visions of drift boats dancing in their heads.

When I saw the boat the next morning, it was love at first sight. It was beautiful, everything I had imagined it would be. The fine, young man who sold us the boat was to accompany us on a short trial run on the first day, and the second day we would be on our own. The first outing was a joy. My son and I got instruction on basic boat safety and oarsmanship, while Jo enjoyed the ride and fished. The boat was nimble and responsive. We took turns fishing and even landed a few nice trout. Soon we were safely back at the ramp, where the truck and trailer were waiting.

The second day, we ventured out on the South Fork to boldly face the river alone. We launched and set forth with such ease that Evan and I were convinced that we were natural rivermen. We set the boat up for runs through ideal sections of the river with such effortlessness that it left us with a feeling that we had finally found our calling in life. By the time we stopped for a shore lunch, we were sure and certain oarsmen. We had caught a few fish in the warm summer water but played them quickly and revived them slowly. After lunch, Evan and I continued to trade with each other on the oars, and neither of us seemed to have much difficulty getting the hang of it on the open, even-flowing river.

Our early success built a false confidence, however. The river that was kind and gentle at the outset was quite different from the river we faced at the conclusion of the journey. The first indication that things were going astray was in our underestimation of the length of the river we had planned to float. I have since learned that this is a common mistake of the uninitiated. It looked like a reasonable distance on the map, but the river opened up into a wider section that was barely moving. Suddenly we were no longer happily being carried along by the current. We were barely moving and the day was waning. We had to turn and row with the river, instead of back-paddling slowly against it. We gave up on fishing. Our trading on the oars became more frequent as we gradually exhausted ourselves. We were glad when the river finally began to gain speed and momentum. Shortly afterward, though, it turned ugly.

We came upon a hydraulic feature near a bridge. There was a strong whirlpool that had to have been a foot lower than the rest of the water. I did not recognize it for what it was until it was nearly too late. We were already in its path when I leaned into the oars. I braced my feet against the foot support and pulled with all I had. It was a test of wills that I nearly lost. When we finally shot out the other side, I had depleted what little reserve I had left and was gasping and sweating as I leaned back in the rowing seat.

Thinking our trials were behind us, I took a break. The water was fast after the bridge, however, and I had to resume rowing before I had caught my breath. The new section of the river was trickier than before, and I had to make constant corrections to avoid trouble. It took more concentration and effort. We tried to cast to trout that had begun to rise but couldn't get the boat into the right position quickly enough in the fast current. We zigzagged across the river in a vain attempt to fish the ideal sections before they whisked by.

After a while, though, we got the hang of this new challenge and resumed fishing effectively. Soon we were ferrying across the river from point to point, and our bruised egos were gradually restored. We were again able to position the boat so that our drifts improved. We caught fish. We congratulated ourselves for having sufficiently met and passed the test. But there's a fine line between being confident and overconfident. There was to be one more trial before this day was over. To sum it up, we zigged when we should have zagged. We were efficiently floating through a nice, deep run along a shady bank when my complacency was shattered. Evan pointed to the opposite bank and said, "Hey, Dad, isn't that the takeout?"

Well, the river was fairly wide at that point, and a sense of urgency turned into fear. Once again, I leaned my back into the oars. We had to race across the entire width of the river to reach the ramp before the current carried us away. We didn't make it. We missed the takeout point by about 10 yards and ended up clutching onto a tree branch in a deep trough of fast water. We all grabbed branches, and then new ones when they broke. We tried to pull ourselves back to the ramp from branch to branch, but most of the branches in easy reach had already been broken off. It seemed that we were not the first to try a hand-over-hand approach to safety. We nearly swamped the boat in the process. It was almost dark, and I had visions of being carried downriver, away from our car and boat trailer. The next takeout point was miles away, and I was too exhausted to dream of making the long hike back. But finally a compassionate angler saw our plight and, taking pity on us, threw a line from shore and dragged us back to the ramp. Thanking him profusely, I offered to buy him dinner. I was tempted to fall to my knees and kiss the ground, but I figured that I had suffered enough embarrassment for one day.

That first trip was an educational experience. Since then, I am a lot more careful when planning float trips, as I don't want to be caught unaware again. I have more respect for the force of moving water and the challenges it creates. Not only do I check the map, but I talk to someone who has floated the section before, specifically asking about difficult areas of the river, so that I have knowledge of the features I'll need to address.

Anglers also must become knowledgeable about the various features affecting the movement of water, and address them, in order to be successful in their presentations. Most of the variations are smaller in scale than the hydraulic feature we encountered, but they are equally important for the impact they have on fly presentations. You also need to be aware of these smaller features in order to improve your angling success.

HELICAL CURRENT

Crosscurrents in rivers and streams can arise from centrifugal force as the water moves around bends in the river. They can also occur as a result of helical currents that may develop in straight stretches of flowing water. In straight sections, two helical currents frequently develop side by side on either side of the center of the river. As a result of these paired helical currents, a relatively thin layer of water at the surface tends to flow from the edge of the river toward the center, where it collides with the surface flow that is traveling toward the center from the opposite bank. This mirrored, bilateral flow from each side to the center at the surface creates a slightly higher point in the middle of the river, much like the crown of a road where the center of the asphalt is higher than the edges, which helps promote water drainage from the surface of the road. If a level laser line were placed across the river where paired helical currents exist, you could see that the surface is higher at the center than it is on either side near the bank.

Once the water meets in the middle, it downwells to the bottom, where it continues across the streambed toward the bank at either side. This creates a second crosscurrent at the bottom of the river moving in the opposite direction from that at the surface. This crosscurrent just above the streambed moves from the center toward each outer bank at the edge of the stream. Once it reaches the edge, the current completes the circular journey by lifting or upwelling to the surface to continue the loop back to the stream center.

This thin, circular, crosscurrent loop spirals like a barber pole because of the net movement of water downstream. The general downstream movement of water causes the loop of circular flow to open into a helix. This continues downstream, spiraling toward the center of the river at the surface and toward the banks just above the riverbed. To illustrate the point, try a simple exercise. Stand with your arms stretched out in front of you, like the caricature of a sleepwalker, but with your hands pressed together. Move your right arm in a large counterclockwise circle and your left arm in an opposite, clockwise manner, slowly tracing a wide circle with each arm as you slowly walk forward. This mimics the continued downstream net flow of water. Both arms should meet high in the middle, then descend together for a short distance while they are directly in front of you, before separating at the bottom and diverging to either side to complete the arc. This movement accurately shows the movement of paired helical currents, which spiral as they move forward.

The combined flow of the crosscurrent and the downstream current yields a net diagonal movement toward the center at the surface and toward each bank at the bottom. The central thread of the three-dimensional water profile seems to be minimally affected by this. In the illustration, the spiral current, V5, is shown looping around the central core of water movement in zones V1 through V4. The spiral thread of current wraps around the central portion like a candy cane as it flows downriver. These spiral currents and the crosscurrents are subtle and often go unnoticed by the angler, but they certainly are strong enough to move displaced or floating insects, which often can do little to resist their effects.

Paired helical currents create two crosscurrents at the surface, one from either side toward the center. Sections of the river with helical currents often have a foam line of flotsam in the center of the stream, which is often the only telltale indication of helical currents. Leaves, sticks, dead insects, foam, and other debris may collect in this lane. Since this is frequently a concentration point for food items, trout often target this area as a feeding lane, especially when they are looking up. They will position

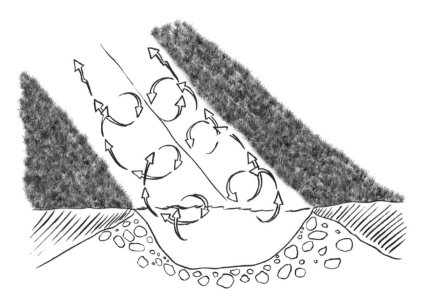

Bilateral helical currents often develop in straight sections of the river as the current follows the curvature of the bank, rolling upward along the bank and across the surface toward the center, where it collides with the surface flow from the other bank, after which it travels downward to the bottom. At the bottom, it flows toward the outer bank. This creates crosscurrents moving toward the center at the surface and toward the outer banks along the bottom.

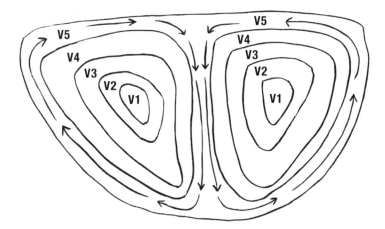

The helical currents involve only a thin portion of the water at the surface and the bottom. The main threads of current proceed downstream unimpeded by crosscurrents, but insects that are often within the thin section of spiral water movement are affected by its properties.

themselves in feeding lies that provide ready access to this current thread. This is always a good place to cast a dry fly following any insect emergence or spinnerfall. Dead and crippled emergers and spinners will accumulate in these lanes, because the bilateral crosscurrents that result on the surface of the stream from helical currents funnel food here.

The crosscurrent at the bottom, from the center toward the outer bank, will have an impact on nymph fishing. The natural insects, if displaced from the substrate, are frequently at the mercy of the current. Some are better swimmers than others, but the overall tendency is that these insects will be concentrated along the outer edges of the stream or the outer slip seam of the thalweg, if it has sharp and defined borders. This is especially true when the helical current pattern continues for an extended distance of the river, such as would occur in a long, straight stretch. This makes the edges and lateral boundaries of the thalweg ideal zones to target for nymph fishing.

The crosscurrent tends to pull the weighted flies and artificial nymphs in the same direction along the bottom, which will place them in the same drift path that the natural insects, under the same crosscurrent influence, have followed toward the bank. While the nymph is gently pulled toward the periphery of the river, however, the strike indicator at the surface will be traveling in a crosscurrent in the opposite direction, toward the center. Thus the leader, as it descends through the vertical water column from the surface to the bottom, will be skewed slightly diagonally. The tension on the flies may inhibit their ability to travel in an unrestricted manner toward the outer bank.

Frequent mending during long drifts, especially on long, straight sections of the river, will correct this influence. It's important to mend the strike indicator, which will be affected not only by the downstream component of vertical drag, but also by the crosscurrent effect from these helical currents wherever they exist. When mending for vertical drag, a slight pull upstream and toward the outer bank may be advantageous to correct the presentation. If you are floating in a boat on the right side of the river, mend upstream and toward that bank in order to reorient the fly and strike indicator so they are vertically aligned. If your position is to the left of center, pull slightly toward that bank as you pull the strike indicator upstream. This may seem like a picky point, but it only takes a minimal effect from drag to spoil the presentation.

As a result of the opposing crosscurrents, your nymph imitation may not always be in the current path where you think it is. Anglers have a tendency to believe that their flies are always lined up under the strike indica-

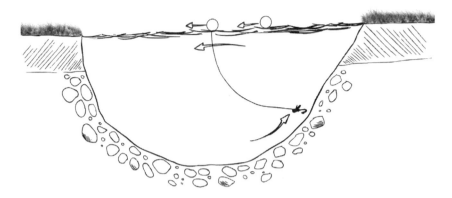

As a result of crosscurrents, there may be a great difference between where you think your fly is and where it actually is, so if you see a fish move to intercept a food particle or even just a flash of white, set the hook. Crosscurrents become especially important while sight-fishing or targeting specific structure. You need to present multiple times to the same structure to ensure adequate coverage.

tor. In reality, however, they might actually be several feet to one side or the other, in an entirely different current thread than the one in which the strike indicator is traveling. Because of helical currents and the competing crosscurrents that result, you can't be exactly certain where your weighted fly is when you are nymph fishing, unless you can actually see it. So if you are sight-fishing and see the white blink of a trout taking a food item, it could be your fly, even if you think it's drifting in a different current thread. Set the hook—you just might be surprised!

Because these crosscurrents are perpendicular to the main direction of flow, the net movement for any object that is caught in the crosscurrent will be in a slightly diagonal direction. However, even with the presence of crosscurrents, the overall movement of the water is still downstream.

Helical currents also can arise at bends in the river. Here, instead of two paired spiral currents, as tend to develop in straight sections of the river, bends have one crosscurrent at the top, moving toward the outer bank, and one at the bottom, moving toward the inner bank. Helical currents at bends usually are not paired.

These helical currents, which are important in the remodeling of meandering rivers, also have an impact on fly fishing. The centrifugal force at the bend creates crosscurrents that travel from the outer bend toward the inner bend along the bottom, just above the streambed, and from the inner bend toward the outer bend at the surface. This influences food distribution, moving food material along the bottom of the stream toward the inner bank around the curve and for a short distance downstream. This tends to create a nutrient-rich thread of food material that extends downstream from the inner bank. There is often a drop-off following the shallow point or finger of sediment that builds up just downstream of the inner bank. This combination of structure and food availability makes this an ideal location for nymph fishing.

The crosscurrents become more pronounced as the water travels farther through the bend and into the tailout that follows. As a result of the surface crosscurrent, there is often a depositional zone on the surface along the outer bank toward the end of the bend and a short section of the tailout afterward. This depositional microhabitat collects enough foam, detritus, and food material to attract the attention of trout. (See the photo on page 30.) Cast your dry fly into these zones, particularly following any insect activity. Sometimes these areas also collect sticks, branches, or other structure. Twitching or swimming a streamer through such cover is often very productive.

Even though these helical currents are subtle and largely unnoticed by most anglers, they have a great impact on your nymph fishing. The same currents that have the power to relentlessly wear away the outer bank and deposit the eroded material along the inner bank, thus widening the river bends and creating meanders, can also relocate insects and affect your fly presentations.

VORTICES AND EDDIES

Vortices and eddies are both characterized by a swirling, circular flow of water around a central point. Vortices may be created by a drop in water level such as is commonly associated with a hole. The most obvious and dramatic example of a vortex is a whirlpool. Many whirlpools are associated with the tidal activity of the oceans. Most are relatively weak and not dangerous, but people have drowned in some of the stronger persistent whirlpools.

Small vortices may develop as swirls on the surface as the water passes an obstruction. If the object is mobile, like a stick jutting up through the water, the back-and-forth vibration of the structure as the water passes often causes minor vortices in the current that follows. These small irregularities in the current may capture your fly as it drifts on the surface and temporarily hinder its downstream progress. Your fly must be able to navigate these inconsistencies in the water in order to closely imitate the natural insect. If there is insufficient slack in the leader, the fly will drag as it is caught in these features.

This whirlpool would be disastrous for any drift boats caught in its clutches.

Eddies also have a swirling flow, but they frequently have a reversing current. They often occur as water flows past a major obstruction, such as a bridge pier or a large boulder that projects above the water's surface. As the water flows on either side of the obstacle, a void of water is created immediately downstream of the obstruction. As water flows into this area to fill the void, it flows backward toward the obstruction. Canoes, rafts, and kayaks often pause on the leeward side of these obstructions, finding respite here from the main current. Trout also take advantage of these current reversals, finding protection from the current here just like the canoeist. Migratory salmonids also rest in eddies on their journey upriver. Since these locations are frequently near rough water, the migrating fish are able to rest from the current while they gather strength for the next part of their journey.

The current reversal creates a recycling loop that captures food particles, causing them to gravitate toward these collection points. Items of food continue to swirl in lazy circles, tempting the trout with each pass. In the protected pockets created by backeddies, trout wait for the aquatic equivalent of Meals on Wheels to deliver food to their doorstep. Called *pocketwater* by anglers, these are ideal feeding lies, often attracting the larger, more dominant trout. Dry flies and nymphs both work well in such situations. Swimming a streamer through these zones can be very productive as well.

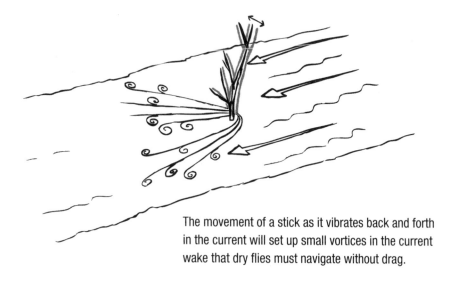

The movement of a stick as it vibrates back and forth in the current will set up small vortices in the current wake that dry flies must navigate without drag.

The eddy behind a midstream obstruction is an ideal holding position for a trout. Behind bridge piers and other obstructions, the current reversals of backeddies create a recycling effect where food collects.

Within the movement of water, vertical eddies and vortices also form, just like the horizontal ones that are noticeable on the surface. As these are frequently below the surface, they may not be visible to the angler and must be inferred from the features that are visible from the surface. Eddies often occur where the water flows over a submerged boulder, rock, or other obstruction. As the water strikes the front surface of the boulder, it is pushed upward into the vertical water column and speeds up slightly to pass over the obstruction. If the eddy created in the leeward space behind the boulder is substantial enough, the current actually reverses, and water

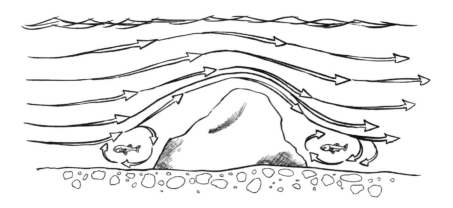

A midstream obstruction often creates a vertical recycling eddy that trout use to their advantage. The layers of detritus that collect in depositional microhabitats attract a wide array of organisms.

is sucked forward to fill the void just behind the obstruction, creating a vertically recycling current. Just like behind a bridge pier, this current reversal recycles food particles and other debris against the back surface of the boulder. This organically rich depositional microhabitat serves as a productive feeding lie for trout, not only for the food organisms that collect here from the current, but also for the insect larvae and other decomposing organisms that prefer to dwell in these areas.

A small buffer zone in front of the obstruction is created as the water recoils from the initial contact with the boulder. This water then collides with the water that is still flowing toward the boulder. The turmoil sends the rest of the water arching over the rock before it actually strikes the surface. If the boulder is large, the zone of current protection will be larger than if the obstruction is smaller. The larger the zone, the larger the trout that will want to occupy it. If it is a small zone created by a smaller rock, the zone of current protection will attract a much smaller fish. Any trout that holds in this lie will get a bird's-eye view of the smorgasbord of food choices that the current is delivering.

A three-dimensional perspective is essential to understanding the manner in which the current relates to structure in the water, not only as it affects trout location, but also as it affects presentation. For instance, the flies that approach a submerged boulder may not pass directly over the obstruction, but may be caught in a crosscurrent that is also created as the current moves laterally across the face of the boulder. In this case, they may be swept to the side of the boulder instead of dropping into the depositional microhabitat created behind it. Although the strike indicator may pass over the obstruction, the flies may follow a different path.

STANDING WAVES AND HYDRAULICS

When fast-moving water comes to an abrupt stop, the recoil that bounces back into the forward-rushing water from behind creates a hydraulic jump. This collision causes the water to rise in a ridge or undulating wave. If the speed of the current is sufficient, the wave will begin to curl back on itself and form a standing wave, which looks like an ocean wave breaking on the beach, but one that does not move. It is characterized by tremendous turbulence, with air entrainment causing a whitewater appearance.

One of the simplest examples of a standing wave can be created in your kitchen sink. Turn on the faucet and watch as the flow of water hits the bottom of the sink and radiates outward in a circular fashion. Initially, as the flow moves outward from the impact point, it is very fast and the layer of water is thin. It slows as it radiates outward and collides with a zone of slower-moving, deeper water, forming a circular ridge or ring. This standing wave has a greater height than either the inner or outer layer. The ring will move inward or outward from the point of impact, depending on the rate of flow from the faucet.

A standing wave is a pronounced hydraulic jump. Naturally occurring hydraulic jumps and standing waves can be seen below spillways, dams, ledges, drops, and falls, where the flow suddenly changes from very fast to slow. They frequently appear where brisk runs empty into slower pools. In these cases, when the water at high velocity crashes into water of lower velocity, the recoil of backflow collides with the forward-moving water,

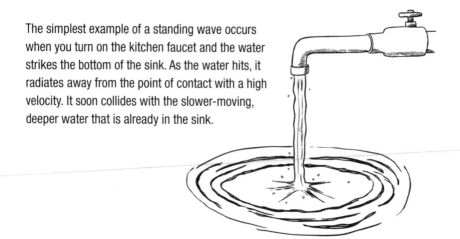

The simplest example of a standing wave occurs when you turn on the kitchen faucet and the water strikes the bottom of the sink. As the water hits, it radiates away from the point of contact with a high velocity. It soon collides with the slower-moving, deeper water that is already in the sink.

Hydraulic jumps have given rise to the new sport of river surfing. Surfers ride small surfboards on top of stationary waves, remaining stationary while the water rushes all around them. Kayak enthusiasts also find entertainment in riding over hydraulic jumps.

and a hydraulic jump forms as a result. If the water speed of the faster section is below the critical minimum, or minimum threshold, the wave may not be completely stationary and may appear as an undulating ridge at the point of intersection. At supercritical flow speeds and above, a standing wave will appear. Since the hydraulic features are dependent on discharge, a small ridge at low flows may turn into a large standing wave during high-water conditions.

Hydraulic jumps are important to anadromous salmonids, which seek out the upward thrusts to give them a boost in leaping up the falls or cascades of water. They can use these stationary launching pads to give them additional momentum to scale the heights. They might not be able to make their spectacular, gravity-defying leaps without the aid of this water feature.

READING THE WATER

The next time you spend time on a river, take a moment to pause and study the water.

The many types of current variations and features add complexity to the rivers and make fishing them a challenge. You need to understand and adapt to these current variations, by reading the water, in order to reach your full potential as a fly fisher.

There is more to reading the water than merely looking at the surface of a stream, although this is what anglers frequently do. At a glance, we assume we know its depth and breadth, and we feel as if this is all we need to know. But we are missing a lot. A river is a three-dimensional entity, and we must learn to appreciate the subsurface effects of current as well. To achieve the greatest success as an angler, you first need to gain a thorough understanding of water movement, as described in this book. Then, when you are on the river, study the water and notice the ways the current interacts with structure. If you read the water carefully and thoughtfully, gleaning as much as you can from the information it offers, you will improve your presentations and become better at predicting trout location. The effort you put into learning to read the water will pay off by making you a more successful fly fisher.

Chapter 5

Turbulence

I f you've ever watched the smoke rising from a burning cigarette or a snuffed-out candle, you've seen one of the best visual examples of turbulence. At first, as the smoke rises with parallel vertical threads, the flow is linear and laminar. As the smoke rises further upward, the flow becomes random and disorganized, mixed with swirls and eddies, as the individual molecules within the plume begin following their own paths. The flow now looks completely different. Laminar flow is predictable and regular, whereas turbulence is not. There are mathematical formulas to describe the laminar flow of a substance, but none that apply to turbulence, which still defies modern physics.

As applied to water currents, laminar flow is regular and well defined, with all of the water traveling in more or less the same direction, although the speed may vary where it is affected by friction. Turbulent flow is complex, with random and chaotic movement of individual molecules or collections of molecules that may be traveling in different directions and at different speeds. Between areas of laminar and turbulent flow, there is a transitional flow that shows the characteristics of both.

In the natural movement of water in rivers and streams, the properties of both forms of flow are present under most circumstances. At normal current speeds and in most rivers and streams, some turbulence is always present. It may be small in scale, but even so, it will disrupt laminar flow. The larger the scale of turbulence, the more disruption there will be. In some cases, the turbulence can be dramatic. Even as the turbulence increases, the horizontal and vertical slip seams still exist. Friction still causes velocity lamination and different zones of current speed.

The smoke that rises from a burning cigarette or snuffed candle wick begins as laminar flow but rapidly becomes turbulent. Conduct your own experiment in a room that is free from drafts. Set a burning cigarette in an ashtray or snuff out a candle, back up a bit so as not to disturb the air around it, and observe the flow of the smoke.

Turbulence serves a number of different roles in the lotic ecosystem, many of which are vital to the health of the plants and animals that live there. Without turbulence, life within streams and rivers would be vastly different.

TURBULENCE AND GAS EXCHANGE

If all of the flow were smooth and laminar, the river would soon be depleted of oxygen. Gas exchange is greatly facilitated by the mixture of air into the water by turbulence. In fact, whitewater is white because of the great number of air bubbles in the water. Oxygen is essential not only for trout, but also for other animals that live in the streams. Some species are more susceptible to oxygen fluctuations than others. Low oxygen conditions will not support trout. Brook trout seem to be the most sensitive of the trout species and are often found only in the upper sections of some streams, where the colder, faster, more turbulent water has a higher oxygen concentration and there is less seasonal variation in oxygen levels than in other sections of the stream.

Turbulence is especially important during the hot summer months, when there is a natural reduction in a stream's overall oxygen levels. The water temperature and oxygen concentration of a stream are inversely related: as the water temperature rises, the concentration of oxygen in the water falls. Warmer water is not able to absorb and carry as much oxygen as colder water, and it carries what it does absorb for a shorter period of time, with the oxygen being rapidly lost back into the atmosphere.

This reduction in oxygen has a profound impact on trout, especially as it relates to the locations they choose. When the water warms up in summer, since turbulence facilitates the gas exchange, trout will gravitate to

Whitewater is white because of the great number of air bubbles in areas of turbulence. This oxygen is thoroughly mixed into the water in these areas and serves as a source of oxygen for the lotic ecosystem.

and just behind areas of strong turbulence to be close to the source of oxygen. Deep runs following sections of rough water, especially those in the shade, are ideal lies for summer trout in warm water.

On warm summer days, I judge the trout's comfort by my own. If I'm finding the spot where I'm fishing to be too hot for me, it's probably also too hot for the trout. This tells me I need to find a shady, cooler place to fish. Chances are good that the fish have already found it. On a blazing hot day, I avoid standing in the middle of sun-bleached riffles, even if they look "fishy." Maybe that fishy-looking spot will be productive after the sun has set, but in the heat of the day, I look for areas that offer the fish some relief from the heat.

Turbulence is important for the exchange of other gases as well. Carbon dioxide, which is essential for many aquatic plants, is also introduced into the water by turbulence. The concentrations of both oxygen and carbon dioxide have a great influence on the flora and fauna of the stream. A very slow-moving river has a vastly different organic biomass than a fast-flowing brook, in terms of the composition of individual organisms as well as their size.

By incorporating air bubbles into the water, turbulence also reduces water density. The amount of entrained air can be up to 60 percent, which can lower the density of the water significantly. This is important to fish, as they will encounter less resistance when they are swimming upstream against the force of the current. If fish had to face strong currents without the reduced density from entrapped air, they would expend a great deal more energy to swim upstream. You may have noticed a similar phenomenon in shoveling light, powdery snow versus extremely wet snow. The powdery snow is mixed with more air and therefore is less dense, so a shovel full weighs less than a shovel full of wet snow.

This reduced water density is particularly important for migrating salmonids. As they launch upward from standing waves, they seek the portions of the waves with fewer bubbles, since the denser water provides greater thrust as they push off from the launching point. After their upstream leap, the less dense turbulent water in which they land allows them to make a rapid escape away from the lip of the drop-off they just scaled and avoid being swept back over the ledge by the water accelerating toward the lip. This less dense water is more easily transited by the powerful fish as they vibrate their tails until they can find refuge behind a rock or boulder. Using this combination of denser water in standing waves to help catapult them upward and less dense water where they land to make their way to safety, they are able to overcome challenges that would otherwise be insurmountable. Anyone who has seen leaping salmon make their way upriver has been awestruck by the experience.

THE MIXING EFFECT OF TURBULENCE

Like a blender mixing margaritas, turbulence does a thorough job of mixing the water in rivers and streams. The churning and tumult ensure complete dispersal and distribution of everything from oxygen and inorganic compounds to the organic biomass and organisms within the lotic ecosystem. The constant buffeting of rocks grinds them together, resulting in a steady release of minerals into the water. These minerals are distributed throughout the ecosystem, affecting water chemistry and pH, as well as the organic organisms that live there. The dispersal of material in the stream is important for natal stream recognition by migrating fish: the current carries the scent of home to distant salmonids as they travel back to the place of their origination. Turbulence also is responsible for much of the large-scale movement of inorganic structure, such as rocks and gravel, aiding the current in lifting and carrying material in the process of bedload transport.

The constant agitation and mixing affect of turbulence helps establish thermal uniformity in rivers and streams. Rivers do not have thermal stratification, layers of different temperatures, as do stillwater or lentic ecosystems. In lakes and ponds, the upper layer of water, called the *epilimnion*, and the deeper layer, the *hypolimnion*, are separated by a region known as the *thermocline*, which allows for an abrupt temperature change between the two layers. These layers differ from each other not only in temperature, but also in many other fundamental respects, such as pH and oxygen content. The epilimnion is generally warmer than the hypolimnion, but depending on the climate at the location of the lake, the thermal characteristics in winter may be different.

The thermal traits of rivers and streams are much more complex because of the current. Shallow, fast-flowing rivers are said to be *isothermal*, meaning that the water at various depths tends to be the same temperature, because of the constant agitation and mixing of water. In sections of the river up to a few feet deep, the water temperature at the bottom of the stream is usually the same as at the surface. The temperature of these shallower sections of the stream doesn't vary to any great extent from top to bottom. Very slow-moving, deep water has more thermal variation, however. The slower current is generally less turbulent, so less vertical mixing of water occurs. This allows a thermal gradient to establish, especially in very deep pools or long slack-water stretches, where the deepest portion of the vertical water column has a lower temperature than the water at the surface. In the deepest pools, the bottom layers may be several degrees colder than the surface temperature, but they still do not develop stratified layers like lakes and reservoirs.

Vertical temperature variation may be introduced by a tributary joining the main river. If a shallow stream joins a larger and deeper river, there is usually a temperature difference between the two waterways before the confluence. Unless it is near its headwater source, a shallow stream is typically warmer than deeper rivers because of the increased surface area, relative to depth, that is exposed to sunlight. After it discharges into the main river, its warmer water frequently accentuates a thermal gradient until it is thoroughly mixed with the rest of the water. Groundwater input can also create a thermal gradient in rivers downriver of this contribution until it is mixed into the general flow. Especially in the summer, this input along the streambed introduces cooler water into the river, which lowers the water temperature along the bottom in the downstream stretch.

Turbulence also plays an important role in the *thermoregulation* of rivers and streams, which is the manner in which they gain or lose heat. In the summer months, turbulence mixes in the cooler air at night, while the stream also radiates heat to the cooler night sky. These factors help the stream dissipate some of the heat it gained during the day and lower the water temperature rapidly and effectively. This provides relief to the trout, which might otherwise suffer during prolonged periods of warm weather.

The thermal characteristics of rivers have a great impact on trout behavior. Because fish are cold-blooded, their internal body temperature varies considerably as the water temperature rises and falls. Thus they must seek sections of the river where the ambient temperature of the water allows them to maintain the closest to ideal internal body temperature. This means that you need to adapt your winter and summer fishing strategies to the thermal activity of the river, and they will be vastly different.

Understanding the thermal behavior of rivers and the impact on the resident organisms also improves the likelihood of predicting trout location and feeding pattern. For example, do trout always hide in the deepest pools in the heat of summer? Not necessarily. Trout react to thermal stress with a number of different thermoregulatory responses. They usually avoid stagnant or slack-water sections where the warm, slow water has been depleted of oxygen relative to areas of faster water. In the summer, oxygen becomes the limiting factor as the water temperature rises. The trout may prefer a deeper pool, but only if the oxygen level is satisfactory. If the pool has a source of oxygen in the form of turbulent, rough water just upstream, it will be more desirable. The fish often establish their resting or nonfeeding lies in deeper water for a number of reasons. Deep water provides safety and security, allowing them to relax their vigilance from predation a little. These waters may be cooler than shallow stretches by several degrees, but the main reason trout seek these locations is the relief from the solar energy of the sun. The energy from the sun diminishes as it passes through the water, and thus the deeper the water, the less heat from the sun.

When you sit in the sun on a hot, sunny day, the sun's rays cause your skin to heat up. If you move to the shade of a nearby tree, you feel much cooler, even though the breeze that blows past you is the same temperature as it is a few feet away in the sun. Your skin absorbs heat from the sunlight, and the same is true for trout. So on hot, sunny days, don't look for trout only in deep pools. They will wait out the heat of day anywhere they can find oxygen, shade, and security. Don't ignore the fast-water runs, especially if they are in the shade. Overhanging banks and streamside vegetation in moderate to brisk current are also choice locations, offering all the elements a trout needs.

THE ORGANIC IMPACT OF TURBULENCE

Another impact of turbulence is that it helps foster biodiversity in the ecosystem. In the lotic ecosystem, turbulence, oxygen, and current strength go hand in hand. Certain organisms thrive in the face of turbulence, while others do not. In particular, some moss species have special features that allow them to live in fast, turbulent water such as rocky chutes and waterfalls. They are tough and have adapted structural features to resist its force, such as a secure holdfast system. Organisms that are less adapted to turbulence are concentrated in other regions. Broad-leaved plants are especially vulnerable to turbulence. Because of the large surface area of their leaves, the constant pounding would shred the leaves or even dislodge the plants. On an even smaller scale, turbulence buffets and concentrates simple life forms like algae, diatoms, and bacteria into small cracks and crevices, and it also disperses these organisms downstream by whirling them into the currents.

Most species of organisms that are well adapted to strong current are also able to better withstand the constant buffeting of turbulence. These include many insects. Stoneflies are especially resistant to the impact of turbulence and can often be found under rocks and in cracks and crevices in fast, rough sections of water. Other insects have adapted to turbulence in the manner in which they feed. Filter feeders, such as some species of caddis, rely on a certain amount of turbulence to dislodge organic debris and other food items. They construct elaborate nets in the downstream stretches following turbulent water, even aligning their nets so that they are at right angles to the turbulence. Still other insects do not withstand turbulence as well and have adapted instead to slower, less turbulent stretches of river. These species have developed elaborate mechanisms to live in lower-oxygen environments.

Different species of trout also vary in the type of water they seek, relative to the combined effect of current strength, turbulence, oxygen, and water temperature. This serves as an effective mechanism of distributing the various trout species within the ecosystem. Brook trout seek colder water with higher oxygen content. This kind of water is typically found near the headwaters, where the stream has not yet gained heat as it flows downstream. The colder water has greater capacity to deliver the higher amounts of oxygen the brook trout need. Brown trout are typically found downstream of the brook trout, in sections of the river where the temperature is a bit warmer and the biomass is greater.

Turbulence thus results in segregation of species within rivers and streams on all scales and levels. From trout to insects to plants and even bacteria, turbulence, especially as it relates to the oxygenation of water, enhances biodiversity. Organisms that have adapted to withstand the effects of turbulence and stronger current are able to survive in this rough but oxygen-rich habitat, while other, more vulnerable organisms are displaced and concentrated in less turbulent portions of the rivers.

THE NATURE OF FLOW

Many factors play a large role in the formation of turbulence, but one of the most important is the slope or pitch of the streambed, which determines the speed of the current. The most extreme pitch is a drop-off or waterfall, which is very turbulent. Gradual, gentle slopes, on the other hand, are less so. Above a certain velocity, known as the *critical speed*, turbulence inherently develops and the flow becomes less laminar. The faster the flow above this critical speed, the greater the turbulence. Most rivers, streams, and brooks travel above the critical speed most of the time, and as a result, some degree of turbulence is usually present in the water flow at all times.

The terrain characteristics of the drainage basin in which a stream is located largely determine the pitch of the streambed, which dictates the speed of the current and thereby influences the amount of turbulence. Mountain streams, such as those found cascading through the Allegheny Mountains of Pennsylvania, typically have a great deal of turbulence. Sure, these streams still have pools and areas of slower movement, but they have more areas of turbulence relative to the total length of the stream. As a result, the oxygen levels are a bit higher and more stable in the summer. Bucolic streams coursing over flat land, such as those in southern Wisconsin, typically have less turbulence, especially where they flow through the valleys. They do have areas of turbulence, but the slower sections with little to no turbulence predominate. This results in variations in oxygen levels along the course of the stream, to which the trout adapt. In summer, the turbulent sections of these streams are trout magnets. In the lowland sections of slow-moving streams, look for the trout to be concentrated in deeper water following turbulent runs anywhere there is shade. They may move upstream or be congregated near the infrequent areas of turbulence, rather than being spread out as would be the case in a stream with a greater amount of turbulent water, where the oxygen content is more uniformly distributed within the stream.

The characteristics of the streambed and banks also influence the amount of turbulence. Water flowing over a rough, irregular substrate, where the streambed and banks are composed of rocks and boulders, becomes more turbulent. Sandy or silty sections with a smooth, even streambed and bank produce less turbulence. Here again, the geologic features that exist in the catchment play a large role.

Water's intrinsic characteristics of viscosity and inertia also influence the nature of its flow, including the degree of turbulence. *Viscosity* refers to the cohesiveness of individual molecules for one another. Fluids with a high viscosity, like honey, tend to exhibit turbulent flow less readily than fluids with a low viscosity, such as alcohol. In fact, the stickiness of honey makes it reluctant to flow at all. Alcohol, on the other hand, is less viscous and flows rather well—especially around fly fishermen! It's the agitation from turbulence releasing the carbonation that causes beer to foam up with a head.

What does this have to do with fly fishing? Quite a bit, actually. Colder water is more viscous than warmer water and resists the development of turbulence to a greater degree. Warmer water is less viscous and therefore more easily develops turbulence, which is important, since it carries less oxygen and more rapidly loses the oxygen it does absorb. The greater tendency for warm water to become turbulent helps offset this loss, as it incorporates additional oxygen into the water on a more frequent basis. This aids in improving the overall oxygenation of the water at a time when trout and other aquatic species need it most.

When the water is more viscous, as it is in the winter, the sediment that is carried in the river is slower to settle out and may be transported farther downstream. During winter runoff, more material is picked up by the higher water flows and is carried longer distances by the more viscous cold water, leading to more change within the river. Thus late winter is the time of river remodeling.

The other intrinsic property of a fluid that influences its flow pattern is *inertia*, which refers to the reluctance of a fluid to accelerate or decelerate when force is applied. Fluids with higher inertia are harder to get into motion when they are stationary and harder to stop when they are in motion. This reflects Newton's first law of motion, which states in part that an object at rest tends to stay at rest and an object in motion tends to stay in motion. Fluids with high inertia favor turbulence, whereas fluids with high viscosity favor laminar flow.

Chapter 6

The Benthic Community

The first time I picked up a rock in the river and looked underneath it, my eyes were opened to a whole new world. As I examined it, I noticed several different creatures of various shapes and sizes crawling or clinging to the underside of the rock. One was broad and flat. Another looked a bit like a miniature roll-up bug that I had played with as a child. Several small, reddish worms wriggled in a bit of mossy vegetation stuck to the rock. What I held in my hand was a world in miniature.

Then I looked at the streambed through the shallow water at my feet. In just a few moments of observation, I saw worms, grubs, larvae, nymphs, snails, and many other organisms. A little crayfish scuttled between the rocks. Interlaced strands of white silk looked like a heavy-duty spiderweb. The scientist within me was intrigued. How could I have been oblivious to all this activity? I stirred up the bottom with my fingers. In the cloud of silt, other small organisms darted to safety. The streambed just beneath my feet contained a microcosmos.

After this eye-opening experience, I started collecting books on aquatic entomology. Rick Hafele became my hero. I read books by Carl Richards, Doug Swisher, Gary LaFontaine, and Ernest Schwiebert. When I traveled, my carry-on began to weigh more than my suitcase, as I jammed three or four textbooks into it. My idea of a little light reading changed almost immediately. Each year, I bought several new books to read during the winter. At the beginning of the winter, they were stacked on my nightstand. By the beginning of spring, they were lined up on the bookshelf, their pages dog-eared and bent.

Looking under rocks in the stream became a regular part of my pre-fishing routine, especially when I visited a new river. I bought a kick net. Closely examining the organisms living in the benthic community allowed me to determine which resident organisms might be available as food sources for trout. By doing so, I was able to answer several questions even before I began to fish: Which insect nymphs and larvae were present, and which ones were in the highest numbers? Which species seemed to be most active and available to trout? Were crustaceans represented? Were other food sources present? I began shaking bushes along the shoreline to see if any insects were clinging to the vegetation. This would tell me what insects might have emerged the day before. With this information, I could make an informed decision as to which fly and manner of fishing might work best.

To be a successful angler, you need to understand the feeding behavior of trout, and for this it is essential to understand the organisms on which they feed. Since trout feed on organisms at the bottom of the food chain, their feeding behavior is largely influenced by the lower-level organisms. Understanding these organisms is the first step on the path to understanding trout.

A WAREHOUSE OF LIFE

The benthic habitat is the zone of organic material, sedimentary debris, and living organisms at the bottom of the stream. This includes the streambed itself, the thin boundary layer of water just above the streambed, and the water in the interstices within the substrate of the bottom. All of these components are interconnected and linked via the water cycle and the flow of water through the storage reservoirs.

Benthos is from the Greek word meaning "from the depths of the sea." This zone is present in marine as well as lentic and lotic freshwater ecosystems. In the ocean, it has been subdivided into different classifications because of the tremendous differences between the benthic community in a shallow reef and in the deepest part of the ocean.

The benthic habitat is an organically diverse and nutrient-rich environment and the foundation of the lotic ecosystem. In a healthy stream, this zone can sustain an extremely large biomass. It is home to a vast array of organisms, from single-cell bacteria to plants and animals. Along the streambed, in the interstices, cracks. and crevices, is a complex world within a world, a dog-eat-dog world where organisms compete for limited resources. This zone is teeming with life as these organisms forage for food, compete, grow, live, mate, and die. For some organisms, their entire life cycle takes place without ever leaving this diverse environment.

Like many other aquatic vertebrates and invertebrates, trout depend on this layer for their sustenance. With the exception of terrestrial insects and small mammals such as mice, most of the organisms that constitute the trout's diet arise from and are nourished either directly or indirectly by the benthic community. It is difficult to overestimate the importance of this habitat to trout, and whatever is important to trout is important to trout fishermen.

The first time I ever went scuba diving in a river, it was like entering a whole new world. Below the water, you are able to see things that are not visible from the surface. The first thing that you notice is that there is a lot of suspended material in the water. Small bits of plants and flecks of algae are drawn into the current. Particles of sedimentary material are lifted from the bottom. Small swirls of current occasionally disturb the gravel at the bottom. Many of the finer particles of the substrate are stirred by the current. Food items are whisking by as well. How trout actually discern the edible from the inedible is amazing, especially with the speed at which it passes them. If you observe the fish for any length of time, you will notice that they make mistakes from time to time. Occasionally they snap up something from the current and spit it out just as quickly. Perhaps they intend only to taste the morsel to see if it is edible. Or perhaps they have the human quality of changing their minds.

From my observations underwater, I noticed the similarity of current and the wind. There is not always a steady and constant flow in either case. There are gusts of current just like there are gusts of wind. Aquatic vegetation waves and undulates in the current much like waves of grain rippling in the breeze. Fish are constantly adjusting, using their fins to hold position. It is surprising how effortless they make this appear. It is like watching a graceful, underwater ballet.

There can be tremendous variation from one section to another, even in the same river and often separated by only a short distance. In areas of swift current, much of the substrate appeared devoid of organic material, almost as if it had been scrubbed clean by the current. But on looking closer, I could see where the current had deposited and concentrated particulate material and organic debris behind boulders and obstructions. In slower current, there was more uniformity along the bottom. The flora and fauna were not necessarily concentrated behind boulders and in the cracks between rocks; they were more evenly distributed. In fact, in sections that were characterized by flat, slow glides, the bottom was often relatively featureless and uninteresting, interrupted only by the occasional rock or log.

EROSIONAL AND DEPOSITIONAL HABITATS

Scientists break down the lotic ecosystem into two main habitat classifications based, not surprisingly, on current. Each has different characteristics and features. The *lotic-erosional* habitat is characterized by faster currents and coarse substrates. The *lotic-depositional* habitat includes pools, backwaters, and stream or river margins. The benthic community of these two habitats also differs. It is present in each habitat, but it is different in character, in both the types of vegetation and the organisms that live there. Each habitat attracts a different population of organisms.

The distinctions between these two habitats are not totally black and white, however. Biological classifications such as these are human constructions to help make sense of the vast complexity that exists in aquatic biology. In reality, in between these two categories are many blended environments with features of both habitats. Transitional zones between riffles and pools are a perfect example. There may also be small areas within one habitat that display the features of the other; for instance, pockets of quiet water may be intermixed in the runs and riffles of lotic-erosional habitat.

Fast-flowing water is the hallmark feature of the lotic-erosional habitat. The typical example is a riffle with a hard, rough bottom composed of cobbles, boulders, rocks, pebbles, or gravel. Soft, loose, and fine sedimentary material is usually lacking, having been removed through the process of bed-load transport and either deposited in depositional zones within the habitat or, more commonly, carried out of the riffles completely and deposited in sections of slower-moving water. Depositional microhabitats are present in the erosional habitat, but these generally are located immediately behind obstructions such as rocks, logs, or boulders. They sometimes also occur near the banks, along the margins of flow. These areas will attract, collect, and concentrate organic detritus, leaf litter, and silt. For this reason, pocketwater areas within riffles are magnets for detritivores, organisms that consume detritus, such as decompositional nymphs, larvae, and scuds, seeking the protection from current. When fishing in riffles, you should target these areas, especially when fishing with nymphs and scuds.

In these faster-water environments, plants that grow tight to the bottom, such as moss and certain types of pondweed, are common. Plants in these habitats have the necessary characteristics to tolerate the rapid flow, such as a low profile and holdfast mechanisms. Diatoms and other plankton are found in the interstices of the substrate and clinging to the back sides of

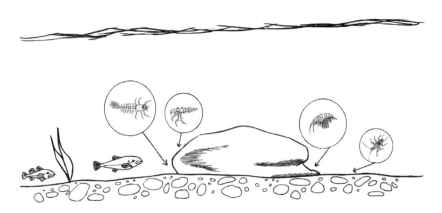

The benthic habitat consists of the boundary layer of the stream just above the bottom and the water-saturated substrate of the streambed. Concentrated here are primary producers (autotrophic) such as diatoms, algae, moss, and other macroscopic plants, and the insects that feed on them thrive. Crustaceans, snails, and other invertebrates crawl along the surface. Trout begin their lives within this zone as eggs and sac fry.

rocks. These habitats generally do not have any broad-leaved aquatic vegetation, save in quiet water along the streambanks, but even here they are rare because seasonal high-water conditions tend to remove them.

The lotic-depositional habitat has slower-flowing water, and the bottom is made up of softer, sedimentary materials that have dropped from the current as the speed and force of the water decrease. Examples include pools, backwaters, and stream or river margins. Sand and silt in flat glides and pools often make the bottom mucky. The vegetation is more diverse and includes broad-leaved plants and other forms of aquatic vegetation. In these habitats, microscopic organisms such as plankton are found suspended in the water, resting on the bottom, or clinging to the other macroscopic plants or rocks. Detritus is more uniformly distributed, instead of being concentrated by the current behind rocks or logjams as in lotic-erosional waters. The aquatic species in this habitat are generally intolerant of strong current and have few modifications to enable them to endure it.

THE FOOD CHAIN

As in all ecosystems, organisms in the benthic layer are arranged hierarchically, according to the nature of their diets, into a food chain. This zone hosts organisms from the beginning to the end of the food chain. Each level in the food chain is known as a *trophic level*.

At the beginning of the chain are the autotrophic organisms, such as diatoms, phytoplankton, algae, and simple plants. Autotrophic organisms

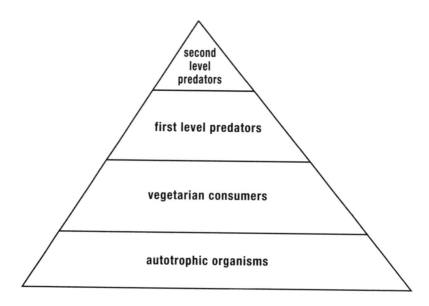

The aquatic food chain shows the interdependence of all the levels of the food chain. Each trophic level depends on the preceding levels. Each builds on the preceding level, and each is smaller than the one beneath it because of the loss of energy between the various layers and because not all of the organisms from the lower levels are consumed by those in the upper levels.

are primary energy producers because they manufacture their own energy. Through photosynthesis, they use sunlight to create biologically available energy for their own use, much like plants do on land. Aquatic herbivores such as mayflies form the next level, known as primary consumers because they feed primarily on the autotrophic energy producers in the first level, much like cows feed on grass.

The third trophic level consists of predators that feed on the organisms from the layer below them. Some caddis and stoneflies are predatory in the immature stages and are examples of predators in the third trophic level. Trout are in the fourth trophic level in the food chain, as they eat foods from all the levels below. They eat mayflies, as do other predators in the third trophic level, but because they also eat third-level organisms such as stonefly nymphs and caddis larvae, they are ranked at the next higher level. Birds of prey that feed on the trout would represent yet another level.

Some animals can be included in the food chain at several different levels, depending on what they are eating. Humans are typically considered to be in the third trophic level, as we eat both plants (primary energy producers) and meats (such as beef from the cows in the second level). A person who is a vegan would be a primary consumer, however, and enter the food chain at the same level as other herbivores. An angler who eats the occasional trout would be considered to be at the next higher level than the trout at this point.

The last organisms in the progression of the food chain are the decompositional species, which break down the organic debris into elemental building blocks to be used by the entire ecosystem. Primary producers and higher-level consumers become the food sources for these decompositional organisms when their bodies decay after they die. In this ecosystem, this would include dead trout as well as decaying leaves that are washed up against the bank. Many insects, such as shredders and detritivores, worms, and bacterial organisms are at this level.

RESPONSES TO CURRENT

In a general sense, the different habitats in the river have been molded by the current; on a smaller scale, the types of individual species that live in the river have also been affected by the current. The current is such a strong determinant that it offers species that live in the aquatic ecosystem a "my way or the highway" sort of ultimatum and is the mechanism by which these organisms are sorted into their various niches in the stream. From an evolutionary perspective, organisms that live in the aquatic ecosystem have two ways of dealing with the current. Either species develop the physical characteristics or behavioral modifications to tolerate and thrive in the current, or they are forced into areas within the lotic ecosystem where the current is more manageable. Sometimes they are even forced out of this ecosystem altogether.

The way this comes about, from an evolutionary standpoint, is as follows: The presence of a strong environmental determinant, such as the current within the lotic ecosystem, places pressure on all of the organisms in that ecosystem. Within each species, any individual that has a trait or characteristic that enables it to cope better with the environmental pressure has a higher chance of survival in that environment. With this advantage, more of the individuals with this trait will survive to reach reproductive maturity, and they will contribute this trait to more of the individuals in the next generation. Of the individuals that lack this characteristic, fewer will survive to reach reproductive maturity and therefore will make less of a contribution, genetically speaking, to the next generation. Over the course of many generations, the trait will become more common and concentrated in the population because of the survival enhancement benefit it confers. In this manner, change is introduced into the species slowly over the course of many generations. Traits are concentrated in the population because they are consistently favored. If a physical feature or characteristic gives certain individuals within a species a survival advantage, this characteristic will eventually become concentrated in the species' genetic makeup as other individuals without the adaptation are culled out and their genes are removed from the gene pool.

This slow, progressive adaptation of a species to its environment occurs through natural selection. Through this process, nature selects in favor of those individuals that are better suited for a particular habitat. Over the generations, this has created the level of species specialization and niche partitioning characteristic of lotic ecosystems. *Niche partitioning* refers to the breakdown of a large and complex ecosystem into smaller subcategories of microhabitat. This selective process favors adaptation of the individual species that live there to the demands of particular niches. The process gradually produces change in the affected species as it is molded to better fit its niche.

Consider this example: What if all the food available to humans were 9 feet above the ground, and each person has to get his or her own food without help from others, tools, or mechanical devices? At the same time, these food items are not unlimited, so every person has to compete for limited resources. Those people that were 7 feet tall would have a competitive advantage. Those that were 5 feet tall would be at a severe disadvantage. Many more of the taller people would be able to survive to reproductive maturity and contribute more, genetically speaking, to the next generation. Since they pass on the gene for tallness, more of the following generation would be taller, and so forth, and each successive generation would grow in height as a result of the selective pressure and genetic advantage of height. Very slowly, over time and many generations, the average height for the population would increase.

Changes within a species may be either morphological changes or behavioral adaptations that have slowly developed over time to enable that species to better survive in that environment. *Morphology* refers to the physical characteristics of an organism, such as its form and structure. For example, as mayflies began to evolve, the first few individuals in the ancestral mayfly group that began to show a flattened body would have had an advantage in the current over other individuals in the species that did not. They would be less susceptible to displacement by the current and less vulnerable to predation. More of these individuals would survive to reproduce than those that did not have this trait. This would lead to a progressive tendency for mayflies to have a flattened body in subsequent generations. Because this morphological feature allows them to better cope with the current, these may have been the precursors to the clinging mayfly group, which favors current. Those individuals that did not have the adaptive feature may have been concentrated in the depositional habitat and progressively developed into the burrowing group of mayflies, which favors that region of the river.

The flattened, wide bodies that clinging nymphs have evolved give them a short, squat stance. Some theories state that this compression and flattening reduces the exposure to current by lowering the profile of the body. As the current flows over the top of the body, the velocity of the water creates lift in much the same way as the flow of air over the wing of an airplane. The lift that is created by the wing of the plane makes flight possible. For the insects, this hydraulic lift created by flowing water is a detriment to survival, because it tends to pull them away from the substrate and set them adrift in the current. Another theory suggests that the flattened bodies permit the insects to escape the current more efficiently by crawling in between crack and crevices in the substrate. Another adaptation in the body of the immature insect is its streamlined shape similar to that of an airplane. This characteristic allows the insect to maintain contact with the substrate by minimizing the tendency of the flowing water to pull it away from the bottom.

The morphology of some insect species takes this to another level, with mechanisms to improve their grip on the substrate. In race cars, airfoils are used to create negative lift to force the cars against the track surface in order to reduce the threat of rollovers; this force is known as aerodynamic

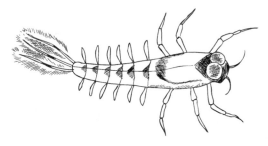

The rounded, blunted head and slender, tapered posterior of the abdomen minimizes the hydraulic lifting effect from current. As the mayfly places its head into the current, the flow of the water along the tapered abdomen reduces the tendency to detach the insect from the bottom. This blunted, cigar-shaped body is as aerodynamically efficient as that of a race car. The fuselage of an airplane is also designed with a taper from front to back in order to make it more aerodynamic.

grip. One heptageniid mayfly species uses a similar concept, positioning the rear legs in such a manner as to create a foil that pushes the insect's body against the substrate as the water flows over it. This allows the insect nymph to thrive in current conditions that might otherwise be unsuitable.

Another physical adaptation of insects is in the form of holdfast mechanisms, including suckers, claws, friction pads, and silk. Stoneflies have tarsal claws, which are like miniature grappling hooks on the appendages that allow them to grab onto the substrate. A few species of insects have developed suckers or other attachment mechanisms. One of the most interesting and common forms of holdfast devices is the use of silk. Species of caddisflies and some blackflies use silk to attach themselves to the substrate. Larvae of these insects use silk strands as holdfasts to maintain their positions in the current. Once it has a silken holdfast, the net-spinning caddis goes on to construct an elaborate net to collect food particles from the current. It then manufactures a fixed retreat made from silk at the base of the net, in which it can hide to escape the current when it is not actively collecting the food particles. It ventures out of its silken home only to "get the mail," so to speak. Case-making caddisflies use silk to make their enclosures and attach them to the substrate. In the process of pupation, the larvae of these caddis construct their cases from benthic debris and silk and attach them to the substrate with the same silk material. Inside these protective cases, the pupae undergo the process of metamorphosis to emerge later as adults. Both the silk cases and attachments protect the vulnerable pupae from the effects of current.

Other adjustments to life in the current take the form of behavioral modifications. Behavioral adaptation to current is generally one of two types: feeding behaviors or strategies to reduce current exposure. Many species of insects have developed unique feeding solutions to the problems posed by current. These organisms require a certain amount of current in

The enclosure of the caddisfly is attached to the substrate by silk that the insect manufactures. This allows the pupal case to remain firmly attached to the substrate during the process of pupation, the period when it is most defenseless.

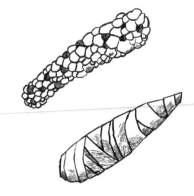

order to feed. Filter-feeding insects use silk to construct nets to filter their food items from the current. These species need current in order to feed. Without current to drive the food particles through the nets, the gathering process would be less efficient. Some mayfly nymphs, such as *Isonychia*, filter suspended particles from the current through bristles on their forelegs that interlock to resemble a mesh filter. They collect food particles from the current with these structures and then glean them with their mouthparts.

The second behavioral modification to current is to use a strategy to minimize exposure to it. All insects and other benthic organisms try to avoid the full force of current. For immature insects, hiding in the protection of the bottom serves to reduce exposure to their other main threat as well: it provides safety from predators such as trout or carnivorous insects.

Whereas some lotic species have adapted to the current and are more tolerant of its effect, others have adapted to the depositional habitats of the river with morphological or behavioral changes. They may have more elaborate gill structures to tolerate lower oxygen levels in slow water. They also may have developed the ability to create their own microcurrent by drawing water, and with it food material, into their burrows, cases, or enclosures. Some species of caddisflies have developed humps that they use to help circulate water through their enclosures. These modifications may help these species feed without the aid offered by the current, or they may be morphological adaptations to allow the insect to tolerate the reduced oxygen content in long stretches of slow-moving water.

AQUATIC INSECTS

When anglers think of aquatic insects, we think of the swarms of aerial bugs we can see. But this stage represents the briefest stage of the insect's life. Long before we notice them in the air, they have completed the majority of their life cycle, having succeeded through several molts to emerge as adults. They have survived the trials of the current and the tribulations of predation. Only a few of the myriads of insects that hatch from the eggs ever make it to the stage that we finally see in the air over the stream. Most are eaten along the way.

The benthic habitat is home to the immature stages of these aquatic insects. For some species, this stage may last for a year or more. Here they live, eat, grow, and compete, and many die long before the few remaining insects emerge as adults to complete the process of procreation. They share their benthic home with a host of other species during this time.

Insects have been very successful in adapting to their environments, whether aquatic or terrestrial. Insects live in all aquatic ecosystems, from strong current to stillwater and everything in between. They are largely freshwater organisms, with a relative scarcity in the marine ecosystems, but the abundance of aquatic insects in essentially all freshwater communities underscores their evolutionary success. Fierce competitors in an ecological sense, they are survivors. They are usually the dominant representative of the macroinvertebrate class of organisms, meaning that they have filled their niche so well that other organisms are less represented in the ecosystem as a result. Even though the aquatic form is the principal stage in the life cycle, aquatic insects retain a link to land in that there is a period in the life cycle, usually the adult or subadult stage, that requires a terrestrial habitat.

Aquatic insects have played a huge role in angling. The marriage of insects and fly fishing has been documented from the earliest writings of the sport. I am amazed by the level of knowledge and understanding that some of these angling forefathers have possessed. In their writings, accurate drawings were often accompanied by detailed text. In 1840, more than half a century before G.E.M. Skues, John Younger wrote in *River Angling for Salmon and Trout* a description of insects swimming in the middle part of the water column, originating from the bottom, "bred up from the grub state on the bottom stones." An avid observer, he also discussed insect emergence: "In half an hour the hurry is over and all stilled again into a dull, calm surface, till another rise of flies from the bottom." Younger explained how to modify existing flies into nymph imitations by mutilating the wings and then recommended letting them sink in the water so that they would resemble the ascending insects. These early pioneers recognized the importance of insects to fly fishing.

At times the role of aquatic insects in fly fishing seems to supersede the role of the trout. Some hatches are so famous that they have become legendary. The Salmonfly, Mother's Day caddis, Hex, and Western Green Drake hatches are well known among most anglers. Each year, many anglers plan trips according to the capricious whims of these insects. I, too, have been guilty of planning trips largely around an expected insect event, sometimes only to be perplexed by their absence.

One such trip involved Jo and me, along with Mary and Terry Pirro, another couple who are friends and fellow anglers. The four of us planned an autumn trip to the Yakima Valley for some fall fishing and a tour of the wine country. Terry and I studied maps and flow charts for the river. We studied hatch charts for the insects. We were targeting the October Caddis, and we were sure we had consulted every expert and authority possible to ensure our success. But we failed to consult our wives and found that they had other ideas. While we were studying river maps, they had been studying hiking maps. We had used insect calendars and hatch charts, whereas they had used calendars for flower and grape harvest festivals. It almost seemed as if they were planning a different trip.

Compromises had to be made. Our trip was moved forward a little, to the last half of September, to accommodate the other activities. The weather was perfect. We all truly enjoyed the Yakima Valley wineries and sampled a lot of fine wine. It was a great trip in all respects but one: there were no October Caddis. Not a one. We missed the hatch completely. But we caught several nice fish in spite of the caddis boycott and enjoyed the beauty of the river. We even used the cool water to chill some recently purchased bottles of wine.

I learned a lot on that trip, though, which is always one of my goals. For one thing, they don't call them the October Caddis for nothing. To expect them to arrive on our timetable was a bit presumptuous. My education did not stop there. I learned a bit about wine tasting as well. I found out that the buckets they give you are so you don't have to drink all the wine they pour into your glass, which you are supposed to only taste. I got that lesson a little late in the game, however, which led to another lesson: it's not a good idea to go fly fishing after a day of wine tasting—a nap is better!

Insects constitute a significant food source for trout, and anglers new to the sport of fly fishing soon come to recognize their importance. Many become amateur entomologists or at least learn the basics of aquatic entomology. While knowledge is power, it is not essential to learn the Latin name of every insect or memorize the peculiarities of each species. There is, however, a tremendous advantage to understanding the basics of aquatic insects. Once you've mastered the basics, it is then easier to dig deeper into entomology with greater understanding. This subject is frequently intimidating at first glance, but a few generalities make it simpler to digest. For anglers, it's important to know which species are found in fast current and which seek a slower-moving water environment.

Although many exceptions do exist, the most common length of the life cycle for an aquatic insect is one year. Some species are capable of more than one generation in a year, and others have a life cycle that is two years or longer, but the average aquatic insect spends fifty-one weeks underwater and one week as an airborne adult.

In general terms, the life cycle of the aquatic insect begins with the egg. This is laid by the gravid female as the final act of her life. At this point, she has already mated and spent a brief period during which the eggs matured and the egg sac developed. The method of egg laying varies among species, but the egg eventually hatches and the immature stage of the insect emerges.

An insect species can have a complete or incomplete life cycle. For insects that have a complete life cycle, such as caddisflies and midges, the immature stage is called a *larva*. The larva grows and develops through several substages, known as *instars*, during which it becomes increasingly larger in size. The larval stage is the longest period in the insect's life, during which time it is a benthic resident. This is the stage when the insect is the most available to trout as a food source. The larva feeds, molts, and grows as it matures. At the termination of the larval stage, the larva encases itself in an enclosure from which it eventually emerges as the pupa, which then rises to the surface to emerge as the adult. Pupation is the same process that transforms the terrestrial caterpillar into the butterfly that flies away from its cocoon. The adults mate and eventually lay eggs to complete the life cycle.

The incomplete life cycle of mayflies and stoneflies is different. The rapidly transformative process of pupation is absent. Instead, the immature stage that hatches from the egg is called a *nymph*. The maturation and transformation from nymph to adult is more gradual and spread out

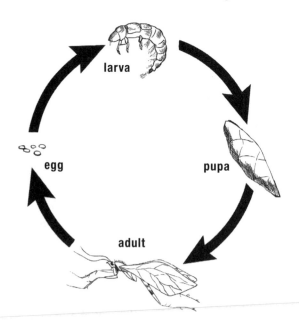

The complete life cycle begins with the egg, which hatches into the larva. At the end of the larval stage, the insect pupates, after which the pupa is released and emerges into the adult.

The incomplete life cycle progresses from egg to nymph to adult. The nymph gradually transforms into the adult without an abrupt change such as occurs with pupation.

over the entire period that the insect is in the nymph stage, rather than an abrupt change that is concentrated at the end of the immature stage by the more immediately transformative process of pupation. For insects without pupation, the immature nymphs undergo a series of instars, each time becoming slightly more mature, both in size and conformation, with each subsequent stage showing more of the developmental characteristics of the adult. As the nymph matures through the various instars, wing pads appear and develop; these are the precursors to the wings of the adult. After the final instar, the winged insect emerges. The winged insect then completes its development, which for the mayfly entails another stage from subadult to adult. The adults then mate and lay eggs into the water in order to complete the cycle of life.

The nymph stage of these aquatic insects is an important food source for trout. The nymphs reside in the benthic layer and become more active as they reach the time of adult emergence. The feeding behavior of trout is often predicated on the activity of these benthic species.

Mayflies

The mayflies are a group of insects belonging to the order Ephemeroptera. They have an incomplete life cycle. The nymphs have abdominal gills, which can often be used to distinguish them from stoneflies. The adults and subadults have upright wings. They are largely vegetarian in their diet, and these herbivores of the ecosystem feed on algae, periphyton, and

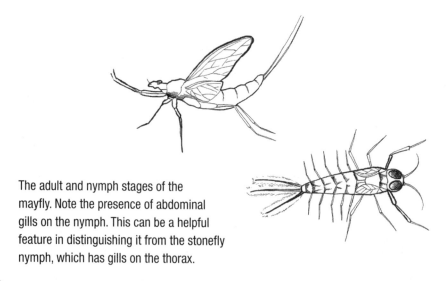

The adult and nymph stages of the mayfly. Note the presence of abdominal gills on the nymph. This can be a helpful feature in distinguishing it from the stonefly nymph, which has gills on the thorax.

fine suspended material. When they crawl on the exposed surfaces of the substrate in the process of foraging for food, they are vulnerable to displacement by the current, which explains why they are often in the drift and subject to predation.

Mayflies live throughout the lotic ecosystem, in accordance with their preference for current. Many favor the faster water and are highly adapted to withstand the effects of current. Some are proficient swimmers; others are ideally suited for clinging to the substrate. Still other species, such as *Hexagenia limbata*, prefer slower water. The Hex nymph burrows into the soft, silty substrate of slow sections of the river. It is capable of creating a flow of water through its burrow to ensure a steady supply of foodstuffs.

Caddisflies

Caddisflies belong to the order of insects called Trichoptera. They have a complete life cycle, undergoing the process of pupation. At rest, the adult holds the wings over the back in a tent shape. The feeding behavior of the larvae varies according to the individual species. Some are shredders or scrapers and feed on plant material such as algae. Other species are carnivorous and roam the benthic layer on the prowl for other insects.

Caddisfly species vary greatly in their preference for current and thus occur widely throughout the lotic ecosystem. Some net-spinning caddis species require a minimum amount of flowing water for their feeding mechanisms, whereas others have adapted to the slowest sections of the river. Caddisflies produce a silk similar to that manufactured by spiders, which helps them remain attached to the bottom and avoid being swept

The larva (left), the pupa (center) and the adult caddis fly. The adult has tented wings over the abdomen which gives it the nickname "tent wing."

away by the current. As a result, many species are often found in faster water. For net spinners, the same silk is used in the construction of the net and the retreat that accompanies it. It is also used in the construction of the shelter for pupation.

Stoneflies

The order Plecoptera contains the insects commonly known as stoneflies. Their life cycle is incomplete and for some species may be three years in length. The nymphs have claws on their legs. The adult rests the wings in a folded position over the back. The mature nymphs migrate to the banks of the river, where they emerge on shoreline rocks and other structure. During the adult stage, the males of some species make a drumming noise before mating by clapping their abdomens on the rocks of the shoreline. This sound is used to locate the females, which answer in a similar fashion.

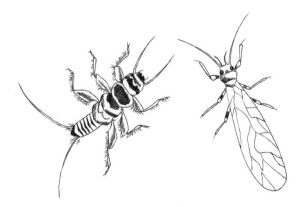

On the left is a typical stonefly nymph, and on the right is a typical adult. The stonefly nymph lacks abdominal gills, which distinguishes it from the mayfly nymph. Instead, when gills are present, they are located on the thorax.

The stonefly's feeding preferences frequently change throughout the maturation of the nymph. Most species begin as herbivores or detritivores, but as their development progresses, some transition to become carnivores and predators, while others become omnivores.

Stoneflies are generally found in areas of stronger current. In fact, most species in this order lack the sophisticated gill apparatus needed to survive in areas of minimal current, and therefore they are sensitive to low oxygen conditions and do not handle the thermal stress of warm water. As a result, they tend to favor clean, cool streams with high turbulence. They are frequently sensitive to pollution.

Stoneflies vary greatly in size. In fact, some of them are huge. The first time I saw a *Pteronarcys* stonefly in the air, from a drift boat on the Pere Marquette River, I thought it was a hummingbird! The river was high, turbid, and fast from the early June rains. After catching this insect out of the corner of my eye as it flew upstream, I did a double take. I have known anglers who have planned their only week of vacation around the salmonfly emergence in Montana. After seeing this one in the air, I can understand why. It is quite impressive.

Midges

The midges, frequently called chironomids, are true flies and belong to the order Diptera, which also includes mosquitoes. This is a widespread and diverse order of insects, found in nearly every aquatic habitat. Midges have a complete life cycle, which for some species can produce several generations per year.

The larvae are free-living and frequently roam about the substrate. They may also swim and burrow into the soft, mucky bottom. Their feeding preference depends on the species, varying from detritivore to herbivore and even to some predatory species. These tiny insects are frequently

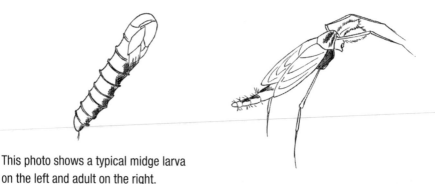

This photo shows a typical midge larva on the left and adult on the right.

an important food source for trout and, as such, they are important to trout fishermen. They are common in the winter diet of trout.

OTHER BENTHIC RESIDENTS

Insects are not the only residents of the benthic community that are important to anglers; if that were the case, patterns like the San Juan Worm would not be so effective. Snails, crustaceans, worms, and other invertebrates are important food sources for trout and are common in most rivers and streams.

Snails are common in many streams and most lakes with favorable conditions of hard water and an alkaline Ph. With a reliable holdfast mechanism in the form of a muscular foot, snails occur less frequently in the drift unless dislodged by boats, high water discharge, flood conditions, or anglers stirring up the bottom while wading. Snails are generally herbivores feeding on the small plant material and algae on rocks and gravel along the streambed. They can also be found attached to larger plants, scraping the smaller plant organisms from their surface. They vary in size depending on specie, some can grow to be very large.

Crustaceans, including crayfish, sow bugs, and scuds, are distant cousins to insects. Crustaceans have many stages of their life cycle, including several intermediate larval stages, a post-larval stage, and the adult. They become larger in size and more adultlike in appearance as they progress. Through molting, the growing crustacean must shed the old exoskeleton and grow a new one at each stage in the life cycle. Some crustaceans are filter feeders, eating plankton, while others are predatory or scavengers. They are a common prey species for trout.

Crayfish, also called crawfish and crawdads, are common in lotic ecosystems. They come in many sizes and colors. They have featherlike gills and resemble small lobsters, to which they are closely related. They are capable of holding tight to the substrate and occur infrequently in the drift. They are competent swimmers, so if they are accidentally displaced from the streambed, they are able to quickly return. As they forage through the substrate, they walk in a forward direction, but when they swim, they move backward. They are capable of lunging forward with the thrust from their tails and can capture small prey species.

Not really a bug at all, *sow bugs* are actually small crustaceans that are closely related to pill bugs that I used to play with as a kid, which were common around damp, rotting wood. In the aquatic ecosystem, they are found in the cracks and crevices of the streambed, eating decaying organic detritus. They are often gray in color with a slightly flattened, segmented body—they look like a miniature armadillo with seven pairs of legs. They are poor swimmers and often roll up when they are detached from the substrate.

Scuds are small crustaceans that spend the entirety of their life cycle in the benthic habitat and are a year-round dietary staple for trout. While fishing in Pennsylvania's Slate Run one day last May with Glen Blackwood, we found that an Olive Green Scud was the only fly that worked. And after sliding down the steep slope to the river that day, I was thankful for every fish we caught. It wasn't until later, when we were safely back at the truck, that Glen told me rattlesnakes are common in that part of Pennsylvania. If I had known that earlier, I never would have left the truck in the first place!

With all the attention that has been focused on aquatic insects, anglers too often overlook the simple scud. Since they are bottom dwellers, they are often unnoticed and underestimated in their important role in the lotic community and their significance as a dietary staple for trout. Not as flashy or ostentatious as the aquatic insects, which have the aerial stage of their life cycle to attract attention to their presence, scuds lead a relatively inconspicuous lifestyle. Nevertheless, these crustaceans are important not only to trout, but to the entire lotic ecosystem. They are frequently so abundant in some rivers that they constitute a significant portion of the trout's diet. When they are available, they are a nutritious food source. They are also a frequent staple for trout in winter.

Scuds lack attachment mechanisms or any other morphological adaptations for life in the current, and therefore they must rely on the avoidance of current to survive in rivers and streams. In other words, they don't handle the current very well. They have no hooks, claws, or other mechanisms with which to hold on to the substrate. Their body shape is not hydrodynamically efficient, offering a fairly large surface area when exposed to the current. Thus they must seek shelter within the substrate and are frequently found in depositional habitats. They are detritivores and scavengers, which means they forage for decomposing organic debris. Pocketwater techniques are ideally suited to fishing with a scud imitation.

There are many different species of *worms* in streams and rivers. Some are aquatic, but many are terrestrial in origin and occur in the stream as they are displaced by the current. Following moderate to heavy rains, the presence of worms will frequently increase due to the runoff that washes them into the river. During and after rainy weather is a good time to use a worm fly. The success of these patterns has led to the popularity of flies like the San Juan Worm and many similar derivatives.

DRIFT BEHAVIOR OF BENTHIC ORGANISMS

The drift behavior of insects is a phenomenon of great importance to trout and therefore to anglers. There is a continuous presence of benthic organisms adrift in the current. Drift studies are a frequent activity of aquatic entomologists and have shown that a considerable number of different organisms make up the trout diet.

In 1965, an entomologist named T.F. Waters divided the drift of insects into three classifications: catastrophic, constant, and behavioral. Although this system describes the activity of insects, it can apply to other benthic organisms as well, such as the scud. *Catastrophic drift* results from disturbances of the benthic layer, such as floods or other activities that lead to the unintentional displacement of insects from the substrate. It might also be caused by wading anglers, drift boats scraping the bottom, anchors, or even animals such as deer and cows crossing the stream. Once displaced, they are entrained in the current. Rick Hafele describes this sort of drift as resembling a herd of stampeding cattle running away from a tornado. Catastrophic drift can occur with changes in discharge in the stream, especially if the changes are profound. Both increases and decreases in stream discharge can cause an increase in the number of organisms entrained in the current.

The impact on benthic organisms can be profound in tailwater rivers with rapidly fluctuating rates of discharge. Many are displaced, but some species that favor the stream margins along the banks can be trapped and die as the water recedes. The desiccated bodies of scuds are frequently found in exposed areas of the streambed during low-water conditions. Since many insects are displaced from the streambed during changing water levels, this often triggers a feeding bonanza for trout and makes this is an ideal time to fish.

Constant drift refers to the continual presence of low numbers of insects in the current. This is caused by the accidental displacement of a few individuals, rather than a larger event. It occurs during the normal feeding or foraging activity of insects and other benthic organisms when they are inadvertently exposed to current that is strong enough to displace them. This type of drift may increase slightly at night as a result of the increased nocturnal activity of many insect species during low-light conditions, which causes more of them to be exposed to the effects of the current.

Behavioral drift occurs when large numbers of individuals intentionally and deliberately detach from the substrate and launch themselves into the current. This behavior is demonstrated by other benthic organisms in addition to insects, including scuds. The exact triggers and mechanisms of this activity are not clearly known. Whether this is an evolutionary call to arms to ensure adequate dispersal and dissemination of the species in an effort to enhance its survival, or a byproduct of overcrowding in order to relieve the pressure of diminishing resources, behavioral drift is a matter of great debate among aquatic biologists. It may also be triggered by rapidly changing water levels and rate of discharge.

For insects that display behavioral drift, it seems that the earlier instars are more likely to participate in this activity than those closer to final emergence. An early theory suggested that this downstream transport of insects during the drift was linked to and perhaps offset the upstream movement of the winged adults after emergence. After mating, many females fly upstream to deposit their eggs in the same section where they began their lives.

Behavioral drift generally occurs in low-light conditions, with peaks at dawn and dusk, and sometimes continues through the night. The trout focus on this feeding opportunity, making nymph fishing highly productive during these drifts. The downstream dispersal of benthic organisms is facilitated by the thalweg, which serves as a conveyor belt for these entrained organisms. At dusk and dawn, you will often find trout stationed in feeding lies along the thalweg. Presenting a nymph, larva, or scud imitation to these lies is often rewarding.

Regardless of the cause or the theories offered to explain the process, the drift of benthic organisms is important in the lotic ecosystem. It may unintentionally arise from the accidental displacement of an organism, or it may be part of a large-scale goal-oriented activity on the part of the insects. In either case, the drift of these organisms ensures a constant delivery of food items to the wary trout. The feeding behavior of trout has evolved in response to the drifting nature of benthic organisms. For this reason, it is important for anglers to imitate this drift behavior with the flies we offer to tempt the trout.

I still look under rocks and shake the bushes along the shore when I visit a river, especially if it's my first visit. And I'm usually the guy stumbling though the water waving his hat through the clouds of darting insects. This is because I have probably left my bug net in the car, but I still have to know what the trout are eating. Just like Nick Lyons said in *Bright Rivers*, "Not only does the bird taking the mayfly signify a hatch, not only does the flash of color at the break of the riffle signify a fish feeding, but my powers uncoil inside me and I must determine which insect is hatching and what feeding pattern the trout has established."

Chapter 7

The Trout Lifestyle

"**W**hat are the trout taking?" asked an old man in the parking lot at Rim Shoals on the White River in Arkansas. He had the wizened look of a veteran angler.

"I don't know," I replied. "I'm just getting started." Even though I had just come up the path from the river, I had yet to wet a line. I was returning to the truck, having once again forgotten something, this time our lunch. My companions had continued down the path to set up and begin fishing while I went back to retrieve the pack.

After putting on his waders, the old man leaned against the bumper of his car and lit a pipe before rigging his rod. The older I get, the more I can appreciate the need to pause once in a while between the various stages of a task. "You should'a been here yesterday," he informed me. "We had a nice caddis hatch about now."

I *was* here yesterday, I thought to myself. But unfortunately, not at the right time. Same old story: a day late and a dollar short. We had spent the early part of the day in Mountain Home at the Sow Bug Roundup, a famous gathering of fly tiers, and arrived at the river in what we thought would be plenty of time for an afternoon caddis hatch. But the hatch went off earlier than we had anticipated, and we missed all the action.

"I think the clouds might put 'em off today," the old man was saying. A cold front had come in overnight, and the temperature was 15 degrees cooler.

He showed me a tattered fly that had produced a few trout for him the day before. "I'm going to give it a try anyway," he said. We both agreed that a caddis imitation might be the best choice of patterns, even if the hatch failed to materialize as well as it had the day before. "But you never know with trout," he said, almost to himself. I stood and talked to the old angler for a while before heading back to the river, this time with our lunch in hand. I looked back at him as I started down the path. He was still leaning on his car with his arms folded, puffing on his pipe. He seemed to be in no hurry to get to the river.

His comment stuck in my mind: "You never know with trout." That pretty much sums it up. Why do they do the things they do? For example, why does a trout eat a tiny Blue-Winged Olive while ignoring a more nutritious meal? Entire volumes of literature have been produced on trout from the distant past up through today. We've come a long way in our understanding of trout and their world. Active research has advanced our knowledge and afforded great insight into their feeding patterns. But there remains a fickle and unpredictability quality that enshrouds them in mystery, and this is both the magnet that draws us and the snare that entraps us. It has us returning to the river time after time. We are intrigued with what we cannot master or subject to our intellect.

Although we may never figure trout out completely, we have come a long way in understanding fish behavior. And although we may never know everything that motivates them or influences their decisions, we can apply what we do know to become more proficient anglers. We have gained enough wisdom to realize that there is a certain amount of predictability in their behavior, and we can exploit whatever we can predict.

So what do we know about trout? Actually, quite a bit. If we borrow what is known about trout from the field of aquatic biology, we find that much of that information is relevant to angling. Their feeding behavior is understandably applicable to the sport of fly fishing, but if we examine them as a part of the whole aquatic environment, we can appreciate their position within the lotic ecosystem—how they have adapted to it and how they respond to the other organisms that share their world. From that perspective, it's easier to understand their motivations, priorities, and preferences, and this knowledge is important to the angler. Since current is the defining characteristic of the lotic ecosystem, its constant presence has molded trout behavior and development. It influences feeding and reproductive behavior. Understanding the trout's interaction with and response to current enables you to predict their patterns and behaviors. Understanding the quarry you seek is essential to success. Sometimes anglers get so caught up with learning about insects that we forget about the trout. We have been busy learning the differences between complete and incomplete life cycles and between nymphs and larvae, but it's also important to learn about the biology, lifestyle, and life stages of the trout.

Reproduction is the ecological goal of every species. From a biological standpoint, the need for the continuation and propagation of its kind is of utmost importance to each organism. Therefore, in order to realize this goal, it is the task of each individual of any species to survive to reach reproductive capability.

In a 1943 article titled "A Theory of Human Motivation," Abraham Maslow described the motivational needs of human beings. His theory became known as "Maslow's hierarchy of needs" and has been depicted as a pyramid, with the most basic needs at the bottom and the higher needs at the top. The lowest level includes those needs that support the essential biological and physiological functions: breathing, food, water, sleep, sex, excretion of waste, cellular activity, and the maintenance of homeostasis. *Homeostasis* can be defined as the constant internal equilibrium or balance that is maintained by metabolic and physiological activity in living organisms, such as a constant blood pressure or internal temperature. It is the internal environment created by the biological processes of life. The needs at the lowest level are those that are absolutely necessary to sustain life. After these needs are met, a person then focuses on the second-level needs, which are those related to personal safety and security, including shelter and protection from harm. The third level involves the need for love, family, and friends. The fourth level includes the need for acceptance, achievement, self-esteem, confidence, and the respect of others. The highest-order need is for self-actualization, which is represented as the apex of the pyramid. It is defined as fully realizing one's potential. It has to do with knowing your place and purpose in the universe. I'm sure that if you asked my wife, she would say that I am self-actualized. She puts me in my place all the time!

The needs for trout can be organized in a similar fashion. At the bottom of the pyramid are the overall goals of reproductive drive and the propagation of the species. Although this need is not always present at all times of year or prior to sexual maturity, when the reproductive urge is present, this need trumps all others. Trout will sacrifice themselves, limit feeding activity, and deplete their body condition and viability in order to reproduce. This innate, instinctive need is powerful, and when it is present, it dominates and supersedes all the other needs.

On the second level for trout are the basic needs essential for the survival of the individual, including oxygen, food, environmental requirements, and anything else necessary to support life in general. Trout need

Maslow's hierarchy of needs is often depicted as a pyramid, with the basic, most essential human needs at the bottom, and other needs ranked above in order of importance. Each level includes increasingly higher-order needs to be met once the more fundamental needs have been satisfied, until the zenith of self-actualization has been achieved.

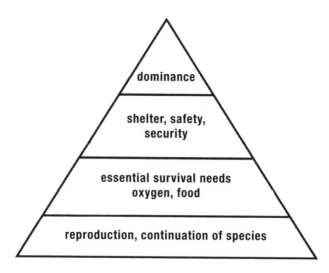

A similar model to Maslow's can be used to illustrate the hierarchy of trout needs, which also are satisfied in order of their importance to the individual. At the bottom of the pyramid are the most fundamental and basic needs, reproductive drive and the propagation of the species, and at the apex is the trout's highest-order need for dominance.

oxygen to support biological functions at a cellular level. Nutritious food sources are essential to provide energy and support growth and development. Environmental requirements include a sufficient supply of water at a suitable and comfortable temperature, as well as appropriate water quality, including the organic and inorganic water composition. If any of these essential needs are lacking for any length of time, the viability of the fish will be at risk.

Once these basic needs have been met, the next focus for trout is on shelter, safety, and security. The fish need protection from predation, especially during the earliest stage of life, when mortality is the highest. They seek concealment, not only from predators, but also from which to conduct their own predatory activities. Trout always have an instinctive concern for security, even after they have reached large size and full maturity.

After these more basic needs have been met, each trout needs to establish its position within the social community, which includes the need for dominance. This correlates with the need for respect and position within the social structure in Maslow's hierarchy for humans. Trout appear unmotivated by needs higher than this, such as status or self-esteem. These tend to be qualities that are more human in nature.

Just as with humans, the needs of trout are satisfied in order of importance. The elemental needs are satisfied first, and then the others at each progressive level. It is for this reason that trout will compromise their need for security and safety to satisfy the more basic and elementary need to feed. They will expose themselves in the shallow water if they are hungry enough. This frequently occurs during times of food scarcity. The hierarchy of needs also explains why trout will deprive themselves of the basic need for nutrition when the opportunity for propagation is present during spawning season, often forgoing feeding opportunities for extended periods of time in order to satisfy the more fundamental need to breed. The activity involved in courtship, competition, and spawning is exhausting, however, and it is often accomplished to the detriment or sacrifice of the individual. Many trout lose weight and condition or even die during the spawning period.

MIGHT MAKES RIGHT: THE ALPHA FISH WINS

The social structure of trout is driven by dominance, which is at the apex of the pyramid. Their social structure rewards dominance in regard to both feeding and breeding. The alpha fish gets the best feeding stations, while the lower fish on the scale have fewer and less desirable opportunities. And the alpha male gets the right to breed to the exclusion of lesser fish.

Dominance is size-dependent and therefore age-related. The larger the trout, the higher that fish is in the social hierarchy. Since trout continue to grow throughout their lives, the larger fish are also the older fish. Dominance behavior is even present in very young fish, which establish a hierarchy in the early stages of life.

Dominance is also species-specific. Some species of trout are more aggressive by nature than others. Brown trout are more aggressive than rainbow trout, which are more aggressive than brook trout. Although these species share habitat in many rivers and streams, the less aggressive species are often at a competitive disadvantage, especially if food is scarce. They may be outcompeted by the more dominant species and sometimes are driven to other, less competitive areas of the ecosystem. Often brook trout move upstream to areas not favored by the brown trout to avoid inter-species competition.

Although male trout are consistently more aggressive than females, even in the juvenile stages, there appears to be no gender bias in the tendency to become socially dominant. Male aggressiveness and dominance become a factor in spawning behavior, but most studies have shown that males and females occupy similar social ranking when it comes to feeding lies. In opposite-sex encounters between like-size fish, females were shown in one study to be dominant about 50 percent of the time. Thus the alpha trout in any section of the river is just as likely to be a female as a male.

Dominant trout, regardless of species or sex, exhibit significantly greater feeding success than subordinate trout. In other words, the rich get richer: by commanding the best feeding stations, these individuals get the best opportunities to grow larger and thus continue to rise in dominance. A fish will always occupy the most desirable site it can actively defend against challengers. The most desirable feeding sites offer the best return on investment in terms of the amount of energy obtained from feeding minus the energy required in the process of obtaining it. The energy a trout invests in the occupation and defense of a feeding station must be offset by the productivity of the feeding opportunities it offers.

THE LIFE CYCLE OF TROUT

The fish we commonly refer to as trout are members of three separate genera of salmonids: *Salmo, Oncorhynchus*, and *Salvelinus*. The brown trout is *Salmo trutta*, and the rainbow trout and steelhead are *Oncorhynchus mykiss*. Those fish that belong to the genus *Salvelinus*, which includes brook trout (*S. fontinalis*), lake trout, bull trout, and Dolly Varden trout, are actually char, despite their common names.

The trout life cycle begins with the laying of eggs during the process of spawning. Prior to spawning, trout move from their usual home range to suitable spawning areas in the stream.

The life cycle is a logical starting point in any discussion about trout. All species of salmonids lay their eggs in fresh water. Even oceangoing migratory salmon return to their natal streams and rivers to spawn. The period immediately preceding spawning activity is associated with movement in all trout species, even full-time river residents. While all trout move to suitable spawning sites, the steelhead and salmon travel much farther than the other species. They move from a different water ecosystem back into the rivers and streams of their birth and are called *anadromous* because of this major migration.

The initial portion of the life cycle is similar for all species, even those that are anadromous, and begins with the laying of eggs. The first indication of spawning activity is the movement of fish in the rivers and streams upstream to suitable spawning areas. The autumn-spawning brook and brown trout move up into the spawning areas in the fall, and the rainbows and cutthroats, which spawn in late winter, move toward the spawning beds just before that time. Anadromous salmonid species migrate from open water to the spawning sites at different times, according to their species and strain.

Once the trout arrive at their spawning grounds, each female selects a suitable site to construct a *redd*, which will serve as a repository and incubator for the eggs, as well as the initial nursery for the newly hatched fish. Sometimes a female constructs her redd on a site that overlaps with another redd already containing eggs, in which case the previous one is compromised. This happens more commonly if there is a limited supply of suitable spawning sites available in the river or stream.

What constitutes a suitable site varies somewhat from species to species, but all have some common characteristics. The current is an important consideration. Redds are sited in lotic-erosional habitats, such as riffles, to avoid the eggs being smothered by the deposition of silt. They are typically constructed in areas with a loose gravel substrate and a constant flow of fresh water that will deliver an adequate supply of oxygen to the eggs. The turbulence that arises from the brisk current ensures adequate oxygenation of the water.

Once she has chosen a site, the female fans her tail to clear an area of debris and make it of uniform character. Her actions easily dislodge the loose and finer material at first, which collects in a pile just downstream of the redd. This pile is called a *tailspill*. Soon she encounters material that is too coarse and large to move. This heavier substrate becomes the bottom of the first egg pocket. The female lays her first batch of eggs, which are immediately fertilized by the male that has won the right to do so. After this process, the female begins a new excavation immediately upstream of the first site. The debris from the construction of the second site covers the

Redds are constructed in briskly flowing current to ensure adequate oxygen for the incubating eggs and avoid deposition of sediment over the site. The eggs are deposited in batches from back to front in the redd. The female covers the fertilized eggs with loose gravel from the upstream excavation for the next cluster within the redd.

newly laid eggs of the first site. The female again lays eggs in this new pocket, which are immediately fertilized by the male. This process is often repeated several times, as the redd is lengthened in an upstream direction. At the end of the spawn, the redd that has been created is usually an oblong-shaped site with a tailspill at the downstream end and a slight depression marking the upstream extent of the site. The redds are usually visible as lighter-colored, circular or oblong areas along the streambed in riffle sections. During spawning season, be on the lookout for them and give them a wide birth. Try to avoid wading or walking through areas where they are located.

For species that spawn in the fall, the redds are likely to be located in sections of the stream where there is groundwater input or upwelling of springs. This input of warmer water through the winter months creates a thermal gradient of warm water near the streambed that provides a more stable temperature for the incubating eggs and minimizes the risk of freezing. The eggs of the autumn-spawning brown and brook trout overwinter in the redds and usually hatch in late February or early March. The eggs of rainbow and cutthroat trout, which are laid toward the end of winter, incubate for a shorter period of time and hatch after those of the fall-spawning species.

The major mechanisms that initiate the spawning process are changes in the photoperiod and water temperature. For brown and brook trout, the decreasing length of daylight and declining water temperature trigger the urge to spawn. For rainbows and cutthroats, the spawn is initiated by increasing length of daylight and warming of the water temperature.

Many of the eggs laid during the spawn are eaten by other fish. Other species of trout often linger just downstream of the spawning sites in the hopes of getting a free meal from the nutritious eggs that may escape the redd. Fishing with yarn-bodied or egg-imitating flies and bouncing them along the bottom is a staple of steelhead and salmon fishermen. Each year during steelhead or salmon season in Michigan, we generally catch a variety of species, from brown trout to bass, suckers, and even the occasional walleye, fishing with these colorful flies. On Alaska's Kenai River last summer, Alan and I were too late for the run of sockeye salmon, but the bright-colored yarn we used to imitate the eggs of the spawning fish were effective for Dolly Varden and rainbows, which were feeding heavily on the eggs just below the spawning sites.

After the eggs hatch, the newly hatched trout are called *alevins* or *sac fry*. They retain a remnant of the egg yolk at the base of the neck. This energy-rich source of nutrition sustains the sac fry for the first several weeks, until they are able to take care of their own nutritional needs, and enables them to remain within the protection of the redd until they are a little older and more self-sufficient. For most species, the sac fry remain in the loose gravel substrate of the redd for several weeks and emerge from its protection about the same time as the yolk sac disappears. Once the yolk sac disappears, the young trout, now called simply a *fry*, must be able to meet its own nutritional requirements from this point onward. The disappearance of the yolk sac is the motivating factor that drives the young fry out of the redd, as they need to find a new source of nutrition.

The emergence of the fry from the redd marks the beginning of the juvenile stage of the life cycle. At first the fry are consumed with the challenge of staying alive. They are focused on meeting the fundamental needs in the first two levels at the bottom of the pyramid: food and security. During this time, they eat plankton and other small organisms. In these early stages, the majority of trout fall victim to attrition or predation, either by other fish or by piscivorous (fish-eating) birds, such as herons. As the young trout grow, they develop dark vertical bars on their sides. At this stage, the trout are known as *parr*, and the vertical bars are called *parr marks*. They begin to eat larger food sources, such as insect nymphs and crustaceans.

It is frequently at this time that the smoltification process begins for those species that will travel to the ocean. This process involves biochemical changes in the young trout, now called *smolts*, that will allow them to tolerate the salinity of seawater. It is estimated that less than 10 percent of salmon reach this age. Those that survive never forget the lessons they learn during this stage of life. The need for protection and concealment make them wary for the rest of their lives.

The parr marks are clearly visible on this young trout. Parr are generally a few inches in length. As the parr grows, the vertical bars disappear, and the trout begins to show a color pattern typical for its particular species. By the parr stage, the trout have begun to feed on small organisms from the invertebrate drift and may find themselves hooked to a fly.

The adult stage is defined as the point of onset of sexual maturity, which varies from species to species. Most male trout reach this point in their second year and females in their third year. Brook trout typically live three to five years, whereas brown trout live up to twice that long under natural stream conditions. Trout continue to grow throughout their lives, and older trout can be huge. A world record class brown trout that weighs in excess of 40 pounds may be nearly twenty years old.

During the reproductive phase of the trout life cycle, the current is important in migration and aids in natal stream recognition as the adult fish return to their home streams. This complex behavior is thought to involve a variety of factors, including olfactory. The current carries the scent of the home stream to the fish and thereby serves as an aid in migration.

ADAPTATIONS TO CURRENT

The Pere Marquette River in Michigan was my first fly-fishing classroom, where I began to observe the behavior of trout. I watched them during feeding activity, and I watched them at rest. I studied how they related to the current. It is where my fly-fishing education truly began. I studied the riseforms that I had read about in Vincent Marinaro's *In the Ring of the Rise*. I still consider this river to be my home waters. I have spent many summer afternoons in the flies-only section near the green cottage access, sitting on the bank. I am still mesmerized by a rising trout whenever I come upon one. I will watch for a while, but often just long enough to identify the form and rhythm. I generally fall to temptation very quickly and pick up my rod. Then I will either catch the fish or put him down in the process.

It did not take me long to appreciate how well suited trout are to their environment. They are born and bred for the current, where they can gracefully hold with just a slight movement of the tail or a pectoral fin. They seem to use their pectoral fins like miniature oars to adjust to the nuances of the current. They make it appear effortless. But they can be lightning quick as well. When startled, they can dart to safety in the blink of an eye, with just a quick snap of the tail. They are like a coiled spring, ready to leap into action at any time.

I had a chance to further my trout education in Bellefonte, a small town in central Pennsylvania that straddles the famous Spring Creek. On a bridge that crosses the creek in the downtown section of the small hamlet, you will find a curbside dispenser that, for a few quarters, will give you thirty minutes or so of delightful pleasure. No, it's not illegal or immoral. Lest your imagination run amok, the vending machine dispenses trout pellets to feed the fish. I went through several dollars one afternoon and consider it to be one of the cheapest educations I have ever received, and one of the more enjoyable as well.

Although those fish were not feeding on a natural food source, many of the behavioral mechanisms involved in the feeding process were the same as under natural circumstances. As a food pellet approached, the fish rose in the current with minimal exertion of their pectoral fins. After snatching the pellet from the surface, they dropped quickly to the bottom and returned to their feeding station. The whole process seemed effortless.

There is a reason the fish seemed to relate easily to the current: they are highly adapted to it. Just like the aquatic insects, which have adapted to suit their surroundings over eons of time, trout also have gradually become modified to adapt to the features of current. The adaptive process of natural selection has produced fish that are ideally suited to live in the flowing water of rivers and streams. Trout have acquired the physical characteristics and made the behavioral adjustments to withstand and flourish in the face of the constant pressure from the current.

Morphological Adaptations

Just like insects, trout have adapted to the current through both morphological and behavioral adaptations. From a morphological perspective, their streamlined bodies, which taper from front to back (cranial to caudal), let the water flow around them in a hydrodynamically efficient manner. Note the similarity in shape to that of an airplane, which is designed to be aerodynamically efficient and stable. Both allow the medium that surrounds them to pass around and along the length of the body with a minimum of turbulence.

Both aviation and automotive engineers must incorporate the concept of aerodynamics when designing airplanes and cars. At high speeds, air resistance, or drag, is an important design consideration that affects acceleration and fuel economy. Cars and planes need to cut through the air with the least amount of drag and resistance possible. For cars, more rounded designs with shapes to channel the air in such a way that it flows around the vehicles have proven more efficient. Engineers previously used wind tunnels to test and improve their designs. They studied how the air interacts with the car and the way it flows over the various surfaces. Now computer simulations have made this evaluation somewhat easier.

For a natural model of efficient design, they should have studied the trout. In fact, for all their effort, engineers have failed to produce a car that is as sleek and effective in its environment as the trout are in theirs. When

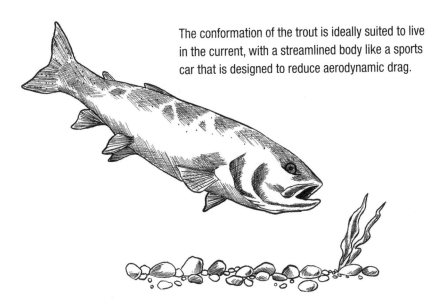

The conformation of the trout is ideally suited to live in the current, with a streamlined body like a sports car that is designed to reduce aerodynamic drag.

they are facing into the current, the water slips over and around their bodies with minimal drag and disturbance. This produces less turbulence, which makes them more stable in the water. It takes less effort for the fish to hold their position in the current. As a result, they consume less energy in the process. If humans had to fight the current all day with our body shape, we would quickly be exhausted and our energy reserves depleted. Trout, with their hydrodynamically efficient shape, can withstand the current and thrive in an environment that would be unsuitable for most other species.

In order to live in the current, trout have developed extremely muscular bodies. Pound for pound, fish have more muscle by percentage of total body weight than most other vertebrates. In salmon, up to 70 percent of their body weight is muscle. The low fat content of fish is one reason why they are a healthy and nutritious food for humans. Fish are also a very nutritious food source for other members of the food chain, including larger fish and piscivorous birds.

The type and composition of muscle tissue in fish are much different than in any other vertebrate. Their muscles must be able to withstand the rigorous demands of swimming against the current for prolonged periods of time, especially when migrating, while maintaining the capacity to achieve bursts of speed for quick getaways from predators or build the momentum to leap over obstacles. If humans had the same muscle capacities as fish, marathons would be hundreds of miles in length, and basketball hoops would be much higher. Runners would be able to run tirelessly without cramping, and then still be able to set a world record for the dash to the finish line. The muscle tone of even the best-trained athlete cannot compare to that of a trout or salmon. How are the muscles of these amazing fish able to work without cramping and fatigue for sustained periods, yet still offer the capacity to contract quickly enough to allow them to accelerate faster than a sports car?

The answer is that they have different types of skeletal muscle tissue that serve very different functions. All of these muscles are involved in locomotion and movement, but they have different capacities and operate under different conditions. Vertebrate animals have three basic types of muscles: skeletal muscles, attached to the bones; smooth muscles, located in the walls of blood vessels and internal organs; and cardiac, or heart, muscles. When skeletal muscles contract, the net result is movement. Land-based animals have only one type of skeletal muscle. In humans, the muscle tissue in your arms is the same as the muscle tissue in your legs, at least from a cellular perspective. The muscles you use to walk are the same as the muscles you use to run. The skeletal muscles of humans are the same no matter where they are located in the body and regardless of their function.

Fish, however, have three different types of skeletal muscle tissues: red, white, and pink. All three are used primarily for movement and swimming, but under different circumstances. Red muscle, also called slow muscle, has a generous blood supply and capillaries. The high concentration of hemoglobin gives it the red color. It is designed for the sustained activity involved in steady, constant swimming without tiring. These are the muscles that enable salmon to swim for long periods of time. The profuse blood supply delivers adequate oxygen to the tissues, which promotes aerobic metabolism while ensuring the removal of the toxic metabolic waste products that might otherwise cause cramping and fatigue of the muscle.

White muscle, also called fast muscle, has less blood supply and therefore less oxygen delivery capability. When these muscles are used, the lack of oxygen causes the metabolism to be anaerobic in nature, which is less efficient than the aerobic metabolism of red muscles and produces a lot of lactic acid as a metabolic waste product. These muscles are able to sustain only short bursts of activity before they are fatigued and depleted. This energy inefficiency results in a high cost to the trout. The buildup of toxins and oxygen starvation when these muscles are used result in a longer recovery time for the fish. But because the individual fibers are thicker, the white muscle can produce contractile forces that are several times as strong as those produced by red muscle. Although they are not useful for prolonged periods of swimming, these strong but inefficient muscles are ideally suited for short bursts of activity, such as darting to safety. The white muscle system gives the trout the capacity for tremendous acceleration and speed for short periods of time. Using the white muscles, adult steelhead are capable of swimming at speeds in excess of 25 feet per second for these short bursts, and brown trout can reach speeds of 12 feet per second, which comes in handy for predator evasion.

The white muscle system is also fully engaged when a trout is fighting on the end of a fly line. When you are reviving a trout you have just caught, it's imperative to take into account the fatigue experienced by these muscles and the toxic aftereffects. A little extra care at this time can increase the survival rate of released fish. Think about a time you underwent intense physical activity or an adrenaline rush from the emotional stress of a "fight or flight" situation. The aftermath no doubt left you weak and depleted, trembling and shaking. This is a postadrenaline response from your body. Imagine what this would be like for a trout that has just fought for his life. The stress and fear factor will have been considerable, but the intense muscular activity also caused a depletion and exhaustion of the white muscle system. The fish is in a state of physiological shock and will be in a vulnerable condition until he can restore his strength and recover from this state.

Unhook the trout and get it back into the water as quickly as possible. If you want to take a photo, get the camera out of the case and have it turned on and ready to go before you lift the fish back out of the water. Take the picture quickly and put the fish back in the water to finish reviving him. Holding the trout in flowing water allows oxygen to begin to be absorbed by the gills and circulated to the muscles. Even more effort is required if the water temperature is high. Hold the trout in the flowing water until he is strong enough to swim away. Notice how upon release, the fish will immediately seek shelter where he can safely complete the recovery process.

Pink muscle has the intermediate features of both red and white muscle. It assists in prolonged swimming activities as well as periods of high demand. Although each muscle system has individual applications, they are used together in a coordinated effort during most situations.

The skeletal muscle tissue of fish is also arranged differently than in other animals. In trout and salmonids, it is layered rather than bundled, as it is in other vertebrates. The arrangement of these layers is evident when you fillet a salmon, with lighter-colored striations visible throughout the pink muscle. If you were to examine the muscle tissue of other vertebrates, you would not find visible stripes like these. Think of the difference between a filet mignon on your plate and a fillet of salmon. There is marbled fat through the beef, but otherwise the muscle tissue lacks the layered effect that is apparent in the salmon and is more uniform.

Another morphological adaptation in trout is their fins, which are advantageous for life in the current. The strong tail, called the *caudal fin*, not only is useful for swimming, but also creates lift to keep the trout from sinking, since the fish's body is denser than water. The upright fin on the back, known as the *dorsal fin*, improves stability in the water and prevents the fish from spiraling or rotating while swimming. The other fins aid in swimming but are more useful for holding or adjusting position. Strong spokes called *finrays* support and add stiffness to the fins.

Behavioral Adaptations

Of all the adaptations trout have made in response to the current, their behavioral modifications are among the most important to anglers. Trout respond to the current with predictable behavioral patterns that we can exploit. The current has had a large impact on their feeding behavior, which is highly adapted to suit the environment in the lotic ecosystem and has evolved in response to the ever-present force of the current. Back in Pennsylvania, watching the fish from the bridge as I fed them pellets gave me the opportunity to study the complexity of their social interactions and other behavior while they were feeding. The fish would line up along a slight drop-off or shelf that offered protection from the current. An alpha fish would move into the prime feeding lie and displace a less dominant fish in the hierarchy, which in turn would move to the next desirable lie. Eventually, the lowest trout on the totem pole, having nowhere else to go, would dart off as if scolded. If the alpha trout failed to return to his feeding post after rising for a bit of food, all the other trout would shift into the next higher position.

The feeding behavior of trout is very complex and could easily be the subject of an entire book, but the basic strategy is simple: the goal is to obtain the most nutritionally beneficial food in the most energy-efficient manner possible. In other words, the fish tries to get the most with the least amount of effort. It is all about feeding efficiency. Trout do not have an internal gauge that measures the cost-return ratio for each feeding opportunity. No internal barometer or alarm warns them that a particular opportunity is not a wise investment of time and effort. They do not have calorie calculators in their heads. Since they lack the sophisticated decision-making capability of higher animals and cannot consult a dietitian, they will make the occasional mistake. The success of their feeding choices, however, is measured in the survivability and growth rate of each individual.

Natural selection is their teacher, and individuals that do not make wise investments are penalized with a net energy loss. If they make consistently poor decisions, they will become less and less competitive than individuals that are more discriminating. Unthrifty trout are weaker, less vigorous, and easier targets for predation from birds and larger fish. They drop in social rank and are offered fewer good opportunities for success. These fish are soon removed from the gene pool, through either starvation or predation. On the other hand, trout that make the best energy bargains are favored with a better growth rate and increased survivability, which allows them to climb the hierarchical ladder of social success and move up to the apex of Maslow's pyramid. They become the dominant fish commanding the best feeding stations and therefore have the best opportunities for future success.

Young trout learn fast or pay the price. Young, inexperienced trout are more likely to chase a food item with a low probability of success or a low return on the energy investment, but they soon become educated. Older and wiser trout are not as easily tempted by a questionable opportunity. They make fewer mistakes or poor decisions. This is a major reason why it's easier to catch a small trout than a larger one. The larger fish are smarter fish, with more experience, and they are less easily fooled. The older trout are older for a reason.

Feeding Strategies

Trout have three common feeding strategies that are of importance to anglers. Their preferred and most common method—especially in the middle portion of their lives, from the early juvenile stage to early adulthood—takes advantage of the drift of invertebrate organisms in the current. Using this tactic, known as *drift feeding*, the fish hold in a stationary position that allows them to view the passing food material delivered by the current. The current therefore is an essential component of this strategy, by which the fish have turned the current from a disadvantage into an advantage. Rather than fight the current by roaming and foraging for food, which would have a high energy cost and therefore a poor net energy return, they remain stationary, conserving energy by holding outside the main flow while waiting for the current to bring their food to them. The benthic community is the smorgasbord, and the current is the conveyor belt delivering a movable feast to the waiting trout. This strategy yields a higher net energy return. The trout thus get the most return on the least investment, which allows them to grow faster than their competitors—other trout.

Because trout are drift feeders, a dead-drift presentation is often a very effective way for the angler to entice them on a fly. This mimics the natural activity of the benthic organisms that make up their diet. They are accustomed to food particles drifting helplessly in the current. There may be some movement in the wriggling of appendages or wings of the natural insect, and this is often imitated by the material from which the fly is constructed. Fly tiers have devised many furry forms of flies, with loose dubbing to give the impression of the minute movements of legs or gills.

The dedication of trout to their feeding lies and use of drift-based tactics are current dependent. The stronger the current, the more committed to their feeding lies the trout become. In the absence of current, with no flow of water to deliver the food material, trout do not use the drift feeding strategy. There also would be no advantage to seek feeding lies, because the fish would not need to seek refuge from the current, and therefore there would be no cost savings in doing so. Feeding lies would be unnecessary and counterproductive. It would be like buying oceanfront property at a premium price, only to have the ocean dry up. Your expensive real estate would then have the same value as any other. One feeding lie would be no better or worse than any other. Thus in the absence of current, trout behave in the same way as lentic fish and have similar feeding strategies. They abandon their feeding lies, collecting near structure and showing schooling behavior.

In heavy current, the trout will be tucked in, out of the force of the current. They will be tight to structure, venturing their heads out only long enough to snatch a choice bit of food. Therefore, when fishing over strong current, you need to keep your presentations close to these lies. The trout cannot afford to chase prey or expose themselves to much of the current's force in order to get a meal. This would lead to a poor net energy exchange. The presentation of your flies must be right on their noses, requiring very little movement on their part, in order to be successful.

This was obvious the first time I tried the Czech nymphing techniques. I had read a book about these methods and purchased the flies online. I even had a short stretch of bright orange leader to use as a strike indicator above the leader. I could barely wait to try them out! When I got to my favorite river, I selected a strong, thick knot of fast-moving water. Facing upstream, I began with a series of short casts near rocks and boulders in the run. It wasn't long before I hooked my first trout.

In the strong current, the trout were tight to the structure, and my casts had to be right on target. If they were even just a little to one side or the other, they were unproductive. Sometimes I had to cast several times to ensure that the flies had drifted close enough to the feeding station. I would drop them into pocketwater, but again the presentation had to be just behind the obstruction in the fast water. The trout were unwilling to waste much energy in moving too far from their protected lies. Errant casts would be ignored.

In light current, the trout hold more loosely to current-protected structure. They may be willing to move somewhat to obtain a meal, even venturing out into the current briefly to follow a morsel. In slower current, the trout will often drift under or alongside the fly, inspecting it in a more leisurely manner. The trout can afford to invest more effort when the current has less force.

As an example of the impact of current on feeding behavior, notice the great difference in the feeding patterns of anadromous salmonids in open water than in the rivers and streams where they were born. As juveniles in the river, they adopt drift-based feeding strategies. Once they migrate to open-water systems without current, their feeding behavior becomes more directed to aggregating around schools of baitfish. In this environment, most make the shift to a piscivorous feeding pattern, eating other fish. When they return to the lotic environment, they once again use drift-feeding strategies, even though they were piscivorous in open water. They will still eat other fish, but they also use drift-based strategies; otherwise, we would never catch them on our egg imitations, Egg Sucking Leech patterns, and other favorite flies.

Trout are drift feeders because of the tendency of benthic organisms to drift in the current, hence the success of drift-based feeding patterns. If benthic organisms were not susceptible to drift behavior, the drift-dependent feeding strategy of trout would fail. Drift-feeding trout have daily peaks of activity at dawn and dusk, which correlate to the increased activity of benthic organisms.

When drift feeding, the trout holds in a position facing the current and identifies drifting invertebrates from the passing milieu. There is a brief time for inspection, which is determined by the speed of the current—and perhaps the hunger of the trout. If the trout commits to taking the food, its exposure to the current is generally minimized, especially if the current is strong. After an excursion to capture the prey, the trout returns to the original position as soon as possible. If it has followed the prey for a while, as trout sometimes do in slow current, it will usually swim first to the bottom and then make its way upstream along the streambed to the original site.

The temperature of the water has a significant effect on the probability of the drift-feeding trout capturing prey. In cold water, the probability is reduced and the trout requires more resting time between excursions. At 43 degrees, the probability of success is only 50 percent; however, when the water temperature is in the mid-50s, the probability improves to over 90 percent. The next time you are fishing in cold-water conditions, if a fish slashes at your fly but misses, it's not always your fault in the timing of the hook set. The trout miss the natural insects 50 percent of the time under these conditions. Give the fish some extra time to rest between casts because of the cold water, and then try him again. If the laws of probability hold true, the next time around should be productive, although there are no guarantees.

A second trout feeding strategy is *epibenthic foraging*, which refers to trout actively seeking a meal directly from the benthic layer. They may move around the stream, looking for opportunities. In this feeding strategy, the trout take food particles directly from the bottom. They may root in the substrate to dislodge benthic organisms on which to feed, or they may actively search along the bottom for suitable prey to capture. This type of feeding pattern is not often used by trout, under most conditions. Sculpins and other bottom foragers frequently feed in this manner. The current plays no role in this type of feeding behavior.

A study compared the stomach contents of trout that had been feeding for an extended length of time with the population of benthic organisms that had been caught from the current in nets during the same time period. The researchers found differences between these two samples, which showed that the trout displayed preferences in their food selection. These preferences were relaxed when the food supply was reduced, indicating a loss of selectivity during periods of food scarcity. At times when the number of organisms in the drift nets indicated a lower amount of available food for trout, the trout stomach contents also contained small amounts of algae and plant material. Thus the fish were eating plant material in addition to the benthic organisms, which indicated that during times of food scarcity, trout were plucking some food items directly from the substrate by epibenthic foraging. Thus epibenthic feeding appears to be more common during times of food scarcity.

Very young trout often use epibenthic feeding strategies, but as they grow, they soon shift to the drift style of feeding. During the first weeks of the trout's life, they are nourished by the yolk sac, and external food sources are unneeded. After the yolk sac has been consumed, the trout begin to forage from the benthic layer. Since their diet is plankton and small vegetative organisms, they frequently graze along the streambed, plucking bits of food from the substrate or ingesting small particulate items drifting near the bottom. As the trout age, epibenthic foraging becomes less common and drift feeding is the norm. By the time the fish reach adulthood, drift feeding accounts for over 85 percent of their feeding pattern, and epibenthic foraging for less than 15 percent.

As the trout reach a certain size and stage of life, their feeding habits change once again. These larger trout need a higher energy return on their investment and turn to a third feeding strategy, becoming *piscivorous* and eating smaller fish. They need a positive net energy balance to ensure continued growth and reproductive development. At some point, larger fish need to satisfy their energy needs with a larger energy source. Continuing to rely on the smaller food sources would be like powering a searchlight on a flashlight battery. The dietary transition for trout resembles the progression from baby food to an adult diet for humans. As the individual grows, baby food no longer meets the nutritional requirements.

This feeding tactic is not predicated on the current as is drift-based feeding. In fact, it is more likely to be employed as the strength of the current diminishes. Marauding trout on the prowl for smaller fish become more common in low-current conditions, and this is the most prevalent behavior on open water with no current. The large trout do not usually establish ambush lies, as do bass and other warm-water piscivorous species, but are more likely to actively search for prey and give chase after a prey encounter. Therefore, they tend to range over a larger territory in search of unwary fish.

For the angler, understanding the various feeding strategies of trout will enable you to anticipate their feeding pattern under different circumstances. There are several variables in determining the feeding behavior of trout. First note the individual's size. The larger the trout, up to a certain point, the less likely it is to engage in epibenthic foraging and the more drift-based strategies will predominate. Beyond a certain size, however, the trout will begin to gradually transition to piscivorous behavior. This behavior has been recorded in trout 12 inches or larger. Another variable that influences feeding tactics is food availability or scarcity. When the food supply becomes scarce, the density of the invertebrate drift falls and the rate of epibenthic foraging increases. This tends to be the case in winter conditions, when the density of the invertebrate drift is at its lowest. Yet another variable is the strength of the current. In sections of strong current, drift-feeding strategies predominate because of the energy cost savings they provide.

One of the most common and potentially frustrating situations for anglers is when there is not an identifiable feeding pattern. It is safe to assume that the trout are still feeding on a regular basis, but they do not feed all the time. Just like us, they have feeding periods as well as resting periods during which they are not actively feeding. Their feeding periods may change from day to day or vary in different seasons, as determined by the availability of food. In the winter, trout spend much less time in feeding activity than in the summer. Knowing what this activity is and when it is occurring will enable you to capitalize on the opportunities. Timing is everything.

On Wisconsin's Big Green River, after a two-and-a-half-hour ride to get there, Terry Pirro and I sat on the tailgate of the Fishmobile, the name by which his beat-up van is known. We rigged our rods and donned our waders for an early April afternoon of fly fishing. We had stolen away from work and felt like two grade school boys playing hooky. It was a last-minute decision to head to the river, and by the time we got there and were ready to fish, it was well into the afternoon. Along the river's edge, we talked to a fly fisherman who had been there most of the day. Evidently, we had just missed a heavy Blue-Winged Olive hatch that had electrified trout and anglers alike. He told us he had caught several nice fish in a short period of time. "Since then," he said as he headed back to his car, "it's been a little slow."

We exchanged a glance that said it all: "Just our luck—we missed the hatch!" Another long drive, only to miss it by an hour. If only we had gotten on the road earlier. This is one major disadvantage of timing my fishing opportunities around my work schedule instead of the trout's feeding schedule. But this was a bonus afternoon, one we hadn't counted on. At least we were on the river. We decided to make the most of it. Now we needed to figure out how to fish to trout that had just eaten.

We tried a variety of flies and tactics. The fish looked upon our offerings with indifference. They were blasé from the piscatorial equivalent of a Thanksgiving dinner food glut. If they had a remote and a sofa, they would have been napping with a football game on the TV. We tried every fly pattern we had with us, to no avail. Despite our every attempt to rouse some interest, the fish remained apathetic.

Finally, after several hours of unproductive fishing, we managed to find a few trout that had recovered their appetites sufficiently to take a nymph. We were using Blue-Winged Olives, figuring these insects would begin to occur in the drift as evening approached. It took a while, but finally we'd been able to tempt enough trout to justify the long trip we'd made to the river. For us, however, it doesn't take many trout to justify a trip to the river. Still, it does pay to be there at the right time, when the fish are feeding actively.

The active feeding cycles of trout mirror the activity of benthic organisms, timed in accordance with their availability, which makes their active periods the best times to be on the river. The trout eat when food is available and fast when it is not. This depends on the variations in food availability from summer to winter, as well as those based on the daily rhythm of the river. Whether a hatch or behavioral drift is occurring, trout take notice. When there is a surge of food in the drift, trout respond with feeding activity, and you will find them in their feeding lies.

Territoriality

Within their home ranges, trout exhibit territoriality over both feeding and refuge lies. A trout will occupy the most advantageous feeding lie that it can actively defend against challenges from other trout. What makes a good feeding lie for trout? An ideal feeding station offers three things: proximity to food, relief from the current, and protection and security from predators. The most desirable feeding lies optimize all three features, assuming that they have already qualified in satisfying the more urgent needs that are lower on the pyramid, such as water suitability. Feeding lies are ranked according to their desirability by trout. Some are better than others. The best ones offer the best energy return and will be occupied by the most dominant trout. The alpha trout will have the best lie, then the beta trout, and so on. Learning to recognize the features of an ideal lie is advantageous to anglers.

If the feeding station does not offer proximity to food, it has no value in the feeding behavior of the trout. This is the most essential factor in the desirability of a feeding station. There is no point in waiting in line at the cafeteria if there is no food. The best lies offer the best feeding opportunities. Often these lies are near the thalweg or secondary current lanes. These channels serve as conveyor belts of food, especially during the periods of behavioral drift, when large numbers of benthic organisms are carried in the current. The larger fish will occupy these stations at these times. These are good lies to fish at dawn and dusk, especially during conditions favorable to behavioral drift activity.

In order to make the most advantageous energy trade-off in the drift-feeding behavior, the ideal lie must offer protection from the current. If the cost of ownership of the lie is too expensive in terms of energy investment compared with the energy return, it will not be suitable. It is the old cost-return ratio. The best lies require the least investment of energy. Trout must occupy lies that are efficient to maintain, since they cannot control the other variable in the equation, that of food abundance or scarcity. They have no influence on the amount of benthic organisms that enter the drift, are entrained in the current, and are available to them as a food source. They can only control their input costs. Minimizing these costs is the key to success for trout.

Security is another important feature of the ideal lie. Fish choose lies that offer minimal exposure to the threat of predation from birds overhead or other fish. This sense of personal security is innate and ingrained in trout from the moment they leave the redd. They prefer not to see or be seen by other trout while they hold in their feeding stations. Trout like to be visually isolated from other fish as they await their next meal. For this reason, areas with coarser features in the substrate along the bottom and banks provide more feeding stations and support a higher population of trout than areas where the bottom has fewer features. Although security is important, it is the characteristic that fish most often sacrifice in the face of food scarcity. Trout will move into shallow riffles in broad daylight if the returns are worth the risks or if they are hungry enough.

Besides feeding lies, trout also need holding lies that provide refuge from risk, safe havens where they can rest quietly and securely. What makes a good holding or refuge lie? In this case, the most important considerations are comfort and security. Peace and quiet. This kind of lie needs to be a location with reduced current and minimal risk from predators. This is where trout go when threatened or to escape pressure. These locations are often in deeper water and associated with protective cover or structure. Here the fish can also rest in comfort away from direct sunlight. The availability of food is not necessarily a factor, although trout may be tempted to feed in these lies under the right circumstances. Imagine lying in a hammock in the shade on a summer day at the beach. It's a nice place for a nap. If a waiter brought a snack to the hammock, it would have to be a tempting morsel or a frozen drink.

Feeding and refuge lies vary according to conditions and circumstance. Periods of extremely high or low flows can alter the suitability of a location. Anything that deviates or redirects the flow of water or the thalweg can rearrange the feeding stations. If structure is added or removed, the locations of feeding stations and refuge lies can be altered. Existing feeding stations can be enhanced or degraded, or sometimes even eliminated altogether. New feeding stations can be created. High water temperatures may change a good feeding station into one that the fish can no longer use until the temperature is more comfortable. Trout are very adept at responding to these changes.

When fishing a particular river or stream repeatedly, you will find over time that some lies almost always produce trout, whereas others may or may not, depending on the circumstances, flow, or season. Just because you caught fish at a particular spot in May doesn't mean that the same spot will yield trout in July, although it is still worth checking out. For rivers that I frequently visit, I remember the locations of the good feeding stations—those few spots that I can usually count on to give up a good fish. These are my go-to secret fishing holes. I make sure to fish each one on every visit. Once you have your own favorite spots, however, don't get into a rut, because the river is constantly changing.

A fish's home range may contain more than one feeding lie but frequently has just a single preferred refuge lie. For brown trout, the home range is established in the first or second year of life and changes little thereafter in terms of location, but it will continue to grow in size. At first the territory may be very limited in size, consisting of one feeding station and one holding area. As a trout grows, it will move upward in the hierarchy to occupy more desirable feeding lies and also expand its territory somewhat. Some individuals, especially older and larger trout, are more mobile and use multiple feeding stations within a given territory. The territory size depends on the size of the fish, the relative food abundance, and the presence of intruders. The largest fish command the largest territories. They will defend a larger geographic area, presumably to gain access to enough food to meet their higher metabolic demands. At this point in their lives, they are largely carnivorous, preying mostly on smaller fish.

For large, mobile fish, there often is some overlapping of territories. This doesn't mean that other fish are not present in these areas; it means that the dominant trout can and will occupy any feeding station that they desire within that area and will chase off any other trout that attempt to occupy feeding sites that they want. These trout frequently range and roam throughout their territory and may move from one feeding station to another, depending on the food availability at each of the various feeding locations.

Increased food abundance reduces the size of territories, as it allows the fish to obtain enough food from a smaller area. The size of the territory is always a trade-off between the benefits of ownership and the cost of defense. Fish density and competition decrease the size of home ranges, as dominant trout are more active in the defense of their territories when intruder pressure increases, and a smaller territory is easier to defend than a larger one.

The predominant use of a single feeding lie is more common for trout through the young adult stage of life. Brown trout embrace this behavior for a longer time than most other species, and for the first few years of their lives, they generally occupy the same feeding station every time they are actively engaged in feeding activity. Some species are more likely to range within a territory, using several different feeding stations, than to occupy a single feeding lie. This is characteristic of larger brown trout, rainbows, and members of the char species. Rainbow trout are more likely than brown trout to have larger home ranges and use multiple feeding stations, which means that they may change locations more frequently.

Life for trout in the home range might be compared to life for a person in a city neighborhood. You visit a bakery in the morning when the muffins are warm and fresh. You eat a leisurely lunch and linger over a cup of coffee. Then you return to your studio apartment for an afternoon nap. Near sunset, you grab dinner once the restaurants have opened. After dinner, you enjoy going out on the town. But you return to the safety and comfort of your apartment each night to rest. The bottom line is that you know your neighborhood. You know the streets of your borough like the back of your hand. You know where to go and when. You know where and when to find the best meals at the best prices. You frequent your favorite haunts, places where you previously had a good meal and good service. The same is true for trout: They know their territory and the natural rhythms and cycles of their river. They know where to be and when to be there.

One of the most notable characteristics of trout is their adaptability. They have adapted to live and thrive in the current. Their feeding behavior is highly modified to suit the lotic environment. Think of how adapted the city dweller is to the neighborhood in the above analogy. If the bakery started serving warm muffins at 8 a.m. instead of 7 a.m., you would change your schedule to fit the circumstances. So it is with trout. In order to anticipate trout behavior, you must understand the world in which they live, the pressures they face, and the actions they take in response to those pressures. They will modify their feeding times around benthic events. They will adapt to daily patterns. They will feed at night if the water temperature is too hot. They will use sun-protected lies in the shade or deeper water. They will seek different lies according to food availability. The feeding patterns of trout will be directly related to the drift activity of insects. They will change tactics according to the pattern of benthic organisms that constitute their diet. Which types of insects and when they appear in the drift are major factors in determining the trout feeding pattern. Trying to understand trout without looking at the whole ecosystem is like trying to understand a tree by looking at a single leaf.

As an angler, you need to understand all the interrelationships within the entire lotic ecosystem that have an impact on trout behavior. You must know how trout will react to a specific pressure or circumstance. What will they do when less food is available? What adjustments will they make when the food source changes? How will they react to changes in discharge and flow? The fish tend to react in a predictable manner to all these kinds of situations, so recognizing and identifying the factors that influence them is essential in order to anticipate their responses. Since trout are adaptive in their behaviors, making the most of circumstances that are constantly changing, you need to be adaptive in your tactics as well. You have to modify your strategies in accordance with the trout modifications. Only then will you have evolved into the best angler you can be.

Chapter 8

Fishing Strategies

By integrating your understanding of the influence of current on benthic organisms and trout, with an appreciation of the effects the current has on presentation, especially in specific circumstances, you can improve your ability to catch trout. One of the challenges of effectively presenting your flies to structure in current is that the very structure you are trying to approach frequently disrupts or deflects the flow of current, which carries your flies away from the very lies you are trying to target.

To be an effective angler, you must think of the river as a three-dimensional entity, with length, width, and depth, and apply this model to the way current interacts with structure, since the feeding positions of trout relate to structure. Your presentations have to be drag-free when targeting these lies. In some situations, drag may completely prevent your flies from drifting in the ideal zones and microhabitats. They might not even get the chance to tempt a trout if you fail to take this drag into account. You might think you have effectively fished an area, when the trout actually may not have seen your flies at all.

While Jo and I were conducting the experiments with the marked leader on the South Holston River in Tennessee, we photographed the interaction of the current with different types of structure in the river. Standing in the frigid water, we used the yarn-marked leader to illustrate the effect that obstructions such as rocks and boulders had on the current. We also documented how the nymph presentations were affected by drop-offs and ledges where there is a radical change in depth. The way current relates and reacts to structure is an important consideration for an effective angling strategy, especially as it applies to specific, commonly encountered scenarios in angling.

Our technique was simple but effective in displaying the complex currents associated with various kinds of structure and situations. Once again, Jo stood upstream with the rod and marked leader and allowed the leader to drift without visible drag on the strike indicator. This time, with care, we were able to avoid tangling the leader, which we celebrated as a major victory. I was back in the water, shivering from hypothermia, positioned adjacent to the structure in order to photograph the presentation as it approached and passed the feature. In most cases, it was necessary to photograph the presentation for a short time after it passed the feature. Part of my mind was concentrating on the task at hand, while the greater part was thinking about a long, hot shower back in the hotel room.

FISHING DROP-OFFS

We first filmed the leader as it passed over a drop-off where the depth of the water changed suddenly from shallow to deeper. As this type of river feature offers abundant feeding lies for trout, we thought it would be an ideal place to start. We found that a tongue of fast current continued well downstream after a ledge or drop-off, extending over the top of the slower-moving water just behind the drop-off. The thread of fast-moving water above screened the soft pocket behind the drop-off and the protected feeding lies, and it prevented our flies from dropping through to present to these lies. The swift current overhead carried the entire presentation in the upper portion of the vertical water column, high over the top of the drop-off and any fish that might have been stationed there.

The cause of this profound effect was simple. As the flies drifted in the shallow section upstream of the drop-off, the shape of the leader assumed the shape of the vertical velocity profile, as it always does, reflecting the fast current of the shallow upstream section. Even after the presentation passed the drop-off, however, the leader retained this same acute shape, which persisted for a considerable distance. This caused the flies to remain at the same height in the vertical water column as if the drop had not occurred. In other words, before the drop-off, vertical drag had lifted the flies at least 6 to 8 inches off the shallow bottom. After the drop-off, they were still traveling in the same vertical position as before, even though the bottom had dropped to a greater depth. The flies did not immediately drop in the vertical water column when they encountered the change in depth.

The drop-off had essentially created two current threads, with a faster current over the top of a second zone of slower, minimal, or even potentially reversed current. These two threads of current were separated by a seam, just like the visible seams we can see along the edges of the river. Above the seam, the upper zone of stronger current held the leader in the shape of the vertical velocity profile it had acquired in the faster, shallow water prior to the drop-off. This current kept the leader well above the ideal holding lies behind the obstruction, and also at the unnaturally faster velocity of the strong current thread. Below the seam, in the current-protected feeding lies, the trout would be little tempted.

The current was not especially swift in the section we studied, but it was strong enough to maintain the acute shape of the leader well beyond the drop. It wasn't until well past the drop-off that the two current threads blended back together, and the shape of the leader gradually began to change into a gentler curve indicative of the slower current of the deeper water. Only then did the flies slow down and drop in the vertical water column to a more appropriate depth. In the moderate current where we were filming, this did not occur until about 6 to 8 feet after the drop-off, by which time the flies were already well downstream of the ideal feeding lies.

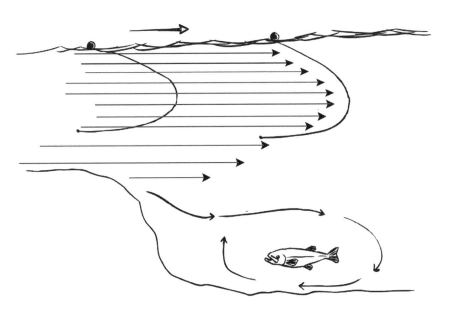

The vertical velocity profile shown to the left represents the effect of current as the water approaches a drop-off. The acute curve of the profile reflects the fast current speed prior to the drop-off. Even after the drift has passed the drop-off, the leader retains that shape as a result of the extension of a faster current thread over the pocketwater behind the obstruction.

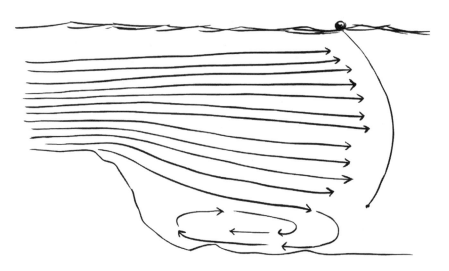

The shape of the vertical velocity profile persisted until well after the drop-off, and only then did the flies lower back to the bottom, near the streambed.

As invertebrate organisms drift in the current, certainly some insects are entrained in the fastest portion of the vertical water column. But the greatest drift density of displaced insects is in the slower section closer to the bottom, for a variety of reasons. First and foremost, this is the water closest to the benthic layer, from which they originated. Second, for insects that are capable of swimming, they are actively trying to reattach themselves to the bottom, especially if they were displaced accidentally. Even during behavioral drift activity, the density is closest to the bottom, and those insects involved will reattach themselves to the bottom at a point downstream from their point of origin.

Those insects that are drifting near the bottom are more likely to enter the backeddy behind the obstruction. Unlike the fly, a natural insect drifting in the current is not tethered to a leader, and as a result, it is not prevented from dropping from the faster current into the dead zone behind the drop-off. Once it enters the soft pocket of current, it can recirculate until it eventually makes contact with the bottom or is eaten by a trout. Unless your flies can imitate this behavior, they will not be as effective as they could be. Trout that hold in feeding lies behind drop-offs are more likely to take an insect that is dropping out of the current than one that is well above the seam in the fastest current. Energy economics again will influence their decision. Insects that drop out of the current offer the best investment opportunities for trout, because this minimizes their energy expenditure. Hence your presentations will be more successful if your flies

Note that the shape of the leader prior to the drop-off matches the vertical velocity profile for the swifter current.

This photo shows the vertical velocity profile of the faster current that the leader acquired prior to the drop-off and retained even after the presentation had passed the drop-off.

The leader experienced a gradual transition in the vertical velocity profile in the slower, deeper water well downstream of the drop-off, which eventually allows the flies to drop in the water column.

are free to drop into the pocketwater behind the obstruction than if they are whisking overhead in the middle of the fast water.

Strategy for Fishing Drop-offs

Vertical drag spoils the presentation by prohibiting the flies from entering the target zone. The flies are also accelerated in an unnatural manner as they are lifted in the vertical water column. The best strategy for fishing the drop-offs is to offset these tendencies, allowing the flies to drop out of the faster current above the ledge and into the pocketwater behind it. A longer leader would help slightly, but it is not recommended because it will impede your ability to detect strikes. The long, continuous drifts from a float boat provide the least chance for the flies to drop into the soft pocketwater behind drop-offs. A strategy from a moving drift boat would be to mend the presentation before approaching the drop-off in order to allow the flies to drop out of the faster current of the upper thread and into the lower current pocket. If this is not done, the flies will pass over the lies and attract little interest from trout. Pausing the indicator will introduce sufficient slack into the leader at the exact time the slack is needed and

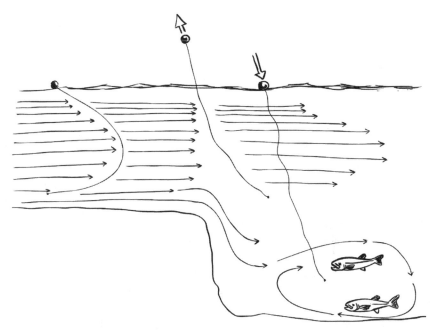

Mending for vertical drag by stopping the progress of the strike indicator or lifting the strike indicator slightly upstream introduces slack into the leader, which allows the flies to effectively target the ideal feeding lies. Managing the slack as the flies pass over the drop-off will improve strike detection and avoid missed opportunities.

allow the flies to pass underneath. They will have the opportunity to drop through the current seam.

You need to adjust the timing of the mend according to circumstances, such as water depth and current speed. A general rule of thumb is to mend at a distance upstream of the drop-off that is equal to half the length of the leader you are using. I hold the strike indicator stationary for a two count, and then release it to continue the drift while at the same time keeping as tight a line to the strike indicator as possible, to the point of pulling it slightly. This tension on the line removes unnecessary slack and improves strike detection.

The length of the leader below the strike indicator needs to be adjusted to accommodate the increased depth below the drop-off. Ideally, you should make this adjustment before the first presentation. When I am nymph fishing, I am constantly adjusting the strike indicator up and down the leader as the circumstance warrants. Any time there is a change of depth, such as occurs with a drop-off, I change the length of the leader accordingly. Additional weight may also help you target this area more effectively.

For the stationary angler fishing a drop-off, the short, upstream casts typical of Czech and tight-line techniques have the best chance of allowing the flies to drop into these subsurface pockets while keeping slack to a minimum to aid strike detection. You need to target your casts to a point just upstream of the depth change. For most situations, I target the cast upstream of the drop-off by a distance equal to half the length of the leader—the same point upstream of the drop where I would have mended from a boat. If you cast much more upstream than this, it will allow vertical drag to spoil the drift and sweep the flies above the target zone after the drop-off. If you don't cast far enough upstream of the drop, the flies will not have sufficient time to sink in the water column. The entire drift should be completed before the onset of vertical drag affects it. The slack at the onset of the drift will allow the flies to drop through the current seam and target those fish holding in feeding stations behind the ledge. Adding an appropriate amount of weight or an anchor fly will allow the flies to enter the backeddy behind the obstruction. Using a tight-line technique from a downstream position will improve the rate of hookups.

Four variables must be considered when fishing a drop-off: current speed, depth of the water before and after, length of the leader below the indicator, and weight of the flies. If you don't feel that your presentation has gotten deep enough to reach the target zone, you can change two of those four variables: you can add weight ahead of the flies to improve the sink rate or lengthen the leader below the indicator to improve the on-target presentation.

It's usually worth the extra time and effort to fish drop-offs effectively, because they offer ideal feeding lies for trout. Fishing the White Hole bend on the White River in Arkansas, R.B. McCallister and I lucked into a group of feeding trout behind a ledge. It took a little extra weight in the fast current, but we were rewarded with several decent trout each. Mending the indicator as the team of nymphs approached the ledge put the flies right on their noses.

FISHING MIDSTREAM OBSTRUCTIONS

A submerged midstream obstruction causes a substantial disruption to the current. To truly appreciate the effect it has, it is essential to visualize this as a three-dimensional structure. As an example, consider a large boulder that is fully immersed in the water. As such, water will flow over it and around it. There is usually a disturbance on the surface of the water that indicates the presence of the obstruction. This disruption of the water at the surface is caused by the hydrodynamic effect created by the boulder. If

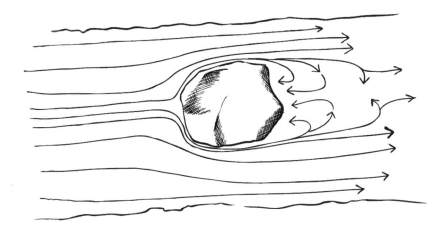

Imagine if this boulder were fully submerged and not projecting above the surface. When viewed from above, the current is vectored around the obstruction, as shown here, which creates a seam separating the faster current from the backeddy pocket behind the obstruction.

the disruption is major, which depends on current strength and discharge, as well as the depth and size of the boulder, the effect could be as dramatic as a standing wave. Where the current is less intense or the boulder is smaller, a more subtle effect might occur, such as a boil on the surface of the water. A subtle surface disruption could also indicate that the top of the boulder is well below the surface.

Looking down on the boulder from overhead, you can see the current flowing around the obstruction as it is deflected to either side. This creates a thread of faster current alongside the boulder and trailing behind it for a substantial distance downriver. A seam separates the faster current from the zone immediately behind the obstruction, where there is less current, no current, or even current reversal.

Viewed from the side, the current sweeps over the top of the obstruction. As the current passes directly over the boulder, the velocity of flow increases from V1 to V2. Downstream of the boulder, the flow returns to the same velocity as preceding the disturbance. The velocity of the current that passed over the obstruction undergoes a gradual reduction, with the eventual development of a velocity profile that is characteristic and representative for that section of flow and with a speed that is indicated as V3. In the backeddy pocket directly behind the boulder, there is minimal water movement. The direction of flow can be in either a forward or reversed direction, depending on the overall strength of the current and size of the

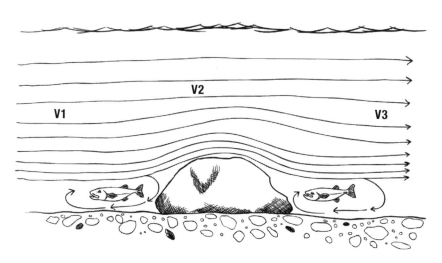

The velocity of the current increases over the top of the boulder and then gradually reduces to a velocity similar to that prior to the obstruction. The vertical velocity profile reflects the changes in current, but it will prevent the flies from reaching the pocketwater behind the obstruction where trout are feeding.

obstruction. A seam separates the faster water overhead from the pocketwater behind the obstruction and trails downstream of the boulder, until it gradually tapers into the streambed and the two sections merge into one. The increased velocity (V2) not only occurs over the boulder, but also persists for nearly the entire stretch over the backeddy, until the two current seams gradually blend together. The current seam is sharper immediately following the obstruction and gradually becomes less distinct as the two zones eventually blend together. The V2 velocity gradually transitions to the V3 velocity as the predominant current thread widens to encompass the entire river depth, which occurs once the flow has passed the boulder and backeddy.

This creates a zone of increased velocity and a seam that trails over the pocket of calm water just behind the obstruction. This backeddy is similar to the one that occurs behind a drop-off. As a result of this velocity increase, the vertical velocity profile changes as your presentation approaches, passes over, and progresses downriver of the boulder. Before the boulder, the vertical velocity profile and the leader assume the shape reflective of the flow in that section of the river. Over the boulder, the profile becomes more acutely curved, reflective of the increased velocity of the compressed current thread. Downstream of the boulder, eventually the current threads blend into one, with a velocity profile characteristic of that section of flow.

This photo shows the persistence of a more acute vertical velocity profile well downstream of the boulder, which prevents the flies from behaving naturally.

As a result, this presentation will be spoiled by vertical drag. As when fishing drop-offs, the acute shape of the vertical velocity profile over the pocketwater accelerates the flies and causes them to pass over the feeding lie behind the boulder. Here again, the flies will not be able to drop into the pocketwater. This presentation will do little to tempt the wary trout, which are discriminating and not enticed by unnatural-appearing flies, as we all know. The shape of the profile will persist well after the obstruction is passed, just as it did after passing a drop-off.

Strategy for Fishing Midstream Obstructions

A midstream obstruction creates two main locations for feeding lies: one just in front of it and the other behind it. Right behind the boulder is an ideal feeding station for trout, and in many cases this is the prime lie because it is a depositional microhabitat. It is a collection and concentration zone for food items. This is usually the location taken by the alpha fish. The fish in this lie are waiting for food particles to settle out of the fast water as it passes directly overhead. These food materials are frequently caught in a backeddy that recirculates the material through the depositional zone until it is swept out of the pocket, settles onto the substrate where the organism can establish residency, or is consumed by a feeding trout. Secondary feeding lies are also created behind the boulder

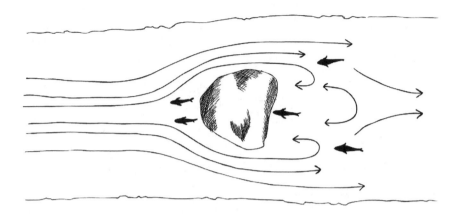

Midstream obstructions create many different feeding lies in two main locations: in front of and behind the obstruction. Fish arrange themselves in these lies according to their social status. When fishing a midstream obstruction, it is important to fish all potential feeding stations.

by the seams of current that trail downstream on either side of the obstruction. Trout often line up along this seam to peruse food materials that are passing in the current.

In front of the obstruction, feeding lies are located in the cushion of water that is created as the current bounces off the face of the boulder and collides with the forward-moving water. The pillow of soft water lifts the flow overhead and offers an ideal protected spot from which trout can peruse the passing food.

When in a drift boat, mending the flies as they approach a midstream obstruction is an ideal way to improve the presentation to the many feeding lies located behind and in front of it. You should identify and target each specific potential feeding lie individually. Mending to introduce slack into the leader will relieve the effect of vertical drag and allow the flies to behave naturally as the presentation passes the boulder. The slack will let the flies drop out of the fast current so you can target the pocketwater in the backeddy behind the obstruction as well as the feeding lie in front of it. The time to mend is before your flies reach the obstruction. In this situation, I usually time the mend at a distance equal to or slightly less than the full length of the leader. I mend a little earlier as the flies approach a boulder than I do when fishing a drop-off so that the flies can swing into the feeding station just in front of the boulder. This places the flies ahead of the strike indicator and gives them the necessary slack to behave in a natural manner. Try to manage this slack as effectively as you can in order to improve strike detection, keeping the line as tight as possible to the strike indicator as you lift and pull during the mend.

If you are fishing from a stationary position, mending is not usually needed in this situation when using the short upstream casts typical of Czech or tight-line techniques, but you will need to make multiple casts to ensure adequate coverage to all potential feeding stations. These casts, if targeted properly, will initiate the drift with sufficient slack in the leader to allow an ideal presentation. Your casts should be directed well above the upstream edge of the boulder to target the holding lies in front of the boulder and also to allow the flies to sink into the pocketwater behind the obstruction. A large boulder that creates a substantial hydrodynamic impact will offer multiple feeding lies for trout, and in such cases, you should address each potential lie. From a downstream position, I usually cast into both trailing seams to the sides of the obstruction as I work my way upstream. Once I am within reach, I target the pocketwater behind it. As I continue to move upstream, I finally target the lies in front of it.

Crosscurrents generally develop in front of obstructions, especially larger boulders with a flat surface facing the current, which can cause lateral deviation in the course or direction of the drift of the flies. As the current hits an obstruction, the water is deflected not only over the obstruction, but also to either side. If the leading edge of the boulder or other obstruction is broad or flat, the crosscurrents can be profound. If the flies are caught in a crosscurrent, they may be swept to the side of your target area. This is not always a bad thing; in less extreme situations, the flies may be vectored into the current that flows in the seam alongside and behind the boulder and target any trout stationed in those feeding lies.

Take your time when fishing to any structure. It is important to cover all the potential lies associated with each structure and feature, and this requires multiple casts to an area to adequately ensure ideal drifts to all potential sites. You might think that your casts have been right on target to the lie behind the boulder, but the flies may actually have been caught in currents that pulled them out of the target zone. Cover each area extensively, repeating the same cast several times before you abandon the site for another.

Fishing to a midstream obstruction that is not submerged eliminates the possibility of drifting over the top of it, since it has no current flowing over it, and this requires less adjustment. In this situation, the presentation will pass around the structure on either side. You still need to mend just before the flies approach the obstruction to ensure that your presentations in the current seams that follow the structure are drag-free. The pocketwater behind the boulder is again an ideal target for feeding lies, but it is easier to achieve an ideal presentation to this zone. Dropping a cast into this area of relatively still water should effectively present to any trout in those feeding stations, since the strike indicator at the surface is also in the softer water and moving at about the same speed as the nymphs at the bottom, at least until the current eventually removes them from the target zone. Get close enough to the target to be able to hold the fly line up over the water, which will allow the flies to remain in the target area for a longer period of time.

FISHING SWEEPERS

A sweeper is a type of structure that frequently holds nice fish. For the purposes of this discussion, a *sweeper* is defined as an obstruction that lies in the water at a downstream angle and serves to deflect the current toward the center of the stream. It does not always have to be a log or tree. By this definition, logjams, rock piles, or other streamside obstructions can become sweepers, especially with the accumulation of debris. Any obstruction that deflects the current toward the center of the stream can have the same sweeping effect.

When Alan Ott and I were on the Pere Marquette, we caught a lot of trout by swinging wet flies across the face of sweepers. We often dead-drifted them in a team or with a nymph and allowed them to swing and lift as they approached the logs or deadfalls. Often we could time the swing to let the flies pass under the sweeper, as in many cases the current had excavated a depression or hollow area near the bottom. If we could keep the flies in the lower thread of current, they would drift under the logs or branches of deadfalls. This technique produced a few fish; however, it also produced a lot of snags!

There are several different types of sweepers, and their effect on the current can be profound and highly variable, depending on the circumstances and conditions. Sometimes an overhanging branch or other structure can lie partially submerged in the water, and it may merely deflect only the surface flow of water toward the center, allowing the deeper flow of water to pass straight downstream, unaffected by redirection. This type of surface sweeper may serve to redirect and concentrate the flow of floating food items, and the trailing edge of such structure may be an ideal habitat for surface-feeding trout during or following surface insect activity. Presenting a dry fly or spinner in this current seam may prove successful, and this is also a great place to float a terrestrial such as an ant or beetle, as many of these insects get swept into the current from the branches or

A sweeper redirects the current toward the center of the river. The force of the current often carves channels in the soft bottom, while the eroded material accumulates in the newly created depositional zone along the leeward side of the obstruction. New gravel bars and sandbars can occur as a result.

leaves of the sweeper. However, fishing a nymph along the bottom underneath this type of surface sweeper may prove no more successful than anywhere else, because the lower portions of the water column are unaffected by the surface influence of the sweeper.

A different type of sweeper may be a log that is lying diagonally along the bottom, from the shallow water at the bank into the deeper water at the center of the river. This type of sweeper has different effects on the current than a surface sweeper. It might deflect all the current toward the center or allow a small amount of water to pass underneath. Sometimes the current and hydrodynamic force of the flow carves out tunnels or channels under logs, especially if the streambed is soft.

Some sweepers that are not solid, such as logjams, fallen treetops, or tangles of branches, can create only partial obstructions. They may deflect some of the current toward the center of the stream but allow the bulk of the water flow to pass through the structure. Although this type of sweeper has less of a tendency to remodel the stream or create depositional zones within and behind the structure, multiple feeding lanes are created along the front, underneath, behind, and along the trailing edges of the deflected current.

Each type of sweeper has a different impact on the current and the immediate area of the river. In general, a sweeper directs the flow toward the center of the stream, concentrating and funneling the food items into a path or lane that extends downstream along the seam. There is usually a zone of quiet current behind the sweeper, which is separated by the seam from the main current thread or thalweg. Since sweepers disrupt the flow of water, the hydrodynamic effect may remodel the immediate habitat through the redirection of the current. This may lead to the creation of a gravel bar or silt bank that did not exist before the obstruction entered the water.

Strategy for Fishing Sweepers

Sweepers present anglers with some of the most diverse and variable fishing situations, but also some of the most potentially productive. With sweepers, it is difficult to predict the effects of the current in the creation of trout habitat as well as on your presentations. In general, the water at the surface that is moving along the face of the sweeper is moving faster than the water near the bottom, which may or may not be moving in the same direction. It is important to analyze each situation individually and develop a fishing strategy tailored to the circumstances.

Sweepers offer a wide range of potential feeding lies. The trout may use a feeding station in front of or behind the diagonal obstruction, along the leading or trailing edge. There are also many potential feeding lies in the depositional microhabitat that is frequently created in the soft water behind the obstruction. The structure may offer protected holding and resting lies deep within logjams, where larger brown trout frequently wait for reduced light to emerge and forage. Sweepers create many potential feeding and resting stations. Take your time when fishing the sweeper, and make presentations to all the potential lies.

The current has dramatic effects on your presentations to the trout in potential feeding stations associated with a sweeper. The strike indicator on the surface will follow the direction of flow at the surface and pull the flies toward the center of the stream, preventing them from targeting the feeding lies along the bottom. This keeps them out of the ideal strike zones.

As your subsurface presentations approach the sweeper, frequent mending is needed before the strike indicator reaches the crosscurrent that flows along the face of the sweeper. This allows the flies to pass underneath the indicator and present to those potential holding stations near interface of the sweeper and the streambed. If you do not mend sufficiently before that point, the crosscurrent may affect your entire presentation. It may keep the subsurface flies from drifting close enough to the potential lies along the leading face to be effective. Mending will allow the flies to drift closer to the log. Not only is this a good way to pick up the occasional fish, but unfortunately it is also a great way to lose flies, which can become tangled in the lower branches of the sweeper if they get too close.

Mend at several points along the face of the sweeper to allow the flies to present at multiple points along the leading edge. This way you will effectively cover the many potential feeding lies. Don't forget to target the trailing edge of the sweeper and the pocketwater that is frequently created behind the obstruction.

Sweepers are also perfect locations to drift a dry fly, especially during insect activity, when the trout are looking up. Allow your fly to drift along the face of the obstruction, as well as the trailing seam of current and the backeddy. The pocket behind the sweeper is a depositional zone that may accumulate dead and crippled flies after insect activity. Streamers and wet flies are effective in front of and behind the sweeper as well. They will target trout that are located within the protected lies.

In the evenings in late May and June, I like to swing large sculpin-imitating streamers across the face of sweepers. The rivers in central Michigan, such as the Pere Marquette and Au Sable, are perfect for nocturnal streamer fishing. Mousing is also a productive way to fish at night for the large carnivorous brown trout that emerge from the depths of logjams and other well-concealed hiding places. It is essential to become familiar before venturing out on a nighttime adventure, however.

One evening, Jo and I drifted down the North Branch of the Au Sable River in a 25-foot, handmade wooden river boat with Jamie Clous. This was Jo's first voyage in a river boat, and she was excited about the prospects of catching a large trout on the "evening swing." We had caught a few small brookies during the late afternoon, but nothing like the big trout she had heard about. Jamie assured her that the big ones come out at night. We had just finished the shore meal for which he is famous when we noticed a pod of rising trout feeding on *Isonychia* mayflies. Jo and Jamie waded over and found a few willing trout. One was a nice-size fish but not substantial. Jo was pleased, but Jamie promised that the best was yet to come.

As the sun went down, the excitement level went up. We waited until the darkness was complete. It is an eerie experience to float down a pitch black river. When Jamie stopped the boat and set up to fish what he said was a prime spot in front of a sweeper, I was completely disoriented and could not see it in the dark, but I took his word for it. Jo was sitting in the front seat as the designated angler, since only one of us could fish at a time. My heart was pounding as Jo sent several casts toward the sweeper. Nothing. We moved to a new place, one of Jamie's favorites, and set up for the next swing. Once again, nothing. Spot after spot produced the same result and had Jamie scratching his head. This occurred repeatedly as we fished all the prime spots one by one. Somewhere along the way, my eyes closed, but Jo remained determined. She was perched in the front of the boat and covered each new site effectively, while I, on the other hand, settled deeper into my seat.

I was awakened when Jamie pointed out the landing a hundred feet ahead. There was a light to mark it. He pointed to a log sweeper on the opposite bank that was faintly illuminated by the light and stopped the boat. "One more cast," he said despondently. "But I have never caught anything here."

With a sound like a cinder block that dropped into the water, the giant brown trout hit the Zoo Cougar that Jo had let swing across the face of the sweeper. The explosion was all the more profound in the silence of night, when previously the loudest sound had been our whispering. I was fully awake at this point. The fish ran straight for the logjam. Jo applied side pressure and kept him in the center. Then he tried to take off downstream. She took line in when she could and gave it back when she had to. Jo played the fish until Jamie finally landed the beautiful trout she had hooked on her last cast.

THE LAST CAST

Although the examples in this chapter do not cover all the various fishing situations you will encounter on the river, you can apply these models of the effects of current to other fishing conditions. The current will behave in a predictable manner, which allows you to develop a sense for when your presentation is compromised and when adjustments in techniques are needed. With experience, your overall fishing strategy will evolve. You will be able to analyze new situations and visualize the effects of the current. With knowledge of current, you can anticipate the effects on your presentations and then mend or adjust to correct them.

This study of current emphasizes the high degree of variation that exists in moving water. Even though Jo and I attempted to re-create the same presentation time after time for the photos, we found that the presentations were different for many of the drifts despite our best efforts. The flies would drift in a different current seam or be swept to the side of the boulder that they had just drifted over in the previous presentation. No two drifts were exactly the same. Sometimes it took several attempts to have the drift follow the path we intended. Small crosscurrents are often created across the faces of many kinds of structure, such as rocks, boulders, and logs, and these crosscurrents can influence flies in an unexpected manner. Sometimes our flies would be caught in one of these crosscurrents and end up far to the side of the structure we had targeted. The current also tends to ebb and flow a bit, much like the wind when it gusts. This also affected our presentations. All of this reinforces that anglers should make several casts to a target before dismissing it as unproductive, because the first few casts may have been pulled off target. It may not be until the third or fourth cast that the flies actually fall to the intended location beneath the water.

A basic familiarity with current also gives new insight into the difficulty of maintaining a dead-drift presentation. The assumption has always been that the nymphs drift under the water in the same manner as the strike indicator does as it floats on the surface. It has also been assumed that if we eliminate drag from the strike indicator, our flies will also be free from drag. The illustrations and photos in this book show that this is far from true. What is actually happening to the flies underwater often is much different than the behavior of the strike indicator on the surface. Not only are the flies degraded by drag even when the indicator is not affected by it, but they also frequently are not where we think they are. Additionally, they often are not as effective in targeting trout locations as we have previously given them credit for.

Fortunately, corrective measures are effective in compensating for vertical drag, which is the main deterrent of a drag-free drift for nymph fishing. Only if our flies can truly achieve a dead drift will they behave in the same manner as the natural insects when they are affected by the nuances of current, especially as it is associated with structure. But the need to achieve a balance in the amount of slack cannot be overstated. Insufficient slack begins to degrade the presentation, whereas too much leads to undetected strikes and failed hook sets. Achieving this balance will make us better anglers.

As anglers, we are salesmen offering our wares to the wary trout. We want to close the deal with them, and we go to great lengths to do so. We devote considerable expense and effort to the process and can only hope that in the end, we will have found success in enticing trout to sample our goods.

Bibliography

Adams, E.S. 2001. Approaches to the study of territory size and shape. *Annual Review of Ecology and Systematics* 32:277–303.

Allan, J.D. 1995. *Stream Ecology: Structure and Function of Running Waters*. Dordrecht, Netherlands: Kluwer Academic Publishers.

Angardi, T.R., and Griffith, J.S. 1990. Diel feeding chronology and diet selection of rainbow trout (Oncorhynchus mykiss) in the Henry's Fork of the Snake River, Idaho. *Canadian Journal of Fisheries and Aquatic Sciences* 47:199–209.

Ayllon, D., Allodovar, G.G., and Elvira, B. 2010. Modelling brown trout spatial requirements through physical habitat simulations. *River Research and Applications* 26 (9): 1909–1102.

Bachman, R.A. 1984. Foraging behavior of free-ranging wild and hatchery brown trout in a stream. *Transactions of the American Fisheries Society* 113:1–32.

Baldwin, C.M., Beauchamp, D.A., and Gubala, C.P. 2002. Seasonal and diel distribution and movement of cutthroat trout from ultrasonic telemetry. *Transactions of the American Fisheries Society* 131:143–158.

Bergman, R. 1938. *Trout*. New York: Alfred A. Knopf.

Biro, P.A., Ridgway, M.S., and Noakes, D.L.G. 1997. The central-place territory model does not apply to space use by juvenile brook charr (*Salvelinus fontinalis*) in lakes. *Journal of Animal Ecology* 66:837–845.

Brewin, P.A., and Ormerod, S.J. 1994. Macroinvertebrate drift in streams of the Nepalese Himalaya. *Freshwater Biology* 32:573–583.

Bridcut, E.E., and Giller, P.S. 1993. Movement and site fidelity in young brown trout (*Salmo trutta*) population in a southern Irish stream. *Journal of Fish Biology* 43:889–899.

———. 1995. Diet variability and foraging strategies of brown trout (*Salmo trutta*): an analogy from subpopulations to individuals. *Canadian Journal of Fisheries and Aquatic Science* 52 (12):2543–2552.

Burroughs, B. 2003. Scientifically speaking. *Michigan Trout*. Michigan Council of Trout Unlimited. April.

Chaston, I. 1969. A study of the exploitation of invertebrate drift by brown trout (*Salmo trutta*) in a Dartmoor stream. *Journal of the Fisheries Research Board of Canada* 26:2165–2171.

Ciborowski, J.J.H. 1983. The influence of current velocity, density and detritus on the drift of two mayfly species (Ephemeroptera). *Canadian Journal of Zoology* 61:119–125.

Clapp, D.F. 1988. *Movement, habitat use and daily activity patterns of trophy brown trout in the South Branch of the Au Sable River*. Fisheries Research Report No. 1907. Ann Arbor: Michigan Department of Natural Resources.

Clapp, D.F., Clark, R.D., Jr., and Diana, J.S. 1990. Range, activity and habitat of large, free-ranging brown trout in a Michigan stream. *Transactions of the American Fisheries Society* 119:1022–1034.

Clapp, D. F., and Diana, J.S. 1990. Range, activity, and habitat of large, free-ranging brown trout in a Michigan stream. *Transactions of the American Fisheries Society* 119:1022–1034.

De Crespin De Billy, V., and Usseglio-Polatera, P. 2005. Traits of brown trout prey in relation to habitat characteristics and benthic invertebrate communities. *Journal of Freshwater Biology* 60 (3):687–714.

Dephillips, M. 2001. *Daily and seasonal movements of large brown trout and walleye in an impounded reach of the Au Sable River, Michigan.* Fisheries Research Report No. 2056. Ann Arbor: Michigan Department of Natural Resources.

Elliott, J.M. 1967. The food of trout (*Salmo trutta*) in a Dartmoor stream. *Journal of Applied Ecology* 4:59–71.

———. 1973. The food of brown and rainbow trout (*Salmo trutta* and *Salmo gairdneri*) in relation to the abundance of drifting invertebrates in a mountain stream. *Oceologia* 12:329–347.

———. 1994. *Quantitative Ecology and the Brown Trout.* Oxford: Oxford University Press.

Elliott, J.M., and Hurley, M.A. 2000. Daily energy intake and growth of piscivorous brown trout (*Salmo trutta*). *Freshwater Biology* 44:237–245.

Farbridge, K.A., and Leatherland, J.F. 1987. Lunar cycles of coho salmon, *Oncorhynchus kisutch*. *Journal of Experimental Biology* 129:179–189.

Fausch, K.D. 1984. Profitable stream positions for salmonids: relating specific growth rates to net energy gain. *Canadian Journal of Zoology* 62:441–451.

Fausch, K.D., and White, R.J. 1981. Competition between brook trout (*Salvelinus fontinalis*) and brown trout (*Salmo trutta*) for positions in a Michigan stream. *Canadian Journal of Fisheries and Aquatic Sciences* 38:1220–1227.

Forseth, T., and Jonsson, B. 1994. The growth rate and food ration of piscivorous brown trout (*Salmo trutta*). *Functional Ecology* 8:171–177.

Galarowicz, T.L., Adams, J.A., and Wihl, D. 2006. The influence of prey availability on ontogenetic diet shift of a juvenile piscivore. *Canadian Journal of Fisheries and Aquatic Sciences* 63 (8):1722–1733.

Giller, P.S., and Malmquist, B. 1998. *The Biology of Streams and Rivers.* New York: Oxford University Press.Giroux, F., Ovido, M., Philippart, J.C., and Baras, E. 2000. Relationship between the drift of macroinvertebrates and activity of brown trout in a small stream. *Journal of Freshwater Biology* 45:1248–1257.

Gowan, C., and Fausch, K.D. 1996. Mobile brook trout in two high elevation Colorado streams: re-evaluating the concept of restricted movement. *Canadian Journal of Fisheries and Aquatic Sciences* 53:1370–1381.

Grau, E.G. 1982. Is the lunar cycle a factor timing the onset of salmon migration? In *Proceedings of the Symposium on Salmon and Trout Migratory Behavior*, ed. E.L. Brannon and E.O. Salo, 184–189. Seattle: University of Washington, College of Fisheries.

Greenberg, L.A., and Giller, P.S. 2001. Individual variation in habitat use and growth of male and female brown trout. *Ecography* 24 (2):212–224.

Griffith, J.S., Jr. 1972. Comparative behavior and habitat utilization of brook trout (*Salvelinus fontinalis*) and cutthroat trout (*Salmo clarki*) in small streams in northern Idaho. *Journal of the Fisheries Research Board of Canada* 29:265–273.

Gunnarsson, G.S. 2009. Territorial and foraging behavior of juvenile salmonids in Icelandic streams. Master's thesis, Universitatis Icelandiae Sigillum.

Hafele, Rick. 1986. *Anatomy of a Trout Stream*. VHS. St. Paul: 3M and Scientific Anglers.

Hudson, J.P. 1993. Seasonal and daily movements of large brown trout in the mainstream Au Sable River, Michigan. Fisheries Research Report No. 1988. Ann Arbor: Michigan Department of Natural Resources.

Hughes, D. 1988. *Reading the Water*. Mechanicsburg, PA: Stackpole Books.

Hynes, H.B.N. 1970. *The Ecology of Running Waters*. Toronto: University of Toronto Press.

Hyvarinen, P., and Huusko, A. 2006. Diet of brown trout in relation to variation in abundance and size of pelagic fish prey. *Journal of Fish Biology* 68:87–98.

Imre, I., Grant, J.W.A., and Keeley, E.R. 2002. The effect of visual isolation on territory size and population density of juvenile rainbow trout (*Oncorhynchus mykiss*). *Canadian Journal of Fisheries and Aquatic Sciences* 59:303–309.

Imre, I., Grant, J.W.A., and Keeley, E.R. 2004. The effect of food abundance and territory size and population density of juvenile steelhead trout (*Oncorhynchus mykiss*). *Oecologia* 138:371–378.

Jenkins, T.M.J. 1969. Social structure, position choice and microdistribution of two species (*Salmo trutta* and *Salmo gairdneri*) resident in mountain streams. *Animal Behavior Monographs* 2:57–123.

Jenkins, T.M., Feldmeth, T.H., and Elliott, G.V. 1970. Feeding of rainbow trout (*Salmo gairdneri*) in relation to abundance of drifting invertebrates in a mountain stream. *Journal of the Fisheries Research Board of Canada* 27:2356–2361.

Jensen, H., Amundsen, P.A., Behn, T., and Aspholm, P.E. 2004. Feeding ecology of piscivorous brown trout (*Salmo trutta*) in a subarctic watercourse. *Annales Zoologici Fennici* 41:319–328.

Jensen, H., Amundsen, P.A., Elliott, J.M., Behn, T., and Aspholm, P.E. 2006. Prey consumption rates and growth of piscivorous brown trout in a subarctic watercourse. *Journal of Fish Biology* 68:838–848.

Jensen, H., Bohn, T., Amundsen, P., and Aspholm, P. 2004. Feeding ecology of piscivorous brown trout (*Salmo trutta*) in a subarctic water course. *Annales Zoologici Fennici* 41:319–328.

Jensen, H., Kahilainen, K., Amundsen, P.-A., Gjelland, K.O., Toumaala, A., Malinen, T., and Bohn, T. 2008. Predation by brown trout (*Salmo trutta*) along a diversifying prey community gradient. *Canadian Journal of Fisheries and Aquatic Sciences* 65:1831–1841.

Jonsson, M., Skov, C., Koed, A., and Nilsson, P.A. 2008. Temporal clumping of prey and coexistence of unequal interferers: experiments on social foraging groups of brown trout on invertebrate drift. *Oikos* 117:1782–1787.

Jonsson, N., Naesje, T.F., Jonsson, B., Saksgard, R., and Sandlund, O.T. 1999. The influence of piscivory on life history traits of brown trout. *Journal of Fish Biology* 22 (6):1129–1141.

Juanes, F., and Stouder, D.J. 1994. What determines prey size selectivity in piscivorous fishes? In *Theory and Application in Fish Feeding Ecology*, ed. D.J. Stouder, K.L. Fresh, and R.J. Feller, 79–100. Belle W. Baruch Library in Marine Sciences, no. 18, University of South Carolina Press, Columbia, South Carolina.

Jude, D.J., Tesar, F.J., Deboe, S.F., and Miller, T.J. 1987. Diet and selection of major prey species by Lake Michigan salmonines, 1973–1982. *Transactions of the American Fisheries Society* 116:677–691.

Keast, A. 1985. The piscivorous feeding guild of fishes in small fresh water systems. *Environmental Biology of Fishes* 12:119–129.

Keeley, E.R. 2000. An experimental analysis of territory size in juvenile steelhead trout. *Animal Behavior* 59 (3):477–490.

Keeley, E.R., and Grant, W.H. 2001. Prey size of salmonid fishes in streams, lakes and oceans. *Canadian Journal of Fisheries and Aquatic Sciences* 58:1122–1132.

Keeley, E.R., and McPhail, J.D. 1998. Food abundance, intruder pressure and body size as determinants of territory size in juvenile steelhead trout (*Oncorhynchus mykiss*). *Behavior* 135 (1):65–82.

Lyons, N. 1977. *Bright Rivers*. Philadelphia: Lippincott.

Maclean, N. 1976. *A River Runs Through It*. Chicago: University of Chicago Press.

Marinaro, V.C. 1976. *In the Ring of the Rise*. New York: Crown Publishers.

Maslow, A. 1943. A theory of human motivation. *Psychological Review* 50:370–396.

Matthews, K.R., Berg, D.L., Azuma, D.L., and Lambert, T.R. 1994. Cool water formation and trout habitat use in a deep pool in the Sierra Nevada, California. *Transactions of the American Fisheries Society* 123:549–564.

Merritt, R.W., Cummins, K.W., and Berg, M.B. 2008. *An Introduction to the Aquatic Insects of North America*. Dubuque, IA: Kendall/Hunt Publishing Company.

Meuse, J.B. 1975. Relation of density to brown trout movements in a Michigan stream. *Transactions of the American Fisheries Society* 104:688–695.

Naesje, T.F., Sandlund, O.T., and Saksgaard, R. 1998. Selective predation of piscivorous brown trout (*Salmo trutta*) on polymorphic whitefish (*Coregonus lavaretus* L.). *Archiv fuer Hydrobiologie Special Issues: Advances in Limnology* 50:283–294.

Nakano, S., and Furukawa-Tanaka, T. 1994. Intra- and interspecific dominance hierarchies and variation in foraging tactics of two species of stream-dwelling char. *Ecological Research* 9 (1):9–20.

Nakano, S., Kawaguchi, Y., Taniguchi, Y., and Miyasaka, H. 1999. Selective foraging on terrestrial invertebrates by rainbow trout in a forested headwater stream in northern Japan. *Ecological Research* 14:351–360.

Nielsen, J.T., Lisle, T.E., and Ozaki, V. 1994. Thermally stratified pools and their use by steelhead in northern California streams. *Transactions of the American Fisheries Society* 123:613–626.

Nilsson, P.A., and Ruxton, G.D. 2004. Temporally fluctuating prey and interfering predators: a positive feedback. *Oikos* 101:411–415.

Ormerod, S.J., Jones, M.E., Jones, M.C., and Phillips, D.R. 2004. The effect of riparian forestry on invertebrate drift and brown trout in upland streams of contrasting acidity. *Hydrology and Earth Sciences* 8 (3):578–588.

Pielou, E.C. 1998. *Fresh Water*. Chicago: University of Chicago Press.

Pyke, G.H., Pulliam, H.R., and Charnov, E.L. 1997. Optimum foraging: a selective review of theory and tests. *Quarterly Review of Biology* 52:137–154.

Regal, G.E. 1992. Range of movement and daily activity of wild brown trout in the South Branch of the Au Sable River, Michigan. Fisheries Research Report No.1907. Ann Arbor: Michigan Department of Natural Resources.

Ringler, N.H. 1979. Selective predation by drift feeding brown trout (*Salmo trutta*). *Journal of the Fisheries Research Board of Canada* 36:392–403.

———. 1985. Individual and temporal variation in prey switching by brown trout (*Salmo trutta*). *Copea* 4:198–926.

Romaniszyn, E.D., Hutchens, J.J., Jr., Wallace, J.B. 2007. Aquatic and terrestrial invertebrate drift in southern Appalachian streams; implications for trout resources. *Journal of Freshwater Biology* 52 (1):1–11.

Schulz, V., and Berg, R. 1992. Movements of ultrasonically tagged brown trout (*Salmo trutta*) in Lake Constance. *Journal of Fish Biology* 40:909–917.

Shetter, D.S. 1968. Observations on movement of wild brown trout in two Michigan stream drainages. *Transactions of the American Fisheries Society* 97:472–480.

Skues, G.E.M. 1921. *The Way of a Trout with a Fly*. London: A. & C. Black.

Stauffer, T.E. 1977. A comparison of the diet and growth of brown trout (*Salmo trutta*) from the South Branch of the Au Sable River. Fisheries Research Report No. 1845. Ann Arbor: Michigan Department of Natural Resources.

Steingromsson, S.O., and Grant, J.W.A. 2011. Determinants of multiple central-place territory use in wild young-of-the-year Atlantic salmon (*Salmo salar*). *Behavioral Ecology and Sociobiology* 65 (2):275–286.

Sweeney, B.W., and Vannode, R.L. 1982. Population synchrony in mayflies *Dolania americana*: a predator satiation hypothesis. *Evolution* 36:810–821.

Swisher, D., and Richards, C. 2000. *Selective Trout*. New York: Lyons Press.

Tippets, W.E., and Moyle, P.B. 1978. Epibenthic feeding of rainbow trout from the McCloud River, California. *Journal of Animal Ecology* 47:549–559.

Utz, R.M., and Hartman, K.J. 2006. Temporal and special variation in the energy intake of a brook trout (*Salvelinus fontinalis*) population in an Appalachian watershed. *Canadian Journal of Fisheries and Aquatic Sciences* 63:2675–2686.

Venables, R. 1662. *The Experienced Angler; or, Angling Improved*. London.

Walton, I. 1653. *The Compleat Angler; or, The Contemplative Man's Recreation*. London.

Waters, T.F. 1965. Interpretation of invertebrate drift in streams. *Ecology* 46:327–334.

———. 1972. The drift of stream insects. *Annual Review of Entomology* 17:253–272.

Wilkison, R.A. 1996. Fish community structure and brown trout predation in upper Silver Creek, Idaho. Master's thesis, Idaho State University, Pocatello.

Wilzbach, M.A., and Cummins, K.W. 1986. Influence of habitat manipulations on interactions between cutthroat trout and invertebrate drift. *Ecology* 67 (4):898–911.

Wooton, R.J. 1998. *The Ecology of Teleost Fish*. Dordrecht, Netherlands: Kluwer Academic Publishers.

Younger, J. 1840. *River Angling for Salmon and Trout*. Edinburgh: W. Blackwood.

Index

Page numbers in italics indicate illustrations.